Judith M. Glassgold
Suzanne Iasenza
Editors

Lesbians, Feminism, and Psychoanalysis: The Second Wave

Lesbians, Feminism, and Psychoanalysis: The Second Wave has been co-published simultaneously as *Journal of Lesbian Studies*, Volume 8, Numbers 1/2 2004.

Pre-publication REVIEWS, COMMENTARIES, EVALUATIONS . . .

"Since *Lesbians and Psychoanalysis* was published in 1995, the small and almost entirely negative literature marked by the intersection of those two nouns has been replaced by a vibrant, interesting, and unprejudiced literature, produced by a community. Taken collectively, the essays in this book are a history of that decade of activity and a map of what remains to be done to assure that neglect and discrimination are never again the fate of 'lesbians and psychoanalysis' and that the new literature continues to grow and influence both lesbians and psychoanalysis."

Elisabeth Young-Bruehl, PhD
Partner, Cherishment Culture
New York City

Harrington Park Press

Lesbians, Feminism, and Psychoanalysis: The Second Wave

Lesbians, Feminism, and Psychoanalysis: The Second Wave has been co-published simultaneously as *Journal of Lesbian Studies*, Volume 8, Numbers 1/2 2004.

The *Journal of Lesbian Studies* Monographic "Separates"

Below is a list of "separates," which in serials librarianship means a special issue simultaneously published as a special journal issue or double-issue *and* as a "separate" hardbound monograph. (This is a format which we also call a "DocuSerial.")

"Separates" are published because specialized libraries or professionals may wish to purchase a specific thematic issue by itself in a format which can be separately cataloged and shelved, as opposed to purchasing the journal on an on-going basis. Faculty members may also more easily consider a "separate" for classroom adoption.

"Separates" are carefully classified separately with the major book jobbers so that the journal tie-in can be noted on new book order slips to avoid duplicate purchasing.

You may wish to visit Haworth's website at . . .

http://www.HaworthPress.com

. . . to search our online catalog for complete tables of contents of these separates and related publications.

You may also call 1-800-HAWORTH (outside US/Canada: 607-722-5857), or Fax 1-800-895-0582 (outside US/Canada: 607-771-0012), or e-mail at:

docdelivery@haworthpress.com

Lesbians, Feminism, and Psychoanalysis: The Second Wave, edited by Judith M. Glassgold, PsyD, and Suzanne Iasenza, PhD (Vol. 8, No. 1/2, 2004). *"This book is the first to set the tone for a lesbian psychoanalytic revolution." (Dany Nobus, PhD, Senior Lecturer in Psychology and Psychoanalytic Studies, Brunel University, United Kingdom)*

Trauma, Stress, and Resilence Among Sexual Minority Women: Rising Like the Phoenix, edited by Kimberly F. Balsam, PhD (Vol. 7, No. 4, 2003). *Provides a first-time look at the victimization experiences that lesbian and bisexual women face as well as how they work through these challenges and emerge resilient.*

Latina Lesbian Writers and Artists, edited by María Dolores Costa, PhD, (Vol. 7, No. 3, 2003). *"A fascinating journey through the Latina lesbian experience. It brings us stories of exile, assimilation, and conflict of cultures. The book takes us to the Midwest, New York, Chicana Borderlands, Mexico, Argentina, and Spain. It succeeds at showing the diversity within the Latina lesbian experience through deeply feminist testimonials of life and struggle." (Susana Cook, performance artist and playwright)*

Lesbian Rites: Symbolic Acts and the Power of Community, edited by Ramona Faith Oswald, PhD (Vol. 7, No. 2, 2003). *"Informative, enlightening, and well written . . . illuminates the range of lesbian ritual behavior in a creative and thorough manner. Ramona Faith Oswald and the contributors to this book have done scholars and students of ritual studies an important service by demonstrating the power, pervasiveness, and performative nature of lesbian ritual practices." (Cele Otnes, PhD, Associate Professor, Department of Business Administration, University of Illinois)*

Mental Health Issues for Sexual Minority Women: Re-Defining Women's Mental Health, edited by Tonda L. Hughes, RN, PhD, FAAN, Carrol Smith, RN, MS, and Alice Dan, PhD (Vol. 7, No. 1, 2003). *A rare look at mental health issues for lesbians and other sexual minority women.*

Addressing Homophobia and Heterosexism on College Campuses, edited by Elizabeth P. Cramer, PhD (Vol. 6, No. 3/4, 2002). *A practical guide to creating LGBT-supportive environments on college campuses.*

Femme/Butch: New Considerations of the Way We Want to Go, edited by Michelle Gibson and Deborah T. Meem (Vol. 6, No. 2, 2002). *"Disrupts the fictions of heterosexual norms. . . . A much-needed examiniation of the ways that butch/femme identitites subvert both heteronormativity and 'expected' lesbian behavior." (Patti Capel Swartz, PhD, Assistant Professor of English, Kent State University)*

Lesbian Love and Relationships, edited by Suzanna M. Rose, PhD (Vol. 6, No. 1, 2002). *"Suzanna Rose's collection of 13 essays is well suited to prompting serious contemplation and discussion about lesbian lives and how they are–or are not–different from others. . . . Interesting and useful for debunking some myths, confirming others, and reaching out into new territories that were previously unexplored." (Lisa Keen, BA, MFA, Senior Political Correspondent, Washington Blade)*

Everyday Mutinies: Funding Lesbian Activism, edited by Nanette K. Gartrell, MD, and Esther D. Rothblum, PhD (Vol. 5, No. 3, 2001). *"Any lesbian who fears she'll never find the money, time, or support for her work can take heart from the resourcefulness and dogged determination of the contributors to this book. Not only do these inspiring stories provide practical tips on making dreams come true, they offer an informal history of lesbian political activism since World War II." (Jane Futcher, MA, Reporter,* Marin Independent Journal, *and author of* Crush, Dream Lover, *and* Promise Not to Tell)

Lesbian Studies in Aotearoa/New Zealand, edited by Alison J. Laurie (Vol. 5, No. 1/2, 2001). *These fascinating studies analyze topics ranging from the gender transgressions of women passing as men in order to work and marry as they wished to the effects of coming out on modern women's health.*

Lesbian Self-Writing: The Embodiment of Experience, edited by Lynda Hall (Vol. 4, No. 4, 2000). *"Probes the intersection of love for words and love for women. . . . Luminous, erotic, evocative." (Beverly Burch, PhD, psychotherapist and author,* Other Women: Lesbian/Bisexual Experience and Psychoanalytic Views of Women *and* On Intimate Terms: The Psychology of Difference in Lesbian Relationships)

'Romancing the Margins'? Lesbian Writing in the 1990s, edited by Gabriele Griffin, PhD (Vol. 4, No. 2, 2000). *Explores lesbian issues through the mediums of books, movies, and poetry and offers readers critical essays that examine current lesbian writing and discuss how recent movements have tried to remove racist and anti-gay themes from literature and movies.*

From Nowhere to Everywhere: Lesbian Geographies, edited by Gill Valentine, PhD (Vol. 4, No. 1, 2000). *"A significant and worthy contribution to the ever growing literature on sexuality and space. . . . A politically significant volume representing the first major collection on lesbian geographies. . . . I will make extensive use of this book in my courses on social and cultural geography and sexuality and space." (Jon Binnie, PhD, Lecturer in Human Geography, Liverpool, John Moores University, United Kingdom)*

Lesbians, Levis and Lipstick: The Meaning of Beauty in Our Lives, edited by Jeanine C. Cogan, PhD, and Joanie M. Erickson (Vol. 3, No. 4, 1999). *Explores lesbian beauty norms and the effects these norms have on lesbian women.*

Lesbian Sex Scandals: Sexual Practices, Identities, and Politics, edited by Dawn Atkins, MA (Vol. 3, No. 3, 1999). *"Grounded in material practices, this collection explores confrontation and coincidence among identity politics, 'scandalous' sexual practices, and queer theory and feminism. . . . It expands notions of lesbian identification and lesbian community." (Maria Pramaggiore, PhD, Assistant Professor, Film Studies, North Carolina State University, Raleigh)*

The Lesbian Polyamory Reader: Open Relationships, Non-Monogamy, and Casual Sex, edited by Marcia Munson and Judith P. Stelboum, PhD (Vol. 3, No. 1/2, 1999). *"Offers reasonable, logical, and persuasive explanations for a style of life I had not seriously considered before. . . . A terrific read." (Beverly Todd, Acquisitions Librarian, Estes Park Public Library, Estes Park, Colorado)*

Living "Difference": Lesbian Perspectives on Work and Family Life, edited by Gillian A. Dunne, PhD (Vol. 2, No. 4, 1998). *"A fascinating, groundbreaking collection. . . . Students and professionals in psychiatry, psychology, sociology, and anthropology will find this work extremely useful and thought provoking." (Nanette K. Gartrell, MD, Associate Clinical Professor of Psychiatry, University of California at San Francisco Medical School)*

Acts of Passion: Sexuality, Gender, and Performance, edited by Nina Rapi, MA, and Maya Chowdhry, MA (Vol. 2, No. 2/3, 1998). *"This significant and impressive publication draws together a diversity of positions, practices, and polemics in relation to postmodern lesbian performance and puts them firmly on the contemporary cultural map." (Lois Keidan, Director of Live Arts, Institute of Contemporary Arts, London, United Kingdom)*

Gateways to Improving Lesbian Health and Health Care: Opening Doors, edited by Christy M. Ponticelli, PhD (Vol. 2, No. 1, 1997). *"An unprecedented collection that goes to the source for powerful and poignant information on the state of lesbian health care." (Jocelyn C. White, MD, Assistant Professor of Medicine, Oregon Health Sciences University; Faculty, Portland Program in General Internal Medicine, Legacy Portland Hospitals, Portland, Oregon)*

Classics in Lesbian Studies, edited by Esther Rothblum, PhD (Vol. 1, No. 1, 1996). *"Brings together a collection of powerful chapters that cross disciplines and offer a broad vision of lesbian lives across race, age, and community." (Michele J. Eliason, PhD, Associate Professor, College of Nursing, The University of Iowa)*

Lesbians, Feminism, and Psychoanalysis: The Second Wave

Judith M. Glassgold, PsyD
Suzanne Iasenza, PhD
Editors

Lesbians, Feminism, and Psychoanalysis: The Second Wave has been co-published simultaneously as *Journal of Lesbian Studies*, Volume 8, Numbers 1/2 2004.

HPP

Harrington Park Press®
An Imprint of The Haworth Press, Inc.

New York • London • Victoria (AU)
www.HaworthPress.com

Front cover image:
"Changes with Heart", a sculpture by Nancy Azara
(Photo credit: Christopher Burke)

Published by

Harrington Park Press®, 10 Alice Street, Binghamton, NY 13904-1580 USA

Harrington Park Press® is an imprint of The Haworth Press, Inc., 10 Alice Street, Binghamton, NY 13904-1580 USA.

Lesbians, Feminism, and Psychoanalysis: The Second Wave has been co-published simultaneously as *Journal of Lesbian Studies,* Volume 8, Numbers 1/2 2004.

The development, preparation, and publication of this work has been undertaken with great care. However, the publisher, employees, editors, and agents of The Haworth Press and all imprints of The Haworth Press, Inc., including The Haworth Medical Press® and The Pharmaceutical Products Press®, are not responsible for any errors contained herein or for consequences that may ensue from use of materials or information contained in this work. Opinions expressed by the author(s) are not necessarily those of The Haworth Press, Inc. With regard to case studies, identities and circumstances of individuals discussed herein have been changed to protect confidentiality. Any resemblance to actual persons, living or dead, is entirely coincidental.

Cover design by Brooke R. Stiles

Library of Congress Cataloging-in-Publication Data

Lesbians, feminism, and psychoanalysis : the second wave / Judith M. Glassgold, Suzanne Iasenza, editors.
     p. cm.
"Has been copublished simultaneously as Journal of Lesbian Studies, Volume 8, Numbers 1/2 2004."
Includes bibliographical references and index.
    ISBN 1-56023-280-3 (hardcover : alk. paper) – ISBN 1-56023-281-1(softcover : alk. paper)
    1. Lesbianism–Psychological aspects. 2. Psychoanalysis and feminism. 3. Lesbians–Psychology. 4. Women and psychoanalysis. 5. Sexism in psychoanalysis. I. Glassgold, Judith M., 1957- II. Iasenza, Suzanne, 1956-
RC558.5.L47 2003
155.3′4–dc22

                                              2003018150

Indexing, Abstracting & Website/Internet Coverage

This section provides you with a list of major indexing & abstracting services. That is to say, each service began covering this periodical during the year noted in the right column. Most Websites which are listed below have indicated that they will either post, disseminate, compile, archive, cite or alter their own Website users with research-based content from this work. (This list is as current as the copyright date of this publication.)

(continued)

Special Bibliographic Notes related to special journal issues (separates) and indexing/abstracting:

- indexing/abstracting services in this list will also cover material in any "separate" that is co-published simultaneously with Haworth's special thematic journal issue or DocuSerial. Indexing/abstracting usually covers material at the article/chapter level.
- monographic co-editions are intended for either non-subscribers or libraries which intend to purchase a second copy for their circulating collections.
- monographic co-editions are reported to all jobbers/wholesalers/approval plans. The source journal is listed as the "series" to assist the prevention of duplicate purchasing in the same manner utilized for books-in-series.
- to facilitate user/access services all indexing/abstracting services are encouraged to utilize the co-indexing entry note indicated at the bottom of the first page of each article/chapter/contribution.
- this is intended to assist a library user of any reference tool (whether print, electronic, online, or CD-ROM) to locate the monographic version if the library has purchased this version but not a subscription to the source journal.
- individual articles/chapters in any Haworth publication are also available through the Haworth Document Delivery Service (HDDS).

This volume is dedicated to the memory of
Adria Schwartz
1946-2003

Her life made lesbians and feminism more visible in psychoanalysis.

ABOUT THE EDITORS

Judith M. Glassgold, PsyD, is a clinical psychologist in private practice in New Jersey and is a contributing faculty member at the Graduate School of Applied and Professional Psychology of Rutgers University. A co-editor of and contributor to *Lesbians and Psychoanalysis: Revolutions in Theory and Practice* (Free Press, 1995), she has written and presented on psychotherapy with lesbian, gay, and bisexual clients from feminist, social constructionist, and psychoanalytic perspectives. Dr. Glassgold is a Fellow and President (08/2003-08/2004) of the Society for the Psychological Study of Lesbian, Gay, and Bisexual Issues (Division 44) of the American Psychological Association. She has an interest in professional ethics and serves on the Ethics Committee of the New Jersey Psychological Association.

Suzanne Iasenza, PhD, is Associate Professor of Counseling at John Jay College-City University of New York and maintains a private practice in psychotherapy and sex therapy in New York City. She is on the faculties of the Institute for Contemporary Psychotherapy and the Institute for Human Identity. Dr. Iasenza is co-editor (with Dr. Glassgold) of *Lesbians and Psychoanalysis: Revolutions in Theory and Practice* (1995) and publishes extensively on sexuality and sexual orientation in professional journals and books. She is contributing editor for *In the Family*, the magazine for lesbians, gays, bisexuals, and their relations. Dr. Iasenza is a graduate and active alumna of the New Directions Program in Critical Thinking and Writing in Psychoanalysis at the Washington Psychoanalytic Foundation. She is also a member of an ongoing study group through the International Institute of Object Relations Therapy.

Lesbians, Feminism, and Psychoanalysis: The Second Wave

CONTENTS

ALL HARRINGTON PARK PRESS BOOKS
AND JOURNALS ARE PRINTED
ON CERTIFIED ACID-FREE PAPER

Introduction:
Lesbians, Feminism, and Psychoanalysis:
The Second Wave

Judith M. Glassgold

Suzanne Iasenza

SUMMARY. This volume presents a collection of psychoanalytically influenced authors writing about lesbian concerns. Profound changes have occurred within psychoanalysis due to the efforts of lesbian, gay, and bisexual scholars and the evolution of psychoanalytic theory away from classical models. The writers in this volume represent a second generation of scholars who have more latitude in using psychoanalysis to study sexual orientation and gender. The article summarizes the major changes in this field and outlines areas where further improvements in psychoanalysis can occur. *[Article copies available for a fee from The Haworth Document Delivery Service: 1-800-HAWORTH. E-mail address: <docdelivery@ haworthpress.com> Website: <http://www.HaworthPress.com> © 2004 by The Haworth Press, Inc. All rights reserved.]*

Judith M. Glassgold, PsyD, is a clinical psychologist in private practice in New Jersey and is a contributing faculty member at the Graduate School of Applied and Professional Psychology of Rutgers University.

Suzanne Iasenza, PhD, is Associate Professor of Counseling at John Jay College-City University of New York. She is on the faculties of the Institute for Contemporary Psychotherapy and the Institute for Human Identity. She maintains a private practice in psychotherapy and sex therapy in New York City.

Address correspondence to: Judith M. Glasssgold, 324 Raritan Avenue, Highland Park, NJ 08907 (E-mail: drglassgold@yahoo.com).

[Haworth co-indexing entry note]: "Introduction: Lesbians, Feminism, and Psychoanalysis: The Second Wave." Glassgold, Judith M., and Suzanne Iasenza. Co-published simultaneously in *Journal of Lesbian Studies* (Harrington Park Press, an imprint of The Haworth Press, Inc.) Vol. 8, No. 1/2, 2004, pp. 1-10; and: *Lesbians, Feminism, and Psychoanalysis: The Second Wave* (ed: Judith M. Glassgold, and Suzanne Iasenza) Harrington Park Press, an imprint of The Haworth Press, Inc., 2004, pp. 1-10. Single or multiple copies of this article are available for a fee from The Haworth Document Delivery Service [1-800-HAWORTH, 9:00 a.m. - 5:00 p.m. (EST). E-mail address: docdelivery@haworthpress.com].

KEYWORDS. Lesbians, feminism, psychoanalysis

This volume presents a new collection of psychoanalytically influenced authors writing about lesbian concerns. In the 1990s, the first wave of women writers, many of whom were lesbian and bisexual themselves, made their first contributions to rethinking sexual orientation, sexuality, and gender (Butler, 1990; Chodorow, 1994; de Lauretis, 1994; O'Connor & Ryan, 1993). By the mid to late 1990s, the works had multiplied and many seasoned educators, researchers, and practitioners published works in this area (Burch, 1997; Dominici & Lesser, 1995; Glassgold & Iasenza, 1995; Gould & Kiersky, 2001; Magee & Miller, 1997; Schwartz, 1998).

Currently, these writers have less of a struggle for legitimacy or a need to focus on debunking older theories. They have found a place at the table as there is a greater acceptance of theories challenging heterosexuality's monopoly on normalcy, and same-sex desire is viewed as part of the continuum of human experience. Many psychoanalytic institutes have abandoned restrictions on accepting openly LGB candidates[1] and some have instituted courses and programs on LGB issues or have open lesbian, gay, and bisexual faculty.[2] The American Psychoanalytic Association has a strong resolution denouncing efforts to use psychoanalysis to change sexual orientation (2000) and has had a resolution deploring discrimination against LGB individuals since 1991. There is a rapprochement between organized psychoanalysis and LGBT issues within psychology and concerted efforts are being made by psychoanalytic psychologists, Division 39-Psychoanalysis, of the American Psychological Association, to focus on issues of multicultural diversity and social justice (Division 39, 2002). These successes are due to the pioneering efforts of many of the writers cited above. Many have written eloquently about their struggles to survive in hostile times (Decker, 1995; Magee & Miller, 1997; Martin, 1995; Goldman, 1995) or described long-held bias against LGB professionals within psychoanalysis (Drescher, 1995).

However, the acceptance of a new view of same-sex desire is due to a profound evolution within psychoanalysis. When psychoanalytic writers first published on lesbian issues (Deutsch, 1932/48; Freud, 1920/61) their writings were overwhelmingly negative and reinforced oppressive stereotypes. This trend only worsened with negative and homophobic distortions of lesbian identity and desire (Eisenbud, 1969; McDougal, 1964/70; Socarides, 1968). However, in the late 1970s, feminists began creating a more accurate representation of female psychology free of misogyny and distortion, integrating ideas from object relations

(Chodorow, 1978; Dinnerstein, 1976), creatively rethinking theory (Irigaray, 1975/87) or challenging Freud's dominance of theory (Mitchell, 1982). Chodorow and Dinnerstein (to name only a few) also rejected some American feminist beliefs that psychoanalysis could not be reclaimed so as to reflect women's lives and attempted to creatively use psychoanalysis to understand human problems. Yet, lesbians were not full beneficiaries of the feminist psychoanalytic revolution as significant works in the 1980s continued to pathologize lesbian development (Eisenbud, 1982; McDougall, 1980; Siegel, 1988) and the new feminist works ignored lesbians almost entirely.

Into the 90s lesbians continued to be marginalized within psychoanalytic institutions, with few affirmative publications, no visibility within training institutes, and few openly lesbian analysts. Within training institutions, homophobia still resulted in the exclusion or harassment of lesbian, gay, and bisexual applicants (Decker, 1995; Drescher, 1995; Martin, 1995). It was in fields such as philosophy, women's studies, and criticism (Butler, 1990; de Lauretis, 1994; Foucault, 1980) where psychoanalysis' relevance to feminist, lesbian, and gay issues first emerged. Poststructuralism, de-constructionism, and postmodernism were critical movements for transforming psychoanalytic theory into an analytic tool to challenge sexism and heterosexism (Butler, 1990; Trask, 1987). These fields incorporated psychoanalysis while transforming it, and when psychoanalysis integrated these new philosophical movements via feminist and postmodernist writers and thinkers, the new formulations of psychoanalysis re-entered the field.

Meanwhile, psychoanalysis had undergone changes in its clinical theories that allowed for new perspectives on human sexuality. Object relations theory and self-psychology presented the beginning of theoretical and therapeutic views that held potential for inclusion, but the ascendance of intersubjective and relational approaches have been extremely important (represented by seminal writers such as George Atwood, Jessica Benjamin, Adrienne Harris, Stephen Mitchell, and Robert Stolorow).[3] These theories have led to the development of new views of humanity that are less focused on determining what is normative and to new therapy practices that resist attempts to make individuals fit prescribed developmental models. This change of understanding of the role of the therapist, the process of therapy and theory has been extraordinarily profound. Many of the authoritarian and pathologizing views (Gould, 1995) that falsely claimed objective scientific status (Lesser, 1995) have no place in these new theoretical viewpoints.

Credit must also be given to the new generation of leaders within psychoanalysis. For reasons perhaps as basic as the evolution of generations, those who are now in senior positions in many analytic institutions are part of a generation whose own life experiences have been influenced by the civil rights movement, the women's movement, and the LGBT liberation movement. These experiences have made them more open to challenging orthodoxy, more capable of creating theories that support new views of identity and sexuality, and more able to be welcoming of those who are different. Ultimately, we are in a period where there is a synergy for the development of new views of gender, sexuality, sexual orientation, and diversities within psychoanalysis.

However, many challenges remain. Progress within psychoanalysis remains uneven. There are still pockets of institutions that are not yet publicly inclusive in terms of sexual orientation. Venues for writing, studying, and training still need to increase and spread beyond the U.S. coasts. Women, in particular, may need support to write and take their place in leadership of institutes and organizations. A recent article in the *Journal of the American Psychoanalytic Association* (JAPA) entitled "Can We Be Both Women and Analysts?" (Wilkinson et al., 1996) discusses the challenges some women candidates still face in becoming analysts, particularly in this example given that the Topeka, Kansas, psychoanalytic institute had not had a woman training analyst for more than 20 years.

Psychoanalysis is still perceived in some parts of the feminist and LGBT communities as hostile, as the damage done to psychoanalysis's credibility by older theories is hard to undo and while a few vocal members of the profession still advocate anti-homosexual practices such as conversion therapy. Thus, a rapprochement between psychoanalysis and feminist and LGBT psychologies through organizational ties, advocacy, and scholarship is still necessary.

Further, ethnic, cultural, and class issues are still underrepresented in psychoanalytic writing, training, and practice. As Greene describes in this volume, issues of privilege still pose problems. Further self-criticism and self-analysis may be necessary to promote more diversity within training institutions and to refocus education so as to be a process of liberation (hooks, 1994), as well as to reexamine the impact of prejudice (Young-Bruehl, 1996). This would require a greater focus in psychoanalysis on the impact of social reality on individuals, particularly issues of power, difference, (in)justice, and (in)equality.

This underrepresentation of diversity and multicultural elements is particularly problematic as the omission of these issues continues to marginalize historically oppressed groups and reinforces stereotypes about elitism within psychoanalysis. Psychoanalysis united with postmodernism and social constructionism provides very powerful theories to understand reality, particularly social reality (Trask, 1987); however, this potential has yet to be fully realized. As psychoanalytic theory is still seen as an individual intervention, its application to social issues and concerns is often doubted. Further changes need to occur in training and practice, so that these areas of diversity are fully integrated into curriculum in psychoanalysis at all levels. It is our hope that even in undergraduate programs, as well as graduate and post-graduate programs, older views of psychoanalysis will become a tiny part of how psychoanalysis is defined and new theories will take their place as the key ideas.

Some clinicians struggle to reconcile the new integration of postmodern theory in psychoanalysis with clinical practice. The postmodern deconstruction of identity and subjectivity may appear to be in conflict with clinical concerns of identity development and self-cohesion (Flax, 1991, 1993; Layton, 1998). We believe that for LGBT people these issues are inseparable, sometimes problematically and sometimes not, as with all those who simultaneously hold memberships in multiple cultures. As Flax (1993, 1991) and we (Glassgold & Iasenza, 1995) previously described (Glassgold, 1995; Stack, 1995) social change, new and fluid models of gender and sexuality can be incorporated into psychotherapy. As Flax (1993) states: "Therapy can make more dimensions of subjectivity available to people. It can encourage the development of the aspects of subjectivity that evoke and enjoy multiplicity. People can develop more tolerance for and appreciation of differences, ambiguity, and ambivalence" (p. 107). These tasks could be seen as part of the strength of psychoanalysis: its rejection of predetermined goals and its embrace of psychic creativity, which inevitably respects an individual's agency in their own self-creation.

We need to be careful, however, that our love affair with postmodernism, which abolishes sex/gender categorization, does not cause us to neglect the particularities of women's sexual subjectivities, especially the continuing influences of sexism, homophobia, and misogyny in many women's lives. Postmodernism and decontructionist theories have been criticized for minimizing issues of power and political oppression (Alcoff, 1988) and de-emphasizing structural inequalities in society.

Some residual issues between heterosexual and lesbian feminists reminiscent of the "lavender menace" days of the 1970s feminist movement are evident in critiques of heterosexist assumptions in contemporary feminist psychoanalytic work (Decker, 1995; O'Connor &

Ryan, 1993; Schoenberg, 1995). These issues have yet to be adequately explored. Is it possible that conflation of feminism and lesbianism caused by societal sexism and homophobia make feminist analysts concerned about being seen as too pro-lesbian and lesbian analysts concerned about being seen as too separatist? How does that affect our work? Can we analysts create honest dialogues about how our own internalized sexism and homophobia operate in the consulting room as well as in our organizations? We need to establish means to discuss and understand these issues and find ways to encourage continuous change and development through new theory and practice that considers both feminism and lesbianism within psychoanalysis.

We conceive of this volume as a way to build on the initial progress of the 1990s as a second wave builds on the one preceding it. Now that lesbians have entered the psychoanalytic field, we now need to expand and deepen our self-examination and our own dialogues. For this volume, we have welcomed those who wish to write and tried to create a more supportive venue than traditional journals. We have tried to present a variety of works that address both new areas and traditional ones by writers who represent a diversity of backgrounds (psychiatry, psychology, and social work), analytic training (formal institute training, study groups, and supervision), and theoretical perspectives (self-psychology, object relations, relational psychoanalysis, feminist theory, queer theory, postmodernism, and Lacanian theory). The one commonality among authors is their belief in the potential healing power of psychoanalytically-informed theory and practice.

This volume includes three sections: Community: Personal and Political, Ongoing Clinical Issues, and New Thinking on Sexuality and Gender. Stressing the importance of documenting our history and the creation of community, Iasenza focuses on training by recognizing the work of lesbian psychoanalytic foremothers, Joanne Spina, Lee Crespi and Judy Levitz, who created safe analytic training environments for the next generation of lesbian (bisexual and gay) analysts by creating LGBT inclusive analytic training programs. Gair illustrates how new conceptualizations of psychoanalytic theory can provide understanding about the role of social factors in intrapsychic development. In an ongoing attempt to consider ethnic and cultural diversity, Greene writes on entrenched problems within psychodynamic theories relating to privilege and diversity, and the limitations and usefulness of psychodynamic therapies for African American lesbians and other culturally diverse people. Decker writes about the impact of Stephen Mitchell's (one of the founders of relational psychoanalysis) early papers on homosexuality on personal and professional development. Bjork further expands our understanding of the therapeutic dyad by examining the clinical impact of a therapist's own experiences with social and cultural influences over the past forty years. Illustrating the utility of psychoanalysis for social problems, Neilson, an expert in domestic violence, describes how psychoanalytic theory can enrich the treatment of volatile relationships between lesbians. Igartua and Des Rosiers discuss transference and countertransference issues with lesbian patients by heterosexual and lesbian woman analysts. Coining a new term "evolutionary butch," Zevy writes about therapy, gender, and the developmental experiences of tomboys who become lesbians. Kassoff discusses how queer theory and relational psychoanalysis have influenced each other and bring new insights into gender and sexuality. Filling a need for debate within the queer theory field, Roth, presents a critique of one of Butler's concepts, the lesbian phallus. Finally, Kiersky offers some new ideas on gender as it is interwoven with identity and desire. We hope this volume creates new dialogues and ways of conceptualizing these above issues, thereby deepening the therapeutic endeavor.

NOTES

1. For instance, the following, amongst others, have nondiscrimination policies that are LGB inclusive: Institute for Contemporary Psychotherapy, New York University Postdoctoral Program in Psychotherapy and Psychoanalysis, San Francisco Psychoanalytic Institute, American Psychoanalytic Association; William Alanson White Institute; National Institute for Psychotherapies; National Psychological Association for Psychoanalysis.

2. Institute for Contemporary Psychotherapy, Psychoanalytic Psychotherapy Study Center, New York University Post Doctoral Program in Psychotherapy & Psychoanalysis, San Francisco Psychoanalytic Institute, William Allison White Institute, Institute for the Psychoanalytic Study of Subjectivity, to name a few.

3. These authors are only some of many, whose work can be found in progressive journals and at many of the newer psychoanalytic institutes. One journal in particular is relevant for this volume, *Studies of Gender and Sexuality*.

REFERENCES

Alcoff, L. (1988). Cultural feminism versus post-structuralism: The identity crisis in feminist theory. *Signs, 13*(3), 405-436.

American Psychoanalytic Association, Committee on Gay & Lesbian Concerns (1991). Position statement on homosexuality. Retrieved December 14, 2002, from <http://www.apsa-co.org/ctf/cgli/position.htm>.

American Psychoanalytic Association, Committee on Gay & Lesbian Concerns (2000). Position statement on reparative therapy. Retrieved December 14, 2002, from <http://www.apsa-co.org/ctf/cgli/reparative_therapy.htm>.

Burch, B. (1997). *Other women: Lesbians/Bisexual experience and psychoanalytic view of women and other women.* New York: Columbia University Press.

Butler, J. (1990). *Gender trouble: Feminism and the subversion of identity.* New York: Routledge.

Chodorow, N. (1978). *The reproduction of mothering: Psychoanalysis and the sociology of gender.* Berkeley: University of California Press.

Chodorow, N. (1994). *Femininities, masculinities, sexualities: Freud and beyond.* Lexington: University of Kentucky Press.

De Lauretis, T. (1994). *The practice of love: Lesbian sexuality and perverse desire.* Bloomington: Indiana Univ. Press.

Decker, B. (1995). How to have your phallus and be it too: Reflections of a Lesbian therapist from Jill Johnston to Judith Butler. In J.M. Glassgold & S. Iasenza (Eds.), *Lesbians and psychoanalysis: Revolutions in theory and practice* (pp. 63-89). New York: Free Press.

Deutsch, H. (1948). On female homosexuality. In R. Fleiss (Ed.), The psychoanalytic reader (pp. 208-230). New York: International Universities Press. (Original work published 1932).

Dinnerstein, D. (1976). *The mermaid and the minotaur: Sexual arrangements and human malaise.* New York: Harper & Row.

Division of Psychoanalysis, 39, of the American Psychological Association (2002). *Psychologist-Psychoanalyst,* 22(3), Summer 2002.

Dominici, T. & Lesser, R. C. (1995). *Disorienting sexuality: Psychoanalytic reappraisals of sexual identities.* New York: Routledge.

Drescher, J. (1995). Anti-homosexual bias in training. In T. Dominici & R. C. Lesser (Eds.), *Disorienting sexuality: Psychoanalytic reappraisals of sexual identities* (pp. 227-242). New York: Routledge.

Eisenbud, R-J. (1969). Female homosexuality: A sweet enfranchisement. In G.D. Goldman & D.S. Milman (Eds.), *The modern woman.* Springfield, IL: Charles C. Thomas.

Eisenbud, R-J. (1982). Early and later determinants of lesbian choice. *Psychoanalytic Review, 69,* 85-109.

Flax, J. (1991). *Thinking fragments: Psychoanalysis, feminism, postmodernism in the contemporary west.* Berkeley: University of California.

Flax, J. (1993). *Disputed subjects: Essays on psychoanalysis, politics and philosophy.* New York: Routledge.

Foucault, M. (1980). *The history of sexuality. Vol. 1: An introduction.* (R. Hurley, Trans.) New York: Random House.

Freud, S. (1961). Psychogenesis of a case of female homosexuality. In J. Strachey (Ed. & Trans.), *The standard edition of the complete psychological works of Sigmund Freud* (Vol. 28, pp. 145-174). London: Hogarth Press. (Original work published 1920).

Glassgold, J. M. (1995). Psychoanalysis with lesbians: Self-reflection and agency. In J. M. Glassgold & S. Iasenza (Eds.), *Lesbians and psychoanalysis: Revolutions in theory and practice* (pp. 203-227). New York: Free Press.

Glassgold, J. M. & Iasenza, S. (Eds.). (1995). *Lesbians and psychoanalysis: Revolutions in theory and practice*. New York: Free Press.

Goldman, S. B. (1995). The difficulty of being a gay psychoanalyst during the last fifty years. In T. Dominici & R. C. Lesser (Eds.), *Disorienting sexuality: Psychoanalytic reappraisals of sexual identities* (pp. 243-254). New York: Routledge.

Gould, D. (1995). A critical examination of the notion of pathology in psychoanalysis. In J. M. Glassgold & S. Iasenza (Eds.), *Lesbians and psychoanalysis: Revolutions in theory and practice* (pp. 3-18). New York: Free Press.

Gould, E. & Kiersky, S. (2001). *Sexualities lost and found: Lesbians, psychoanalysis, and culture*. Madison, CT: International Universities Press.

hooks, b. (1994). *Teaching to transgress: Education as the practice of freedom*. New York: Routledge.

Irigaray, L. (1985). *This sex which is not one* (C. Porter with C. Burke, Trans.). Ithaca, NY: Cornell University Press. (Original work published 1977).

Layton, L. (1998). *Who's that girl? Who's that boy? Clinical practice meets postmodernism gender theory*. Northvale, NJ: Jason Aronson.

Lesser, R. C. (1995). Objectivity as masquerade. In T. Dominici & R. C. Lesser (Eds.), *Disorienting sexuality: Psychoanalytic reappraisals of sexual identities* (pp. 83-96). New York: Routledge.

Magee, M. & Miller, D. C. (1997). *Lesbian lives: Psychoanalytic narratives old and new*. Hillsdale, NJ: Analytic Press.

Martin, A. (1995). A view from both sides: Coming out as a lesbian psychoanalyst. In T. Dominici & R. C. Lesser (Eds.), *Disorienting sexuality: Psychoanalytic reappraisals of sexual identities* (pp. 255-264). New York: Routledge.

McDougall, J. (1970). Homosexuality in women. In J. Chasseguet-Smirgel (Ed.), *Female sexuality*. Ann Arbor, MI: University of Michigan Press. (Original work published 1964).

McDougall, J. (1980). *A plea for a measure of abnormality*. New York: International Universities Press.

Mitchell, J. & Rose, J. (Ed.). (1982). *Feminine sexuality: Jacques Lacan and the ecole freudienne* (J. Rose, Trans.). New York: Norton.

O'Connor, N. & Ryan, J. (1993). *Wild desires and mistaken identities: Lesbianism and psychoanalysis*. New York: Columbia University Press.

Schoenberg, E. (1995). Psychoanalytic theories of lesbian desire: A social constructionist critique. In T. Dominici & R. C. Lesser (Eds.), *Disorienting sexuality: Psychoanalytic reappraisals of sexual identities* (pp. 203-226). New York: Routledge.

Schwartz, A. E. (1998). *Sexual subjects: Lesbians, gender, and psychoanalysis*. New York: Routledge.

Siegel, E. (1988). *Female homosexuality: Choice without volition*. Hillsdale, NJ: Analytic Press.

Socarides, C. (1968). *The overt homosexual*. New York: Grune & Stratton.

Stack, C. (1995). The lesbian patient: Narratives of subjectivity, gender, and sexual identity. In J.M. Glassgold & S. Iasenza (Eds.), *Lesbians and psychoanalysis: Revolutions in theory and practice* (pp. 327-344).

Trask, C. (1987). *Feminist practice and poststructuralist theory*. New York: Basil Blackwell.

Wilkinson, S., Peebles-Kleiger, M.J., Buchele, B., Bartlett, A., Nathan, S., Benalcazar-Schmid, R., Mintzer, M., & Everhart, D. (1996). Can we be both women and analysts? *Journal of the American Psychoanalytic Association, 44*/Supplement, 529-555.

Young-Bruehl, E. (1996). *The anatomy of prejudices.* Cambridge, MA: Harvard University Press.

COMMUNITY AND HISTORY: PERSONAL AND POLITICAL

Lesbian Psychoanalytic Foremothers Making Waves: Interviews with Joanne Spina, Lee Crespi and Judy Levitz

Suzanne Iasenza

SUMMARY. The progress lesbians have made within psychoanalysis is in its infancy since the first wave of gay/lesbian affirmative literature be-

Suzanne Iasenza, PhD, is Associate Professor of Counseling at John Jay College-City University of New York. She is on the faculties of the Institute for Contemporary Psychotherapy and the Institute for Human Identity. She maintains a private practice in psychotherapy and sex therapy in New York City.

Address correspondence to: Suzanne Iasenza, PhD, 26 West 90th St. #1, New York, NY 10024 (E-mail: siasenza@aol.com).

[Haworth co-indexing entry note]: "Lesbian Psychoanalytic Foremothers Making Waves: Interviews with Joanne Spina, Lee Crespi and Judy Levitz." Iasenza, Suzanne. Co-published simultaneously in *Journal of Lesbian Studies* (Harrington Park Press, an imprint of The Haworth Press, Inc.) Vol. 8, No. 1/2, 2004, pp. 11-43; and: *Lesbians, Feminism, and Psychoanalysis: The Second Wave* (ed: Judith M. Glassgold, and Suzanne Iasenza) Harrington Park Press, an imprint of The Haworth Press, Inc., 2004, pp. 11-43. Single or multiple copies of this article are available for a fee from The Haworth Document Delivery Service [1-800-HAWORTH, 9:00 a.m. - 5:00 p.m. (EST). E-mail address: docdelivery@haworthpress.com].

Digital Object Identifier: 10.1300/J155v08n01_02

11

gan to surface in the early 1990s. The author stresses the need to document the history of the development of this long overdue movement. Three lesbian psychoanalytic foremothers are interviewed who offer glimpses into the psychoanalytic community from the early 1970s to the present giving us a deeper understanding of courageous acts that helped create gay and lesbian affirmative space within psychoanalysis. *[Article copies available for a fee from The Haworth Document Delivery Service: 1-800-HAWORTH. E-mail address: <docdelivery@haworthpress.com> Website: <http://www.HaworthPress.com> © 2004 by The Haworth Press, Inc. All rights reserved.]*

KEYWORDS. Lesbian foremother, psychoanalytic training, gay/lesbian affirmative psychoanalysis

INTRODUCTION

On the occasion of the recent death of Harry Hay, Richard Goldstein wrote an Op-Ed article in the *New York Times* (10/30/02) advocating the need to document gay history, not just for members of the gay community, but for all of our citizens. Educating our children about gay history, he asserts, is the single most powerful tool with which to combat homophobia. It is a compelling argument.

Hays was "the first American to imagine a gay community." In the spirit of not letting our history remain invisible, I embarked on this interview project to begin documenting stories of how the first wave of lesbian affirmative psychoanalytic work came into being.

All three of these lesbian psychoanalytic foremothers, like Hays, were some of the first American lesbians to imagine a gay and lesbian affirmative psychoanalytic community. They set their minds, talents, and energies to creating safe psychoanalytic spaces on both interpersonal and institutional levels.

Joanne Spina

Joanne Spina is a graduate of Hunter School of Social Work and the Institute for Contemporary Psychotherapy (ICP). She cofounded GALA (Gay and Lesbian Analysts) for which she served as Chair for 10 years and GLAP (Gay and Lesbian Affirmative Psychotherapy) division of ICP. She is a recipient of a GALA distinguished contribution award. She was member of the Board of Directors of ICP for 15 years and presently is a faculty member and supervisor. Joanne maintains a private practice in NYC.

S–Tell me how you got interested in psychoanalysis in the first place.

J–This is a hard question.

S–Why?

J–Why, because I got into psychoanalysis as probably most people do, as a patient.

S–Not knowing that you were going to practice it.

J–I was involved in a lot of community work. Most of the community organization and outreach work I was doing was about taking care of others. I was working with drug addiction and community building. I found my work very gratifying. My first job was in Puerto Rico and then for the Lower East Side Service Center where I worked with a drug-addicted population. After that, I went to Hunter School of Social Work and after I graduated, I worked on the Lower East Side for many years in a city hospital. My life felt turbulent. There were a lot of things I was going through emotionally. I gravitated to therapy and in the process found that it was something that I would like to do myself. I continued working while I attended analytic training.

S–Did your therapist suggest that you go for analytic training?

J–No. I think the reason I chose analytic training was because a friend of mine who was in graduate school with me had a very dear friend who was starting an institute, which was the Institute for Contemporary Psychotherapy. I was one of the first patients at that institute in 1971. I was also in a woman's group that was connected to the Institute and Hunter College. So I began to know about the Institute, and I was encouraged to train there.

S–So you were there as a patient around 1971, when did you start training?

J–1973. One year after I graduated from social work school.

S–And two years after you started your own therapy. That was pretty quick.

J–Yes. I was older, in my early thirties, and I appeared to be competent and unflappable, as they say, but internally it was another story. I also started to come out, which was a whole other process.

S–At that time, most training institutes would not accept people who were out. In 1973, did you apply as an out lesbian?

J–No. I wasn't quite out myself. It was the end of 1973 or in 1974 when I lived with someone for the first time. I switched analysts to somebody who was a bit Freudian and a bit homophobic. Her office was on Christopher Street and Oscar Wilde bookstore was down the block. I would go for my sessions with her and then I would go to Oscar Wilde to shore up my own identity and calm myself about what I was doing in therapy.

S–So, why wouldn't that have turned you off about doing analytic training, if you were having a therapy experience with an analyst who was a bit homophobic?

J–I think there is such value in psychotherapy. I was in such desperate need. There were many things going on besides my sexuality that I needed to work on and the work itself was terrifying but challenging. I don't think it occurred to me not to be in analytic training.

S–That is interesting because that is what some lesbian therapists say about why they stuck with analytic training or theory even with all the homophobic parts, that the process of psychoanalytic work is compelling. They feel that other forms of training are not as deep, not as involving . . . exploring the unconscious, dream analysis and other ways we examine issues in psychoanalysis. Some people just don't want to throw out the baby with the bathwater.

J–My institute was an eclectic institute–it wasn't just Freudian, but certainly in those years being a lesbian was not a good thing.

S–So, in 1973 if you applied for admission as an out lesbian you probably would not have been accepted.

J–Probably not. But I came out right before I graduated. I started to come out to the people in my class and the head of the institute.

S–That was in 1974-75?

J–Yes–I graduated in 1976. So between '75 and '76.

S–How was that received?

J–Very lovingly I would say when I think of Mildred Schwartz [the director of the institute at the time] and with great shock. I had started to drop out of social events and people thought I was seeing either a black man or a divorced person. It never occurred to any of them that it would be a woman in those days. Now I think we are a little more sophisticated. Around that time we started an Institute Society. One of the things about me is that whenever I get involved in professional activities I get into a leadership role. I was quite involved in the Society when I met a woman who was a staff member at ICP who I thought might be a lesbian.

S–Was she trained at ICP?

J–No, she was not. I am not sure how I figured out that she was a lesbian, but in conversation we used the general pronoun for our partners and finally got around to asking each other. I think we were the first two people who were out at ICP.

S–Who was she?

J–April Martin.

S–What about Lee Crespi? You had mentioned to me about her impact on you.

J–Yes, once I was established at the institute by '78 I began to get involved in different committees at ICP, one of which was the intake committee. Involvement in that committee was important because as gay patients came for intakes having a gay person sitting on the intake committee softened some of the remarks that were made. I also directed patients to therapists who I thought would be gay friendly. I had access to candidate records probably from being on the training committee. I would sometimes screen the records to see who might be a gay or lesbian person coming in and I would approach them, sometimes gently, sometimes not so gently, and ask them if they were gay or lesbian. Of course, I would tell them right away that I was. So we developed a gay affirmative reputation. Lee Crespi was one of the people who came to ICP who was out early on. There were others, Vivian Roll and Susan Gair. Marty Frommer was another.

S–What year was that?

J–It was probably the late '70s. Some were more out than others, but Lee was someone who seemed very comfortable being out. I remember overhearing her talk on the phone to her partner one day. There she was in the receptionist's office out in the open where therapists were walking in and out and she was clearly talking with her partner, Judy, and was very natural and open about it. She was an important role model for me. She was outgoing and well-rounded.

S–Do you think she was out as she was going though the application process?

J–Possibly.

S–At that point people could be out and be accepted?

J–Possibly. It was becoming much more acceptable. In fact, at ICP the important factor was how well you could develop a relationship. It was a relational institute even back then before Relational Psychoanalysis became a movement. You would score more points if you had an established relationship, whatever the gender of your partner, then if you didn't.

S–So, it was the quality of the relationship not necessarily the gender of the partner.

J–Absolutely.

S–That was progressive at the time.

J–It was very progressive.

S–There were other people–Bev Decker for one–who when I shared with her some of the ICP stories, she actually wondered why she didn't go to ICP. She went to another institute where she had to stay in the closet even in the early '80s. But she didn't know how lesbian affirmative ICP was at the time. ICP did not advertise to the gay community that they were happy to take gay and lesbian candidates?

J–I don't think at that time anyone even thought about advertising to the gay and lesbian community. But gays and lesbians gravitated to institutes where they felt there was some basis for connection. I wouldn't say that the content of the courses was always so gay or lesbian friendly. You can't change everybody and certainly Freudian theory was problematic. There was always that developmental question about whether you were good enough or adequate or whether homosexuality was regressive. But in terms of feeling supported by the heads of the institute and by the student candidate body, for the most part, there was a group of us that created an atmosphere of acceptance.

S–It sounds like you were one of the first.

J–I was the first.

S–You may have been the first openly gay candidate to graduate and the first openly gay staff and board member at an analytic institute in New York City. You helped to create a context for ICP to be in the forefront of gay affirmative analytic work.

J–You are probably right.

S–As other gay and lesbian people came in, you were pretty friendly and open.

J–I made it a point to ensure that people experienced an accepting atmosphere by knowing that I was there. As the gay group became stronger and people felt safer, they began to challenge some of the rhetoric in the classes.

S–You were truly a grassroots activist in two ways . . . you came out very early on and you would not let a homophobic comment pass. You challenged the canon in class.

J–Yes, I'm probably one of the least tolerant people when it comes to prejudice or homophobia.

S–Was it the '80s by the time a core gay group was present at ICP?

J–I believe so. It's hard to believe that in 30 years, we have gone from one lesbian candidate to a whole program called GLAP–Gay and Lesbian Affirmative Psychotherapy. We now have over 90 patients, including couples.

S–How many staff members?

J–15-20 active therapists who are in supervision groups discussing gay and lesbian issues. We have approximately two to four seminars per academic year on these issues as well as the summer sexuality course given by you. We have several grants that enable us to offer low-cost therapy starting at $20 as needed.

S–Any guess why ICP of all places was so open and accepting to you and the new gay and lesbian candidates. In other institutes you would have been repressed or threatened once you started coming out.

J–The founders of ICP, Mildred Schwartz and Fred Lipshitz particularly, were very far-sighted and accepting, and had a wonderful philosophy. Some of the gay and lesbian candidates were very intelligent, articulate, and community minded. They contributed a lot to the growth of ICP, both academically and in spirit. They gave to the Society, became teachers and supervisors. They were quite visible. They became a strong part of ICP and were respected members of the community.

S–So out gays and lesbians were involved at every level of the institute.

J–Yes.

S–Besides the fact that you and a few candidates began to come out, what else happened early on that created such an accepting community?

J–There was openness among the analytic candidates in general about wanting to know more about gay and lesbian issues. The Society of ICP gave weekend workshops and invited several of us to present a workshop on Gay and Lesbian Issues.

S–That was the first gay oriented program given at the Institute?

J–I believe it was, on that big a scale. It wasn't the first because we had Hetrick and Martin come to give a lecture on gay male issues in the late '70s or early '80s. We also had a workshop on AIDS. We had an AIDS division in the early '80s. Our workshop was later–in the late '80s. It was a whole weekend. It was out of that weekend that Marty Frommer, Susan Gair, others and I decided to find out what was going on at other institutes. We set up a general meeting at my home and out of that developed the Gay and Lesbian Analysts Group (GALA). We just had our 10th anniversary. So our small gay and lesbian group at ICP has always been a strong part of ICP and a force within the greater analytic community.

S–It seems like your LGBT program developed out of the cumulative impact of the earlier events. The Henrick and Martin lecture was the first time you had someone outside the institute come in to do something on gay issues. It sounds like another influential factor was the AIDS crisis. This is a common story. The AIDS crisis was so devastating and challenging on many levels, medically and psychologically, that people had to start dealing more with homosexuality since gay men were so deeply affected.

J–We set out not only to treat AIDS patients but also to train institute members about AIDS. We had an enormous turnout for that program. We had to rent a hall. It was an all day affair. We had experts from GMHC and Bellevue. They were fabulous teachers about the illness itself and about the psychological complications.

S–Did they talk about homophobia and the gay population in particular?

J–I believe they did. I think we had two whole day workshops and then we had a follow up one later on. Afterward, we ran a couple of supervision groups for people who were interested in treating the AIDS population.

S–The institute was quite in the forefront–if you are talking about the early '80s–that was right at the beginning of the AIDS crisis. How was the reception for Hetrick and Martin?

J–Packed and I cannot remember how we decided to do that. I remember I was the one who got them, but it was through the Society.

S–They talked mostly about gay men. They did not talk about lesbians, did they?

J–No, they didn't.

S–I assume that when you presented the first gay issues weekend workshop you and Susan [Gair] made sure that lesbian issues were represented.

J–My paper primarily focused on Freud's case where a young woman falls in love with an older woman and Freud describes her as an independent thinker, having a mind of her own. I also focused on the idea that gay and lesbian therapists should be out to their patients.

S–That was probably controversial.

J–It was very controversial. I am not saying that people shouldn't explore the meanings involved, but if a gay or lesbian patient comes to you and wants to know your sexuality, they have every right to know your sexual orientation. Every gay and lesbian person should have the right to see a gay or lesbian therapist if they want.

S–Did they give you a hard time when you said that?

J–I get a hard time every time I say it now but I make it a rule that you can't be a GLAP therapist unless you are willing to be out whether you are straight or gay.

S–Sounds as if the workshop you gave was groundbreaking also because of the deeper clinical issues you raised.

J–Yes. The other groundbreaking event, which you reminded me of, was the O'Connor and Ryan lecture. It was co-sponsored by ICP and GALA.

S–What year was that?

J–It was the early '90s. Why was it so groundbreaking for you?

S–When I was coming out as a lesbian in the early '80s I was subjected to graduate education and analytic writing that was either anti-homosexual or just plain silent on the topic. I was starving for lesbian analytic role-models. I was suffering from the McDougall-Siegel syndrome, I'll call it, trying to reconcile horribly pejorative analytic writing about lesbians while at the same time struggling with my own internalized homophobia in therapy. My only life preserver at the time was Martha Kirkpatrick's 1984 paper on lesbian mothers in which she questioned the pathologizing of lesbians as regressed or fixated at infantile levels of development. I read and reread her paper for comfort throughout the '80s. O'Connor and Ryan's work was the first book that was clearly lesbian affirmative and challenged the canon. It was monumental. Remember, Joanne, you grew up in the ICP community much of which was remarkably tolerant and supportive of gay and lesbian issues. By the time O'Connor and Ryan came in the early '90s you were already out for almost 20 years at the Institute, you helped train numerous gay and lesbian candidates, and you had already had your earlier workshop experiences. You were spoiled by being in a very precious and unique analytic institute environment compared to others of us who had different training experiences.

J–You are right. Nevertheless, I was thrilled with their book because up to that point there wasn't one that spoke to lesbian women in such a comprehensive way.

S–What was missing from your introduction of them, their presentation, and from the discussion afterwards, was what a groundbreaking experience it was. No one mentioned the historical significance of that event. And no one mentioned that they were lesbian women. Do you remember that?

J–No, I don't.

S–You didn't discuss what it meant to have lesbian analysts write such a book or to have such an event sponsored by a mainstream psychoanalytic institute. They didn't discuss how it was for them, as lesbian analysts or therapists, to write it, and nobody in the audience, including myself, said how it felt as lesbian analysts or therapists to receive such a book.

J–I think partly it was because they had a very difficult time in England with the book and who they were. If we think we have a hard time in the U.S., they have a harder time in England. I remember their talking about that. So I don't think it was quite natural for them to get up and say "as lesbian analysts." I think I just assumed people would know they were lesbians since they wrote such a lesbian affirmative book. Do you think that it would have been important for them to have said so?

S–Well, yes. At that time for the term "lesbian analyst" to be uttered in a public forum at that point in history would have been ground-breaking. That was before any lesbian affirmative books existed. I say this as someone who was not at ICP. For you, you were already experiencing a revolution happening while from my viewpoint I considered that lecture major because it was the first time lesbian affirmation and psychoanalysis were together in the same time and place.

J–In some ways ICP created a false cocoon. Not that every course was on target, they weren't. And gay and lesbian candidates struggled with some instructors about their insensitivity, but the atmosphere in general was accepting. I wasn't as aware of what was happening elsewhere.

S–This goes to show how theory lags behind practice. You were out in an analytic institute 20 years before the first lesbian affirmative book on psychoanalytic theory came out. You could be a member of the board of an institute where McDougall and Socarides' work was still being taught.

J–And for all of the acceptance you still wonder and think about how many patients you don't get, how many supervisees don't come to you.

S–Those are versions of subtle homophobia. There can be such a mixture of experiences.

J–You reminded me when you said about the Institute–when I graduated in 1976, my partner at the time and I came to the graduation as an openly lesbian couple. It was only the second graduation there and we danced together. It was a wonderful experience.

S–How did people react?

J–My analyst at the time was there and I introduced her to my partner. It was fine. I remember it being a joyful experience. Your face looks shocked.

S–I remember attending a graduation in the early '80s–we will not name the institute. There was no way at that institute that anything remotely similar could have happened. There were 3 or 4 gay people who knew each other–nobody was out. It was the only way they could get through that institute. So look at the difference. At about the same time in history, two entirely different experiences were going on at analytic institutes in the same city.

J–I know from my GALA involvement that people have such different experiences with coming out. You can't assume that anyone is safe.

S–Even now?

J–Yes, there still is a lot of homophobia around. And although I think things are changing a lot still is hard. Homophobia now is more subtle. For example, one of my supervisees was talking about a case where a male patient was sleeping with both men and women. I brought up that he could be bisexual. But I could see how some therapists privilege heterosexuality. My fear is that if a patient experiences any heterosexual feelings, some straight analysts would secretly feel that it would be better if the patient were heterosexual, that it would make life easier.

S–Let's talk a little bit more about the GLAP program. Once you, Frommer and Gair gave that workshop–was that the beginning of GLAP?

J–No, but GALA formed. And it gave all of us a feeling of being validated and having a community. It was extremely nourishing to have regular meetings. We had discussion groups, supervision groups, and reading groups. We started a networking brunch. All of it empowered me personally to be even more comfortable in my role as a lesbian analyst. The development of GALA coincided with some shifts in gay and lesbian foundation donors. We applied for a grant to start a gay and lesbian affirmative treatment service (GLAP) at ICP through the New York Community Trust and were awarded a grant.

S–The year was . . .

J–1996-97. That was when we applied and it started in '98. We were awarded a $300,000 grant–$100,000 each year.

S–That must've given you credibility at the Institute.

J–Absolutely. That particular grant made us all even more focused because we had to decide what type of division we wanted, how we wanted to influence the Institute. We felt it was important for it to be institute wide. So we worked toward educating from the top down and bottom up. We met with all of the heads of every division once a month and discussed readings. We also had an umbrella committee–we wanted every division involved–the 2- and 4-year psychotherapy and analytic programs, adult treatment, eating disorders, family and couples, children's, group, and so on.

S–How was your effort received?

J–Excellently. Every division sent somebody. The meetings were very heated. At the readings people were very open. We would sometimes go home pulling our hair out at some of the things people said. Nevertheless, they were saying them and we were able to make a big difference. Along with that we started supervision groups and we started advertising for low-cost therapy. We practically doubled our treatment population.

S–That is incredible. In 30 years you went from being a lesbian patient, to being a candidate, then a staff member, to Director of a whole division.

J–Right.

S–One last question, Joanne. What do you think really has changed as it relates to lesbians and psychoanalysis?

J–I think that many lesbians in my practice do not come in questioning their sexuality as much. Not that people don't have some internalized homophobia and maybe it is more subtle but people are more proud of being who they are. That is one major change. People are not sneaking around. They are out about who they are in the psychotherapy context and at psychoanalytic institutes.

S–What do you think hasn't changed?

J–What I don't think has changed is that women still are not strong enough. I come from a Catholic background and I can see that men are so dominant even now. So many more gay men speak out. Lesbians need to have more of a voice within psychoanalysis.

S–This is really an important point because one of the things I am asking people as I talk to them is a set of questions. I ask them, "Can an open lesbian be an analyst, a supervising analyst, or a training analyst?" Most say yes, absolutely. Then I ask them, "Can a lesbian feminist be an analyst?" It is an interesting question because the term "lesbian feminist" is not embraced by most lesbian analysts in the literature. And this is not because they don't consider themselves feminists but they don't use that term. I think that partially reflects how feminism has changed over the years and how central we feel it is to what we do. When you say women need to have a greater voice or how do we get a greater voice–it is very often through feminist ideas or experiences–safety in numbers, power in numbers, feeling comfortable with power and taking it, not letting men take over. You are talking about the way we present ourselves.

J–I know that at ICP over the years people seemed to like me and accept me. I had no idea what people really thought of me.

S–Regardless of what they really thought of you, they didn't prevent you from doing what you needed to do there. The biggest challenge now is giving candidates the tools, the therapeutic and theoretical tools to be able to view the homosexual experience as nonjudgmentally as possible. Everybody has internalized homophobia. I think what is different now is that we have texts that teach new theories on gender and sexuality. Candidates at ICP now get a kind of training that folks in the '70s and '80s did not get.

J–Right.

S–Beyond a GLAP program, gay issues need to be integrated across institutes and within curricula everywhere.

J–Yes. Even major conferences now present about gays and lesbians in ways that don't focus on homosexuality as pathology. We are truly making progress.

S–Are you aware that people see you as key to making that progress happen? If people like you weren't in the trenches coming out and creating safe spaces for gay and lesbian analysts and patients, we wouldn't be where we are now. You are a lesbian analytic foremother. Is that an unusual way for you to think about yourself?

J–Absolutely.

S–Why?

J–Because I just perceive myself as rolling along doing what I have to do. I have gotten wonderful feedback from gay people about how ICP and GALA are a comfort. But it is a mutual feeding of each other, a way that helps everyone feel better and become stronger in their own voices.

* * *

Lee Crespi and Judy Levitz

Lee Crespi is a graduate of Stony Brook School of Social Welfare and The Institute for Contemporary Psychotherapy. She is an Executive Committee Member, teacher and supervisor at the Psychoanalytic Psychotherapy Study Center. She is the author of a number of articles, including "Countertransference love" (*Contemporary Psychotherapy Review*, 1986, Vol. 3), "Some thoughts on the role of mourning in the development of a positive lesbian identity" (in T. Domenici & R. Lesser [Eds.], 1995, *Disorienting sexuality*, NY: Routledge), "From baby boom to gayby boom: Twenty-five years of psychoanalysis in the lesbian community" (in E. Gould & S. Kiersky [Eds.], 2001, *Sexualities lost and found*, Madison: IUP), and "And baby makes three: A dynamic look at development and conflict in lesbian families" (in D. Glazer and J. Drescher [Eds.], 2001, *Gay and lesbian parenting*, NY: Haworth Press. She is in private practice in New York City.

Judy Levitz is a graduate of NYU, the Philadelphia School of Psychoanalysis and a member of the National Association for the Advancement of Psychoanalysis. She is the Founding Director of the Psychoanalytic Psychotherapy Study Center and serves on its Board of Directors as well as its Executive Committee. She is the recipient of the 2001 GALA award for distinguished contribution to the Gay and Lesbian Psychoanalytic Community. She maintains a private practice in NYC.

S–I'm thinking about what analytic training programs created space early on for gays and lesbians when most doors were closed and one place was ICP [Institute for Contemporary Psychotherapy].

L & J–Right.

S–And now they have a gay and lesbian psychotherapy program there.

L & J–That's right.

S–I interviewed Joanne Spina to give me the early history of ICP since she's been affiliated with them for almost 30 years and she was the first openly lesbian person at ICP.

L–I think she may have been. She and April Martin was one of the first, too.

S–Yes.

L–Martin Frommer was I think the first gay man and then I came in after him.

S–What year did you enter ICP, Lee?

L–I entered in '79.

S–Was Joanne already on the faculty when you entered ICP?

L–She was a faculty in training. She was co-teaching with Mildred Schwartz, who was the Director. She co-taught a first-year class.

S–When you came into the program did you know Joanne was gay?

L–Not immediately but I found out within the first year. There was another lesbian in my class who I met on the first day of orientation.

S–Another person in your class?

L–Yes, Vivian Roll. I don't know if that name means anything to you. I am sad to say she died in a car accident shortly after we graduated.

S–Oh.

L–So I was delighted when I got there to find that I was not alone in the class–that was a great feeling and we discovered the first day that not only were we both lesbians, we had the same therapist.

S–Who was that?

L–Jean Millar, who is also now deceased.

S–Yes.

L–She was also a foremother.

S–Why?

L–Because a lot of people went into treatment with her because she was one of the few analytically trained lesbians around at that time. I learned that Joanne was an out lesbian analyst within my first year at ICP. In fact, at my graduation in 1983, she danced with you. Right? (Speaking to Judy).

J–Yes.

S–Who danced with whom?

L–Joanne danced with Judy. Slow dance, I think.

S–It was a slow dance?

J–It was a slow dance or fast dance, I don't remember now. But that was probably for me one of the first experiences of being out in a psychoanalytic community because it was at that graduation where Joanne made a statement by coming over, pulling me out of my chair and dancing with me.

L–That's right–with all of the other couples on the dance floor.

J–We were in a restaurant, the waiters were looking and smiling and, of course, at first I thought they were looking and laughing, but afterwards I realized they were enjoying it and were probably gay themselves.

S–Did Joanne come out wherever she was?

L–She didn't make a big thing of it in general. We knew she was a lesbian. We were all out at that point at ICP.

S–That was remarkable, wasn't it?

L–Yes, but that was '83. Early on, in 1979, things were more uncertain. For example, I was nervous when I first went for my interview. I had never made a secret of my sexual orientation, but at the same time I was concerned about whether I would be accepted into a psychoanalytic training program if I were out. I really debated whether to come out in the interview and as it turned out it never really came up. Nobody asked me anything specifically about my personal life, so I didn't bring it up. I just thought, "Well, I don't have to volunteer it unless I'm asked." But I came out right away once I was in the program. I told my supervisor early on because I work with many lesbians so I talked in supervision about being a lesbian.

S–How did your supervisor react?

L–She didn't seem bothered, at least as far as I could tell. She also interestingly supervised Vivian [Roll]. Vivian was more vocal than I was. Vivian was the one in class who spoke up. Vivian challenged anything that offended, including Freudian theory. I was still getting my bearings. I was quietly feeling my way in class but continually coming out outside of class to fellow candidates, supervisors and faculty. It was my way of educating others–of making a difference by coming out–by being who I was.

S–Did Vivian challenge homophobic comments directly?

L–No one ever said anything overtly homophobic. It was a liberal atmosphere. That's not to say that there weren't people who had negative thoughts or feelings about it but it was never made an open issue. The reading material sometimes was homophobic. There was one teacher who taught in our first year. She was a Freudian, she was teaching development, and she made a big speech at the beginning of the term in which she let it be known that she really didn't want to hear anybody's issues, not just on gay issues but also feminism. She just didn't want to hear it. I found out later that the year before many of the women in the class who were feminist had challenged her so much that she didn't want to get into it. But that was a very bad way, obviously, to run a class.

S–It certainly discourages discussion and open dialogue.

L–Yes. It had a big impact on her teaching style.

J–We have people at our institute [PPSC] now, I am sure they do at ICP too, who teach Freudian theory and are much more with it, who attempt to talk about what fits and what doesn't fit, how we think about theories now. One of the things that was necessary for the teachers at PPSC to know coming in was that such an awareness was expected of them. When questions came up, they had to talk about it.

S–So you told your staff this when you hired them, that it was part of . . .

J–It didn't necessarily come up specifically in the hiring but it would usually come up when we would invite someone on the faculty to teach a particular course. We would discuss, for example, some of the issues about narcissism, pre-oedipal relationships, and homosexuality that are going to be discussed in class and we'd tell faculty that there would be gay, lesbian and straight students who are going to be raising questions so they had to be prepared.

S–Right.

J–So from the teacher's side it was discussed. From the candidate's point of view even though it wasn't always discussed directly, just by virtue of the fact that they came to an institute where they knew there were gay and lesbian faculty and administration, there was inherent permission for those who were more inclined to speak up to do so, not like a "Vivian" who would speak even if it wasn't safe. People who didn't necessarily feel safe had the protection of the institute as a whole to know it would be okay.

L–It's a safe place. When I was in training at ICP at that point, we didn't know how safe it was, you had to feel your way still. It turned out to be safe but . . .

S–You didn't choose ICP then because you thought it would be safe around gay issues per se?

L–I thought it would be safe because of its theoretical orientation. My analyst's orientation was similar, more interpersonal. I also knew a couple of straight people who were in training there so I had the feeling that it would be okay. I didn't see it as a stuffy, conservative or rigid place. The fact that it wasn't a Freudian institute made me feel safer. The whole atmosphere seemed more open but I was also very intimidated then by the fact that it was a psychoanalytic training program and I was just a little candidate. I didn't know how things were going to work out but it was fine. I came to feel that people judged me on my merits and that, in itself, dispelled people's stereotypes about lesbians. I don't think I encountered much directly in the way of prejudice but I remember at one point I had several female supervisors and I thought I really better get a male supervisor or people are going to think I am avoiding having male supervisors, which sometimes was the way subtle prejudice would work. Sometimes candidates would say something challenging. I remember once discussing a case about a lesbian and one of my fellow candidates asked a question about why I thought the patient was gay. The teacher intervened saying she didn't think that was something that anybody actually knows about–that we can't make that kind of assumption that there's a psychological reason–that there were many possibilities.

S–Good for that teacher. That was 20 years ago before gay and lesbian affirmative analytic literature existed.

L–Many of the faculty members were very progressive people. Most of them came from either [William Allison] White or NYU. They were liberal but that's not to say that some didn't hold questionable views about homosexuality and pathology.

S–The only literature then was Socarides and McDougall.

L–Right. But homosexuality wasn't discussed much. It was a period when people felt there was very little to say about it. No one knew what to say about it. The only theory I remember reading at the time was a Ruth Jean Eisenbud article that I held on to as the only positive discussion on lesbians. It wasn't until much later that people started formulating interesting and different ways of talking about homosexuality. The student who asked the question wasn't necessarily being homophobic. I think she really wanted to understand but nothing could be said. Now that question could be answered differently.

S–Why did you two get interested in psychoanalysis anyway given its awful history at the time you went for training?

L–I think we both had good psychoanalytic experiences.

S–It started with treatment. That's an old story but you probably didn't pick therapists necessarily because they were analysts. They just happened to be analytically oriented?

L & J–Yes.

J–I was already a psychology student before I went into treatment. I wanted to be a therapist.

S–Were you in your doctorate then or your masters?

J–I was just beginning my masters. I was also engaged to be married. I was working in a program with disturbed children when one of my friends and co-workers was talking to me and picked up that I was not very happy about getting married. She said, "Why don't you see somebody and talk about it? I'm seeing this great guy, why don't you see him?" So I did, and he turned out to be a Modern Analyst. In my first session, I reported a recurring dream: that I was walking down the aisle and at the end of the aisle was a door. I would open up the door and I would plummet into a black abyss. He simply said, "When in doubt, don't." That was his first intervention. I postponed the engagement. I just needed somebody to give me permission to think about it. So there was this convergence between entering psychoanalysis and exploring my sexuality right then. I came out in my analysis, got further ensconced in the field of psychoanalysis, and ultimately wanting to do it my way, branched out into another direction altogether.

S–What made you want to branch out Judy? I thought you co-founded PPSC with Lee.

L–I was part of the group that worked with Judy in the founding of the institute. But it was really Judy's vision and her idea.

S–Tell me·how that started.

J–It began as a convergence of a number of different issues. We were working together at South Beach Psychiatric Center. We would always present cases to each other and we all had different orientations. It was so exciting and rich. I always thought, "Why can't I do this in training?" I joined the training institute that was founded by my analyst because that seemed to make sense. But I also had this craving to learn other ways of doing things.

L–I remember we went to a seminar on Self Psychology, which neither of us trained in. We went to one of those week-long workshops at the beach with the Ornsteins. I remember both of us comparing Self Psychology to what we were learning in training and finding all the ways in which the theories were the same and different. The language was different but the ideas were the same. It was just very exciting to think about all the ways theories interfaced.

J–It was very challenging and stimulating to think of it that way and yet when we arrived at that Self Psychology conference, I was greeted by someone who said, "What are you doing here? Aren't you a Modern analyst?

L–So there still was the camp idea by some people.

J–My God, the whole notion of avoiding narcissistic injury is so central to both Modern and Self Psychology. "How could you say that?" I said to myself. And that always bothered me. Looking back on it, I think there may have been some other issue going on which had to do with sexuality that I really was not aware of. I was one of the only gay people in my institute.

S–When you were being trained?

J–When I first started training. With the exception of one gay man, no one else was out.

S–What year was that?

J–I started in '79.

S–Oh, that's about the same time as you, Lee. Didn't you start the same year?

J–We were training at the same time.

S–Were you a couple then?

J–We got together in '77. So I think many of the feelings that I had about being marginalized and isolated, some of which included issues about sexuality that I wasn't dealing with head on, I displaced onto my feelings about theoretical orientation camps.

S–That's interesting.

J–I know I had an extreme sensitivity to whenever I heard somebody say, "Oh, that's not the right way, you don't do it that way, or you should do it this way." That was much of what drove my interest in forming another institute, in founding PPSC.

S–Because your vision was what, Judy?

J–I wanted to have a place where people could go and regardless of their orientation, could co-exist and exchange similarities and differences on an equal footing. It would be a win-win situation for everybody to break down barriers in a comfortable place.

L–At the time, places like ICP, which had started out as interpersonal, the Sullivanian school, had already started to embrace and integrate theories like Self Psychology and Object Relations, but they were taught, even at the Modern Institute, as individual courses. No one had yet integrated them. A lot of this was done by baby boomers forcing our way into the psychoanalytic world in that way we have in everything else in this culture, forcing pluralism into it. Judy's vision was to say we are an institute in which you can learn Modern, Self Psychology, Freudian or Object Relations and that we recognize that these are the four contemporary important orientations that currently exist in psychoanalysis. We are not making any one of them the main one. You can decide what you want to integrate or specialize in. But we recognize them as having something to say to each other and that was really a first.

S–Is it safe to say this was the first institute that had that kind of vision?

J–Yes, I think so.

S–Isn't PPSC the only institute that integrates the Modern perspective?

J–At this point, that's true. I think it's a little bit less marginalized than it used to be. People no longer raise their eyebrows the way they used to. I think Larry Epstein had a lot to do with that.

L–Larry Epstein is someone from [William Allison] White who is very respected and editor of Contemporary Psychoanalysis. He has been running supervision groups for years with people like me, graduates of ICP, Adelphi, White and NYU. People who trained and knew him became interested in the approach and have integrated it, but as far as a school offering it, I think we are still the only one.

S–So your conscious vision was to integrate different theoretical orientations within psychoanalysis, including the Modern perspective. I heard through the grapevine years ago when you started PPSC that it was teaching about homosexuality from an affirmative perspective–that you could be out and that there were gay teachers. Was that a conscious part of the mission of the institute too?

J–It's also about relationships–people I knew who I was close to and I respected, who had a lot to offer–straight, gay and lesbian from other institutes. We wanted them to be at PPSC. I didn't have to consciously recruit gay and lesbian instructors.

S–You must have created an environment in which teachers and students knew they didn't have to be closeted.

J–And some students came here for that very reason. Here's where transference comes in on some level–transference relating to politics. If a lesbian is the head of an institute, some believe that you don't have to put anything in your nondiscrimination statements, although we did because we thought it was important to say something about nondiscrimination based on sexual orientation. We were the first institute to include sexual orientation in its nondiscrimination statement.

S–What year was that?

J–1988.

J–It's not been a secret that the director is a lesbian and that some of the faculty are gay and lesbian. I don't think we ever actually had a reputation for being a gay institute but I think that people recognize that we are completely integrated.

S–But you are a gay affirmative psychoanalytic institute.

J–Giving it a name doesn't feel right, but it is reality. These things happened because we wanted them to happen or maybe certain things were unconsciously enacted. But the things that were not unconscious were, for example, sitting down with the admissions committee and talking about what people's experiences were when they were admitted to their own institutes. What kind of questions were asked. We came up with a consensus about what we were not going to ask.

S–Like?

L–We were not going to ask, "Are you married?"

S–You mean they used to ask about marital status?

L–Are you kidding? I knew somebody who was asked why she wasn't married and she was not a lesbian. But analytic interviews were stress interviews. They wanted to see how stable, self-aware, analyzed, and defended someone was. They would really push you.

J–And it was diagnostic to assess your level of object relations to see if you were in a relationship and of course, they weren't going to ask if you were in a gay or straight relationship. So they asked if you were married. That was a sign of your maturity. Do you have children? If you're 35 or whatever, why are you not married.

S–That must have been very rough for gay candidates.

L–It was rough for everybody, even straight people, if you think about it. Who wants to be asked about it?

S–Sounds like every level of planning at your institute was consciously done in a way that differed from other institutes at the time.

J–Probably in that regard. When we would review the curriculum for the personality development course or the Freud course, we'd pay particular attention to whether certain developmental theories were even-handed in how they treated development and oedipal theory and so forth. In one course of Freud which we had agreed was going to be a historical presentation one first-year lesbian candidate met with me to question why contemporary theories on sexuality and development were not included right away in the curriculum since much of the early material was not accepted anymore. I was so pleased that she was aware enough and felt comfortable enough to knock on the door and say, "Hey, I want to talk to you about this," and then we started to address that in the curriculum committee.

S–So how did you address it?

J–Even though we still had some resistance from faculty who felt we have to cover these papers first and chronologically, we addressed it by doing away with a contemporary theorists course where all of the current material was covered and said that from now on each of the courses, the course on Freud, on Self, and so on, was going to have a certain amount of the contemporary theories starting in the first semester.

S–Did students know you were gay, Judy?

J–Yes, Lee and I would go to events together. We would be on committees together.

S–Did you have any concerns that it would hurt you in any way?

J–That's why I was the boss. The only person who could get rid of me was me.

S–So you didn't have to deal with much homophobia among faculty or students?

J–I am still dealing with homophobia but not in terms of how I am perceived. What challenges me are the more subtle issues. I am open to all different orientations–theoretical orientations and sexual orientations. But when you get into the work, into the curriculum and supervision, more subtle biases come up which even the teacher and the supervisor don't always realize they have. That's the interesting part of the work of this institute–how to take something which would never be talked about elsewhere, but has to be talked about here otherwise the hypocrisy would be too glaring.

S–Did you ever get any complaints that it isn't talked about enough?

J–No. I have on occasion, more recently, been made aware of something you were referring to earlier, that even though we aren't a gay institute some heterosexuals hear that about the institute and do not want to apply.

S–Because they think it's a gay institute?

J–Because they think they would feel like the minority in the class.

L–But that's not true, in fact, number wise, they are not in the minority in the school.

J–It is another aspect of prejudice which is so unfortunate because the goal is to break down prejudice.

S–Isn't it safe to say that you probably are the only openly lesbian director of an analytic institute in New York City?

J–I don't know.

S–You might be the first openly lesbian director in history and still the only one.

J–And I think that the word "open" is what's key. Because there have been many other gays and lesbians in the field who were closeted, usually out of necessity, but who really made tremendous contributions, some in leadership positions, some behind the scenes.

S–Who inspired you two lesbian analytic foremothers?

J–I was inspired by her. (Laughs)

L–We used to fight about our approaches and orientations when we first got together. I'm not a Modern and I was one of those people who thought it was a crackpot theory, actually, so we used to get into arguments.

S–Did you go to couples therapy to deal with that?

L–Not to deal with that. Judy won me over gradually to appreciate the Modern approach. We met at Mapleton Outpatient. She was the director of the program and I was in supervision with her. I gradually came to be influenced in my theoretical approach. I came into the relationship with more political activist leanings.

S–Did you always have an identity as a feminist?

L–Always?

S–When you entered ICP was that a word you would have used to describe yourself?

L–Oh yes. I was an activist in my 20s. I came to the field by way of activism. I went to Stony Brook social work school which was a hotbed of activism in 1973. It was mostly about civil rights and feminism, not gay rights as much. However, I was told that I was the first out lesbian who was accepted into social work school at that time. I applied as an out lesbian at the urging of Bernice Goodman who knew that Stony Brook wanted to increase student diversity. A lot of the faculty were leftists or Kennedy liberals, progressive people who were interested in community organizing and policy. The students came in wanting to train as therapists and they didn't know what to do with us. We all learned to integrate our perspectives. So I think I influenced Judy in a political consciousness way.

S–Would you use the term feminist to label yourself Judy as you were training in psychoanalysis?

J–I think so but I have to preface it by saying I never really focused on the world of politics and social issues except for how they manifested in my little room. My style was not exactly head buried in the sand but more nose to the grindstone. I always thought, "What do I have to do now? What should be done now?"

S–You practiced practical feminism.

L–Right. She is "the personal is political."

J–That's a nice way of putting it.

S–Who inspired you in psychoanalytic writing? And how did you deal with the homophobia in earlier literature?

L–I just avoided homophobic material. That was my way of dealing with it. That's why I trained in the interpersonal school rather than the Freudian because I didn't want to be in a homophobic situation. Interpersonalists were not primarily concerned with sexuality and sexual orientation at the time. I'll tell you someone who made a big impression on me. Around 1976 Stephen Mitchell came to South Beach. There was a great intellectual and educational environment there. He presented a paper about homosexuality. He presented his theory that you could talk about, analyze and understand a person's homosexuality in psychoanalysis without pathologizing it.

S–That was groundbreaking at the time. That must have been remarkable for you to hear someone speak about homosexuality in that way. How did the crowd respond by the way?

L–Very positively, although it was a small turnout. My guess is that most of the people who came were gay. Those who were not gay were interested and open. He was a wonderful presenter and writer and his thoughts were very organized. They made a tremendous impression on me.

S–What about you, Judy? Given all of the homophobic literature at the time, it doesn't sound like you came into your development of PPSC in a rage against the injustices of gay people per se.

J–No, that wasn't my focus.

L–Judy is a doer. She is the kind of person who, if there is a problem or an injustice, she is going to figure out what to do about it.

J–That's different from anger. It's "let's see what I can do here."

S–Let me ask one last question. What do you think has really changed with lesbians and psychoanalysis and what still needs to change?

L–One of the most wonderful and dramatic changes over the last 10 years or so starting with the publication of your book is all the literature that is now available for people to read that just didn't exist before. This is huge. We're starting to develop new and different theory. The literature has so normalized things and influenced straight therapists in the community who wanted to be able to think about homosexuality differently but who didn't have any other material or ideas than the old canon. I get calls every now and then asking for a copy of my Mourning paper. I just got a call the other day from a woman who I have known for many years but rarely see. We saw each other at a conference and she asked if she could have a copy of my paper for a study group she's in. She's straight. I think that people want and need it.

S–And we have it now.

L–And it's had an effect across the board. It's made it more possible for people to go to training institutes and be out, even in institutes that are more traditional. I think it has made more lesbians come into the field. I was joking with one of my supervisees when she was asking me about building a practice. I told her how it's good to have a niche like maybe substance abuse or eating disorders. She asked, "What was your niche when you were starting out?" I said, "My niche was that I was a lesbian." That's not a niche anymore.

S–And that's a change that reflects something positive, doesn't it?

L–Yes, there are so many lesbian therapists. If somebody calls for a referral, you don't have just one name anymore who you hope will be a good fit. You know many different people with different approaches. That's expanded across the board because psychoanalysis has become a more hospitable place for lesbians than it was back then.

S–Anyone want to comment on what needs to change?

J–It's all connected because when I was first thinking about the question the only thing I came up with was just doing more of what we're doing–more writing, more openness, more dialogue. And a certain kind of dialogue–not just one that brings together gays and straights but one that includes a discussion of all the issues, including the harder ones like how homophobia still operates clinically, institutionally, and in the therapy community.

L–It makes me think of the conference in '93 that Ronnie [Lesser] and Tom [Domenici] organized that came about because gay students at NYU Post-Doctoral Program felt that there was a problem in how psychoanalysis treated homosexuality. Participants tried to talk directly about the issue of homosexuality in the psychoanalytic world and Roy Schaefer did a wonderful keynote in which he talked about his own development and feelings. But there was, continues to be, a defensiveness on the part of some straight analysts–a "stop picking on us" type of thing. They claim, "We're okay, we accept everybody, everything is fine, get over it." They were saying it in '93. Someone stood up and made a long statement about how he wasn't prejudiced. The question is are we going to talk about this and acknowledge that there needs to be an ongoing dialogue about how we deal with each other and think or are we just going to pretend that everything is wonderful and that we all get along.

J–The proof ultimately will be how many of the articles in Jack Drescher's book, your book, or Deborah Glazer's book will end up in the mainstream curriculum? How many people putting together courses will go to the gay and lesbian journals and bring that material into their coursework and writing?

S–Some of them already are. But a danger now is, as sexuality and gender are becoming hot topics some analysts who aren't that well read in gay and lesbian analytic literature write about these issues without acknowledging the earlier literature.

J–People often say the same things repeatedly but who gets the credit is the person who . . .

S– . . . has access to the discourse–the power to shape the discourse.

J–That's right, yes. I don't think that any analyst will claim, "I'm the only one who's ever done this" but it can become that if people who are reading the present discourse don't also read the earlier writers. And it's important that whoever is writing on these topics now should read the earlier work and cite them.

S–And this will likely happen if we have more ongoing dialogues about sexual orientation as a matter of course at our institutes and in the psychoanalytic community–not waiting until some disagreement shows up–

including dialogues not just on sexuality and sexual orientation but on homophobia as well.

L & J– . . . yes, that is what's needed.

CONCLUSION

These two interviews contain some noteworthy similarities. All three foremothers credit positive psychoanalytic psychotherapy experiences for motivating them to pursue psychoanalytic training at a time when psychoanalysis was anything but hospitable. All three foremothers created safe space for colleagues and future generations of therapists by coming out early in their careers as well as through teaching, writing and supervision. Finally, their suggestions for the future focus on the need to not only create dialogues about sexuality and gender within the psychoanalytic community but, more importantly, to resist the temptation to feel that we've fully arrived at the analytic table. They urge us to be conscious of subtle forms of homophobia and heterosexism that co-exist with progress. Their lives and work have created a path for those of us who follow to travel a safer route. We owe them, and so many other lesbian psychoanalytic foremothers, a great debt. Let us continue to pay tribute to them all.

It Takes a Community

Susan Gair

SUMMARY. Most lesbian and gay people are traumatized by being raised in a society that denigrates and devalues their sexual orientation. Experiences of trauma during identity development are non-mirroring and can be psychic assaults. The ever-presence of the trauma renders it hidden and difficult for the patient and therapist to address. This paper will examine the psychic impact of this trauma and treatment concerns, particularly problems of shame, hiding, and empathy. Special attention will be paid to finding external communities that support and give recognition to lesbian, gay, and bisexual identities and internalizing this influence into psychic "internal communities." *[Article copies available for a fee from The Haworth Document Delivery Service: 1-800-HAWORTH. E-mail address: <docdelivery@ haworthpress.com> Website: <http://www.HaworthPress.com> © 2004 by The Haworth Press, Inc. All rights reserved.]*

KEYWORDS. Lesbian, gay, trauma, shame, homophobia, internal community

---

Susan Gair, CSW, is in private practice in New York City. She is Clinical Director of the Gay and Lesbian Affirmative Psychotherapy Program at the Institute for Contemporary Psychotherapy (ICP), where she is a faculty member, training analyst, and supervisor. She is also the author of "The False Self, Shame, and the Challenge of Self-Cohesion" in *Lesbians and Psychoanalysis* (J. Glassgold and S. Iasenza [Eds.], Free Press, 1995).

Address correspondence to: Susan Gair, CSW, 330 West 58th Street, Suite 514, New York, NY 10019.

[Haworth co-indexing entry note]: "It Takes a Community." Gair, Susan. Co-published simultaneously in *Journal of Lesbian Studies* (Harrington Park Press, an imprint of The Haworth Press, Inc.) Vol. 8, No. 1/2, 2004, pp. 45-56; and: *Lesbians, Feminism, and Psychoanalysis: The Second Wave* (ed: Judith M. Glassgold, and Suzanne Iasenza) Harrington Park Press, an imprint of The Haworth Press, Inc., 2004, pp. 45-56. Single or multiple copies of this article are available for a fee from The Haworth Document Delivery Service [1-800-HAWORTH, 9:00 a.m. - 5:00 p.m. (EST). E-mail address: docdelivery@haworthpress.com].

Digital Object Identifier: 10.1300/J155v08n01_03

INTRODUCTION

When individuals are raised and live in communities and cultures that shame and despise their sexual orientations, continuous traumas can occur. This constant trauma and abuse–by its familiarity–too often remain hidden and outside of awareness. What needs to be considered in working with individuals who have been living with this silent traumatization? What are the ongoing traumas? How do they go unnoticed? What are some of the ways we can be more attentive to considering this a significant aspect of our work?

Both therapist and clients, who are lesbian, gay, and bisexual, are frequently traumatized by these circumstances and live in fear of being found out. Finding communities that support, accept and validate suppressed differences can be extraordinarily difficult. Nevertheless, when and if these new communities are found, the acceptance of those aspects of oneself perceived as unacceptable and shameful provide a significant opportunity to mitigate trauma.

I have often heard it said, who you are has more to do with your environment. In this paper, I will describe the impact communities that are negative to lesbians, gays and bisexuals have on their coping mechanisms throughout their development. Although support systems for people with same sex attractions and/or questioning have been available since the 1980s, the stigmatization around sexuality remains powerful and pervasive. Sexuality is a powerful part of identity. Scaer states that the family and society provide us with the most basic sense of ourselves and teach us by behaviors, inferences, and words that sexuality is private and central to the core of who we are (2001, p. 5). Unlike members of other marginalized groups whose parents are also in their group, our core selves do not fit our families' or society's teachings, and are devalued, entirely unmirrored, and invisible. This fosters such a deep and intense shame, and traumatizes the self.

Many hide. When we hide, even in situations without a realistic risk of harm, we associate the need to hide with being wrong or bad. This is especially true if we are hiding from our own family, friends, and the very communities in which we reside. When as children we hide something and are found out, the consequences are often dire, affecting our own self-esteem as well as the esteem we are held in by the other. Scaer says, "Trauma is most devastating when it comes from persons or events surrounding those persons who are the primary source of our safe boundary formation, our primary caregivers" (2001, pp. 6-7).

In a previous work, I summarized the intrapsychic impact of the shame-inducing dissonance of being lesbian, gay or bisexual in an unsupportive family and society and its effects on self-structure:

> The anticipation and experience of shame are generated and rein-forced by a combination of internal and external factors resulting in a vicious cycle of shame. Contempt produces and reinforces shame . . . This contempt, when internalized, accentuates . . . the feeling of being a defective woman. To protect herself from being overwhelmed by her negative introjects, she may split off and pro-ject those unwanted aspects of herself onto others. Although the splitting process may be psychically efficient, it weakens the self-structure and self-esteem remains low. (Gair, 1995, p. 114)

When we hide aspects of ourselves, it is difficult to embrace recognition when it is finally available because being known may evoke emotional memories that are associated with the original trauma. Thus, being known can actually be retraumatizing, especially early in recovery from the initial trauma. For instance, a lesbian client, who is a successful corporate execu-tive, believes that whenever people are talking quietly, it is somehow nega-tively related about her. She in turn keeps her distance, remaining unapproachable, thereby sustaining her beliefs. She is convinced she has nothing to offer and is unable to embrace her success. She believes that if people at work knew she was a lesbian, she would be scorned.

Over time, hiding may cause difficulty in forming intimate and com-mitted relationships. A lesbian woman I work with commented, "Every time I think about being in a relationship, I'm terrified. I feel that when she finds out who I really am, she will leave me. Intellectually, I know otherwise, but it doesn't help." I wondered if getting close was a trigger for a reoccurrence of the feeling of unacceptability to her parents–a type of feeling memory that triggered retraumatization. Because her parents were so disappointed and hurt about her orientation, she believes that she was unacceptable to them. Thus, being in a relationship was unac-ceptable to her as well because being in a relationship made it harder for her to deny her lesbian orientation.

Case Example

For some, hiding may result in clinging to harmful relationships to get some form of acceptance. A gay client who grew up in the South was called a sissy throughout his childhood and adolescence. The kids at school made fun of him daily and often taunted him physically. His siblings and parents did not treat him much better. He claims that since he moved to New York City his whole life has changed and he is not troubled by his past. Yet, his intimate relationships have been abusive. He has been with men who are dependent victim-bullies, probably both to perpetuate the community he is used to, and because he does not acknowledge those aspects in himself. He finds himself being harshly critical of any number of things about his partners.

According to Jody Davies, one of the ways trauma survivors avoid experiencing painful object loss is to identify with the victimizing aspects of the abusers (Davies & Frawley, 1994, p. 132). This client re-enacts the role of the defective one through reincorporating his partners' demeaning attitudes and treatment of him. Davies says ". . . the self destructiveness, in fact, assumes both continued bondage to the abuser and identification with the abuser's ruthlessness" (Davies & Frawley, 1994, p. 130). The abusers in the context of this paper remain his community, family, and society.

WHAT IS COMMUNITY?

I would like to consider some notions of community. How do we define community? It is past and present, imposed and selected, internal and external, intimate and distant. What are the effects of community on us? How important is it for us to have–and feel we have–an impact on community? Community is a mate, is family, is neighborhood, and is a place of worship, school, and any type of group, place of work, society, and political organization. These all significantly influence and are part of our internal community. Yvonne Agazarian (2000), a beloved mentor, in her theory on Systems Centered Therapy, believes all human systems are driven towards survival, development and transformation. And these drives are governed by discrimination and integration of information. "Discrimination is the ability to see differences in the apparently similar and similarities in the apparently different. Integration is the process by which information is organized within the system so that it is available for work" (2000, p. 24).

While we may exist in communities that appear similar, on an intrapsychic level they may be intolerably dissimilar. I believe it is essential for everyone to seek communities with enough intrapsychic and interpersonal similarities to themselves so that the community is able to provide the atmosphere to make it possible to internalize new beliefs about oneself. For if, communities are to bring out and enhance a stifled vitality and creativity, the communities must provide enough recognition and acknowledgment of who we truly are.

When a validating, reparative community is not found until adulthood, the internal intrapsychic communities have become quite fixed and difficult to let in new attitudes. Patterns of self-regard and perception are entrenched from the early and ongoing negative messages; we develop significant self-destructive styles of relating that maintain these negative beliefs about the self; we find ourselves projecting our beliefs onto our current environment thereby reinforcing our attitudes. Being marginalized by society may foster defenses that aid survival, such as isolation, hiding or defiance, which tend to restrain us from reaching out to affirming communities. The example I gave of my male patient's denial of past traumas is understandable. Without yet having developed or found affirming supports to counter the internal community, it is virtually not possible to reflect on the past with a perspective that can convert trauma into understanding and empowerment. When he is helped to find a community that he respects and that accepts him as a gay man, he will hopefully be better able to tolerate his emotional memories without reenacting self-destructive patterns. The hurtful socialization of lesbian, gay and bisexual individuals, in most societies, is itself an example of trauma and as such, needs to be considered in terms of trauma work.

In *The Traffic in Women: Notes on the "Political Economy" of Sex* (1975), Gayle Rubin elaborates on the kinship system. Every culture has social, sexual, marriage, economic, political status rules and categories. These are imbedded and passed on through generations. Rubin quotes Lacan:

> In Lacan's scheme, the oedipal crisis occurs when a child learns of the sexual rules embedded in the terms for family and relatives. The crisis begins when the child comprehends the system and his or her place in it; this crisis is resolved when the child accepts that place and accedes to it. Even if the child refuses its place, he or she cannot escape knowledge of it. Before the Oedipal phase, the sexuality of the child is labile and relatively unstructured. Each child contains all of the sexual possibilities available to human expression. But in any given society, only some of these possibilities will be expressed, while others will be constrained. When the child leaves the oedipal phase, its libido and gender identity has been or-

ganized in conformity with the rules of the culture which is domesticating it. (1975, p. 189)

We may intellectually know better, but because of these early repeated and intense messages, we are emotionally stuck in our own internal struggle to ward off those damaging messages about ourselves. Karen W. Saakvitne states, "Finding community transforms the existential isolation that comes with despair and grief. Communities offer connection with shared visions, beliefs, hopes, dreams, and goals. They speak to the potential creativity and constructive outcomes that result when humans work together to bring about positive change" (2002, p. 448).

We need to remember that our internal community, consisting of attitudes, beliefs, and coded messages, continually attempts to recreate itself consciously and unconsciously. Everyone wants to fit in, while being admired and recognized for unique qualities. When this type of recognition is not possible, blame is often used against oneself or others. This idea is further supported by Scaer when he states, "Even in adulthood, the meaning of those individuals in our life remains as it was as a child . . . The most devastating form of traumatic stress, therefore, clearly occurs when caregivers, the intrinsic safe haven, the providers of our basic sense of boundaries, become the existential threat" (2001, p. 5). Those who have experienced this trauma must find communities that understand and approve of them.

Herbert Rosenfeld (1971/1981, p. 249) uses the terms "gang" and "Mafia" when describing the extraordinary power of early internalized attachments in the form of beliefs and attitudes. He holds that internal gangs/ Mafias maintain their superiority over any new attachments (and messages) through inducing self-sabotaging mechanisms in a client that often appear to be narcissistic attachments to the belief in the superiority in the older and known internalizations. If the culture (gang/Mafia), in this case, refuses to set aside its heterosexual superiority, it does not allow for the creation of an equal lesbian, gay, or bisexual culture. This is maintained, subtly or not so subtly, by the continued marginalization of lesbian, gay, and bisexual individuals through lack of access to privileges and acknowledgments. Marginalized cultures are forced to adapt to the superior gang and, therefore, are not incorporated fully as part of the community.

AS THERAPISTS

Practicing in New York City, I have heard many tales of why people migrated here. Some who are lesbian, gay, or bisexual seek anonymity.

However, most would say that they are here to live in an atmosphere of tolerance, with the hope of acceptance and self-recognition. Jessica Benjamin (1995) emphasizes the essentialness of mutual recognition between two people. Attunement is an end in itself. She further indicates that in order for the capacity for mutual recognition to exist "we must stretch to accommodate the necessary tension of difference, the knowledge of conflicting feelings" (1995, p. 42). Accordingly, a reciprocal influence and respect must occur between therapist and client in order to acquire a sense of recognition.

As therapists, we have so many different theoretical points of view with a myriad of techniques and approaches. We pay attention to patterns of behaviors and relationships with clients who have come from impoverished and traumatized backgrounds. This is necessary to encourage and skillfully decipher if our clients are finding appropriate communities to enhance their esteem. Linda Pollock and Jonathan Slavin (1998) reflect, "We also understand our patients' decision to seek treatment as a consequence of their unsuccessful struggles to find recognition in the relational world, to find their own place, to discover their true selves, to acquire a sense of their own validity" (1998, p. 371). Thus, in this perspective in order to remedy this failure, therapists must attempt to help our clients be able to form successful ties to affirming communities.

Case Example

A lesbian woman I work with complained about her frustration that she and her spouse were not able to be "out" in her neighborhood or in her apartment building. I asked, how come? As she spoke, it was not clear what the dangers in the community might be. In this community, were there other gay people? How did she know? How did she think she and her spouse would be treated? What means did she have to find out? Did her hiding reflect the reality of her new community or did her fears reflect the perseverance of old intrapsychic communities? She became annoyed with me for spending so much time exploring this when it wasn't that important to her. She and her spouse were fine with it, she said— even though there was tension between them due to the frustration. Why was I pushing my agenda on her? I asked if she could tolerate a bit more exploration in this direction, and she gave permission. I asked her to think of communities where she has stopped hiding who she is, and to notice how being known has affected how she feels about herself and her relationship with her partner. How do those compare with communities in which she is still hiding? She is initially annoyed with me each time I do this, but afterwards she describes how different and more connected to herself she feels. I remind her of this, and I remind her that the purpose of the exploration is not always to come out, but to consider each situation separately, remembering the prior successes while sizing up each new situation.

It is helpful for therapists to take every opportunity to decipher the difference between realistic danger and unfelt shame in statements such as, "Other people at work talk about their weekends but I don't because I'm a private person," or "No one in the neighborhood knows we are domestic partners; they think we are just roommates, and I don't correct them because it's none of their business anyway."

As therapists, we need to pay attention to the retraumatization of hiding. Hiding, by its very nature, often is not obvious. As is the case with other "phobias," homophobia is characterized by giving in to the anxiety and preventing the incorporation of new behaviors that might neutralize the fear and end the phobia. There is an aspect of circularity and repetition in this dilemma. The trauma forms patterns of behavior that prevent the very changes that would heal the original trauma. Fortunately, in therapy the hiding may be disclosed directly or indirectly.

FINDING COMMUNITY

Traumatized individuals need to be part of one or more communities where same-sex desires are the norm, where there is no marginalization for being lesbian, gay or bisexual. In order for a community to provide sustaining nourishment, the individual should feel proud of and identified with the community. But finding community when we are lesbian, gay or bisexual is not so simple. Communities are usually formed from school, work, or other generally heterosexual networks. Seeking a community outside of these settings requires being somewhat comfortable with being out. When heterosexual people want to meet potential partners, they can go just about anywhere they like to meet other heterosexuals. Lesbian and gay people, on the other hand, must go to places they might not otherwise be interested in merely because those place offer opportunities to find others who are gay or lesbian.

It may take many communities to help us heal from the traumas of hate, fear, and shame. The difficulty of finding those communities and individuals that will not continue the negative patterns is often exacerbated because we project our beliefs into most situations until we are helped to learn how to do otherwise. It is vital for lesbian, gay and bisexual people to have a base or anchor community that permits authenticity as well as a created family community where each individual feels well-known and valued. In its most productive role, a community can counter not only the harshness of earlier messages, but also the continuing daily reminders of marginalization. Much work lies ahead to stop the retraumatizing hate messages that keep many people frightened and hidden.

A challenge to many therapists is to be able to empathize, despite differences. Being willing and able to know and feel one's own traumas is essential in order to help the client experience a sense of being understood that allows for the possibility of a healing therapeutic community. Apprey's (2000) concept of "horizonality" is relevant here. Apprey describes how one person's trauma may be understood by another who has experienced a different, yet significant, trauma: "For example, the enslavement of African-Americans, with all the murders, rape, and pillaging that went with it, and the Holocaust of the Jews are not interchangeable but horizonal. They are horizonal in the sense that they both give us an idea of what humans are capable of doing to each other" (2000, pp. 119-120).

Accessing our own parallel experiences facilitates our clients' feeling known and recognized, and believing that we are able to recognize their humanity. The effectiveness of this therapeutic action depends on our willingness to know these emotional states–our own and our clients'–and have the fluidity to move in and out of them.

The therapist and client form a community in which the client can not only be validated, but also can practice his or her impact on others. Neville Symington contends, ". . . the inner act of freedom in the analyst causes a shift in the patient and new insight, learning, and development in the analyst . . . the essential agent of the change is the inner act of the analyst and that this inner act is perceived by the patient and causes change" (1983, p. 286). When clients sense their impact on the analyst, recognition and mutuality are enhanced. We may need also to consider that client "resistance" may be a function of the analyst's unwillingness to be affected by the client. This has relevance to the situation of gay/ lesbian therapists working with heterosexual clients as well.

Case Example

Several years ago a young married man I was working with let me know he was having difficulty bringing up something about me that had been troubling him for a few weeks. Clearly, he felt safe enough to confront me. I took advantage of the situation and encouraged him to elaborate and explore his thoughts and feelings further. He said he had learned from an acquaintance that I was involved with a woman, that I was a lesbian. Why had I not told him? How could a lesbian woman understand a heterosexual man? He appeared hurt, angry and ashamed.

Fortunately, for both of us, I was not struggling with any of those feelings at that moment. I say fortunately because it would have been difficult to attend to his feeling if I were stuck in my own homophobic shame. As we explored what it meant that I had hidden this from him; what it meant that I chose a woman instead of a man; that he found out the way he did, the work deepened. Over time, by my being less hidden, which this may have been symbolically keeping out of the treatment, seemed to have the effect of making him less afraid and less ashamed to explore hidden aspects of himself. This brought us both more fully into the room and allowed for more intimacy and less shame. The less shame I have in relation to my sexual orientation, the less it is an issue for the client.

Case Example

A client struggling within the community of my office feared that I would not understand, or judge negatively, something from which she was gaining much affirmation. She attended gay AA and was amazed at how great the meetings made her feel. Prior to going to these meetings, she thought the concept of higher power was silly; now, though able to embrace it on her terms, she was afraid I would think it silly. Did I think it was foolish or was I threatened by the positive effect it was having for her? What were my attitudes and beliefs about religion and spirituality? She wanted to know whether I could tolerate an opening up of the space between us, a triangular space. This client wanted a community in me that could tolerate, embrace, encourage, enjoy, recognize, and learn from her and her other, new community.

As Judith Glassgold writes, "Recognition and assertion of the self in the mutuality of the therapeutic relationship encourages lesbian and bisexual women toward the next step of self-assertion: insisting on recognition from the outside world" (1995, p. 207). Further, "self-disclosure expressed spontaneously allows for the development of the experiences of mutuality, trustworthiness, and feeling valuable" (1995, pp. 215-216).

As therapists, we need to know about the particulars of the external communities our clients are embracing. If we do not know, we need to be curious. Ignoring these issues perpetuates the lack of attunement and the client's experience of invisibility and insignificance. Knowing about our clients' communities is essential to understanding their internal communities and an important piece of information about the depth of trauma that our clients still experience. The process of inquiry about this important aspect of our clients' lives allows us to be educated by our clients; this furthers the development of mutuality and recognition. Through recognition, appreciation, respect, and encouragement, we can help our clients and ourselves gain the courage to find what is similar in what merely looks different.

REFERENCES

Agazarian, Y.M. (2000). Autobiography of a theory. In Y.M. Agazarian & S. P. Gantt (Eds.), *Developing a theory of living human systems and its systems-centered practice* (pp. 221-254). London: Jessica Kingsley Publishers.

Apprey, M. (2000). From the horizon of evil to an ethic of responsibility. *Mind and Human Interaction, 11*(2), 119-126.

Benjamin, J. (1995). *Like subjects, love objects: Essays on recognition of sexual difference*. New Haven: Yale University Press.

Davies, J.M. & Frawley, M.G. (1994). *Treating the adult survivor of childhood sexual abuse: A psychoanalytic perspective*. New York: Basic Books.

Gair, S. (1995). The false self, shame, and the challenges to self-cohesion. In J.M. Glassgold & S. Iasenza (Eds.), *Lesbians and psychoanalysis: Revolutions in theory and practice* (pp. 107-123). New York: Free Press.

Glassgold, J.M. (1995). Psychoanalysis with lesbians: Self-reflection and agency. In J.M. Glassgold & S. Iasenza (Eds.), *Lesbians and psychoanalysis: Revolutions in theory and practice* (pp. 203-227). New York: Free Press.

Pollock, L. & Slavin, J. H. (1998). The struggle for recognition, disruption, and reintegration in the experience of agency. *Psychoanalytic Dialogues, 8*(6), 857-873.

Rosenfeld, H. (1988). A clinical approach to the psychoanalytic theory of the life and death instincts: An investigation into aggressive aspects of narcissism. In E.B. Spilliers (Ed.), *Melanie Klein today: Mainly theory (Vol. 1)*. New York: Routledge. (Original work published 1971).

Rubin, G. (1975). The traffic in women: Notes on the 'political economy' of sex. In W. Kolmar & F. Bartowski (Eds.), *Feminist theory: A reader.* New York: Mayfield Publishing Company, 2000.

Saakvitne, K.W. (2002). Shared trauma: The therapist's increased vulnerability. *Psychoanalytic Dialogues, 12*(3), 443-449.

Scaer, R.C. (2001). *The body bears the burden: Trauma, dissociation, and disease.* New York: Haworth Medical Press.

Symington, N. (1983).The analyst's act of freedom as agent of therapeutic change. *International Review of Psycho-Analysis, 10*, 283-291.

African American Lesbians and Other Culturally Diverse People in Psychodynamic Psychotherapies: Useful Paradigms or Oxymoron?

Beverly Greene

SUMMARY. The treatment of African American lesbians and other culturally diverse people in psychodynamic psychotherapies has been challenged as inappropriate. The Eurocentric, sexist, and heterocentric origins of these therapies have been viewed as intrinsically insensitive to the unique needs of diverse group members. Moreover, they have been viewed as pathologizing of nondominant cultural values and behaviors, while legitimizing the social pathologies of dominant groups. This discussion, however, argues that there is great diversity in the theories and practice of psychodynamic therapies, that they have undergone signifi-

Beverly Greene, PhD, ABPP, is Professor of Psychology at St. John's University and a practicing clinical psychologist in New York City. Licensed in New York and New Jersey, she is a Fellow of the American Psychological Association and six of the associations divisions, the Academy of Clinical Psychology and a Diplomate in Clinical Psychology. She received her PhD in clinical psychology from the Derner Institute at Adelphi University in 1983.

Address correspondence to: Beverly Greene, PhD, Department of Psychology, St. John's University, Jamaica, NY 11439 (E-mail: bgreene203@aol.com).

[Haworth co-indexing entry note]: "African American Lesbians and Other Culturally Diverse People in Psychodynamic Psychotherapies: Useful Paradigms or Oxymoron?" Greene, Beverly. Co-published simultaneously in *Journal of Lesbian Studies* (Harrington Park Press, an imprint of The Haworth Press, Inc.) Vol. 8, No. 1/2, 2004 pp. 57-77; and: *Lesbians, Feminism, and Psychoanalysis: The Second Wave* (ed: Judith M. Glassgold, and Suzanne Iasenza) Harrington Park Press, an imprint of The Haworth Press, Inc., 2004, pp. 57-77. Single or multiple copies of this article are available for a fee from The Haworth Document Delivery Service [1-800-HAWORTH, 9:00 a.m. - 5:00 p.m. (EST). E-mail address: docdelivery@haworthpress.com].

Digital Object Identifier: 10.1300/J155v08n01_04

cant revisions since their origins in classical theory, and that there are minority and majority opinions within the "culture" of psychodynamic and psychoanalytic theory and practice. I also propose that the prevalence of dominant cultural identities among psychodynamic theoreticians and therapists is a significant factor in the practice of therapy and the development of theoretical paradigms. The usefulness of innovative psychodynamic paradigms in addressing some of the unique challenges associated with socially disadvantaged group membership is also explored. *[Article copies available for a fee from The Haworth Document Delivery Service: 1-800-HAWORTH. E-mail address: <docdelivery@haworthpress.com> Website: <http://www.HaworthPress.com> © 2004 by The Haworth Press, Inc. All rights reserved.]*

KEYWORDS. African American lesbians, cultural diversity, psychodynamic psychotherapies

This discussion examines the persistent notion that psychodynamic theoretical approaches are mutually exclusive to successful psychotherapy with members of culturally diverse populations that can be exemplified by African American lesbians. My analysis takes place in the context of a belief in the meritocracy myth, and some of the dynamics that are intrinsic to historical and contemporary social injustice. Mental health institutions exist as a part of a broader culture that verbally espouses pride in its "melting pot" of different cultural groups while practicing cultural insensitivity and a denigration of group differences (Strickland, 2000). Acting in accordance with the practices and values of the dominant culture, institutional mental health in the United States has historically conceptualized differences from the dominant cultural norm as deviant and pathological. Only recently have psychological paradigms come to view human development and behavior as something that can have many different trajectories that are not inherently pathological simply because they are different from those of dominant cultural groups. These ideas formed the core of the development of multicultural and diversity initiatives in contemporary psychology and psychotherapy.

Diversity and multiculturalism are socially constructed concepts that are used to describe the study of ethnoracial, gender, sexual orientation, age, disability, and other cultural differences between groups and the descriptions of those differences. Possessing little meaning in and of themselves, the social context in which these dimensions are perceived, experienced, understood and defined is what renders them salient (Greene, 2003). In western culture, these aspects of human diversity are deemed of great importance by social scientists and they are often viewed as both explaining and justifying the positions people hold in the social hierarchy. In the context of psychotherapy, their salience must be determined by how much of a difference these differences actually make in people's lives, at a given time, how they are understood and what they come to mean to the client. This naturally leads to questions about how these relative statuses in and of themselves contribute to the client's position in the social hierarchy and what the client must do to negotiate the social barriers associated with disadvantaged status. Given the relational nature of social status, it also raises questions about the effects of the theoretician or clinician's position in that hierarchy.

How does the theoreticians' subjective social positioning, their awareness of it or lack thereof effect their conceptualization of the psyche and how it works? Furthermore, how does it affect their view or awareness of the social hierarchy and their understanding of their place in it? Beyond these issues, we must ask what is reenacted in the therapy process itself when the clinician is a member of or strongly identifies with a privileged and dominant group and the patient is/does not. I contend that there is the potential for the normative social power relationship to be reenacted.

Theoreticians have and continue to get their information about others from the same places that their clients get that information. Our beliefs about others and ourselves are shaped by many complex sociopolitical and economic variables and realities that may have little to do with locating the true nature of identity. Our descriptions may be designed and used to serve other than noble purposes in a larger system of dominant/ privileged and subordinate/marginalized relationships. Both therapist and client alike are all affected by a cultural mythology that has been developed to explain differences in our relative positions in the social hierarchy, as well as to justify social injustice by creating and maintaining discrepancies in social power.

In the myth of meritocracy, achievements by members of privileged groups are usually attributed to individual efforts and rewards for those efforts are seen as having been earned and deserved. Jordan (1997) observes that a myth of earned power and meritocracy was developed by the members of the dominant culture to justify their right to discriminate against and limit social opportunities for people who were different. When these myths are accepted, all people are viewed as getting whatever they deserve. People who are in positions of power are seen as deserving of the privileges associated with their position. People who are powerless, disadvantaged, vulnerable, *and exploited* are presumed to be getting what they deserve as well. This includes blame, punishment, and contempt for their condition. Both client and therapist have their own personal stake and role in these beliefs. The reality of life against a backdrop of dominant and subordinate relationships extends to the practice of psychotherapy, institutional mental health, and the development of psychological theories. This naturally includes psychodynamic paradigms.

CRITIQUES OF PSYCHODYNAMIC APPROACHES WITH CULTURALLY DIVERSE POPULATIONS

Because of their ethnocentric, androcentric and heterosexist assumptions about development and behavior, psychodynamic paradigms have been assailed as mutually exclusive to the treatment of diverse ethnoracial group members, women, and lesbians (Abramowitz, 1997; Mattei, 1996). African American lesbians as clients are individuals who represent the convergence of 3 major identities that have been pathologized by institutional mental health. Abramowitz (1997), Adams (2000), Altman (1996), Jackson (2000), Moncayo (1998), and Leary (2000) critique psychodynamic theories for limiting the definition of a normal family or marriage to the Western nuclear model, for defining normal psychosexual development as having only heterosexual outcomes, for an exclusive focus on the individual and on individuation, and for minimizing the importance of relationships and connections. Additionally, these critiques fault psychodynamic theories for failing to analyze the real, not just the symbolic, sociopolitical context of the patient's life, and thus assuming that actual sociopolitical issues have no effect on patients' intrapsychic development or assuming the effects must inevitably render the patient a psychological cripple. Leary (1997, 2000), Mattei (1996), and Thompson (1996) argue that these ideas are attributable to early classical formulations that viewed people as if their culture was not a core piece of their psyche, or for examining these issues in terms of culture's symbolic and not realistic aspects. This failure to name and critique social pathology and the interactive relationship between the individual and a hostile social milieu was correctly assailed as a glaring omission. It was, however glaringly omitted from most mainstream psychological analyses of behavior.

When psychotherapy paradigms that include psychodynamic theories simply legitimize the social status quo rather than examine it critically, they become witting or unwitting instruments of social oppression and control. In this context, people who step outside of their socially proscribed, limited roles are pathologized and may even be deemed dangerous. In this context, women whose primary erotic attractions are to other women are deemed "ill" when normal gender is defined in part by erotic attraction to the other gender (Glassgold, 1992). Hence, socially oppressed people, lesbians for example, were given labels in the form of diagnoses that blamed them for their misery. Specific ways that this applies to African American lesbians may be found in Greene (2000). This process also failed to identify the real and not symbolic socially constructed barriers associated with race, gender and sexual orientation African American lesbians must negotiate. The failure to do this made it less likely that they and members of marginalized groups like them would look outside of themselves for causes of their misery and seek social change by challenging the status quo. Furthermore, their appropriate rejecting responses to social injustice are cited as more evidence of their intrinsic pathology. That evidence is used to justify the continued scapegoating of marginalized group members as well as their exclusion from social opportunities granted to members of dominant/privileged groups. This process is facilitated by organizing behavioral and cultural norms around the dominant cultural group. Doing so serves to obscure both the pathology of the dominant group as well as the socially constructed nature of one's placement in the social hierarchy.

PSYCHODYNAMIC THERAPIES AS USEFUL PARADIGMS

Despite these legitimate assertions, many clinicians have expanded, transformed and modified psychodynamic theories and techniques in ways that address their intrinsic biases and are useful in the treatment of African American lesbians as well as other clients who are members of socially marginalized groups. Over 30 years ago, Schachter and Butts (1968) were among the early professionals who introduced the need to recognize the reality of race in psychoanalytic discourse. Over the years, I have learned a great deal from many colleagues who practice using this modality in creative ways that maximize its use in integrating race, gender, and lesbian affirmative perspectives into the therapy dialogue. In a recent volume (Jackson & Greene, 2000) a group of African American women, all psychodynamic psychotherapists and/or certified psychoanalysts, describe innovations they have developed over years of practice successfully using psychodynamic theories in therapy with diverse groups of African American women. Glassgold and Iasenza's (1995) volume on psychoanalysis with lesbians also illustrates the many ways that old heterosexist biases inherent in psychodynamic theories can be addressed with new theoretical modifications. A detailed analysis of these works is beyond the scope of this discussion; however, the reader is referred to Abramowitz (1997), Altman (1995, 1996), Berzoff, Flanagan and Hertz (1996), Chodorow (1989), Foster, Moskowitz and Javier (1996), Greene (1997, 2000), Greene and Boyd-Franklin (1996), Hall (2002), Jackson and Greene (2000), Jordan (1997), Leary (1995, 1997, 2000), Moncayo (1998), Ratigan (1995), Thompson (1987, 1989, 1996), and Yi (1998) for examples of innovations.

Despite these innovations, psychoanalysis and psychodynamic therapies are still often assailed as being intrinsically unsuitable for psychotherapy with clients of color as well as women and lesbian, gay, and bisexual clients. When we examine the aforementioned works, as well as many others, and when we consider what takes place among many of our colleagues in practice, we see there is great diversity in the way that psychodynamic models are taught and are practiced. In this paper I will explore some of the factors that contribute to the perception of the unsuitability of psychodynamic therapies for culturally diverse people, I challenge some of the misconceptions about psychodynamic theory and practice, and I examine why some practitioners are complicit in practicing in ways that deserve critical commentary. I end with some suggestions about how to make psychodynamic therapies more inclusive.

MISCONCEPTIONS ABOUT PSYCHODYNAMIC THEORIES

One misconception about psychodynamic theories is the assumption that there is one unified theory upon which everyone agrees when in fact we are talking about a constellation of different theoretical trajectories that have common origins in Freud's psychoanalytic theory of neurosis. Leary (2000) describes psychoanalysis as a method of inquiry that raises questions and seeks through the patient's narrative to determine the unconscious meanings of developmental and social experiences. Mental operations are presumed to function in such a way that feelings and impulses that would be anxiety provoking or unacceptable to the ego if consciously experienced will be kept out of awareness or disguised by unconscious psychological defense mechanisms. As a part of this framework, affective processes are presumed to be endowed with an autonomy that permits them to be detached or displaced from or onto objects of greater or lesser significance (Campbell, 1989; Greene, 1997). Psychodynamic methods of inquiry rest on interpretive theories of mental processes that are unified primarily around the notion that unconscious processes exist and can be important determinants of behavior and affect (Greene, 1997).

Psychodynamic formulations commonly assume that clients can change their behavior if they understand their unconscious contributions to that behavior. Despite many common theoretical elements, however, the practical application of diverse theoretical approaches that can be appropriately labeled psychodynamic range from the most orthodox to those heavily influenced by feminist theory. Furthermore, the salience of intrapsychic dynamics does not lessen the importance of understanding the way that gender, sexual orientation, and ethnocultural identities are directly relevant to the shaping of the patient's intrapsychic elements and their social world, particularly, but not exclusively, when they are tied to social disadvantage. Specifically, we need to know how the patient interacts with and understands her social world, what it elicits in her, and what the patient's identities elicit in others in her world, and how they all reciprocally influence and shape the intrapsychic world. Patients who are different in ways that are disparaged by society face a range of additional psychological tasks and challenges that must be understood by the therapist. This understanding cannot be accomplished if the therapist focuses exclusively on intrapsychic mechanisms at the exclusion of the aforementioned realities. Furthermore, the exclusive focus on the intrapsychic is not a requirement of psychodynamic therapy. This raises an important question as to why many practitioners and theoreticians continue to practice as if this were so.

Critics of psychodynamic and psychoanalytic theories also object to them as if they have remained unaltered for the last century. It is rather like suggesting that modern chemists who choose only to use the periodic table of 1926 are exemplars of their discipline or as if their doing so indicates no acquisition of new knowledge since. Critiques of early work such as classical theory ignore numerous new formulations such as intersubjective (Yi, 1998), contemporary object relations (Adams, 2000), relational and feminist (Jordan, 1997; Leary, 1997, 2000) analyses of theory. Many of these innovations in theory seek to apply a broader range of possible meanings to any patient's behavior, as well as different potential outcomes from the same developmental circumstances. However, they do not limit themselves to analyses of behavior as a function of the patient's personal psychology alone. They include an analysis and consideration of the integral effects of the larger societal and cultural milieu in which identity and relationships around race, sex, sexual orientation, and class are shaped. Perhaps what is most important is that new approaches presume that the positioning of the therapist is not objective or neutral, rather that therapist and client each view the world via their own subjective cultural lens. Their analyses are also situated in the explicit consideration of the effects of sociocultural variables on the shaping of theoretical paradigms of pathology and health, as well as diagnostic nosologies. Hence, anything that influences a person's characteristic ways of being in the world, how they come to see who they and others are or can be is "grist" for the mill. In contemporary paradigms, the therapist seeks to understand the client's experience with the view that differences are seen as different perspectives rather than "right" or "wrong."

THE THERAPIST'S SUBJECTIVE CULTURAL POSITIONING

Psychodynamic psychotherapists are influenced by their own personal cultural identities as well as the culture of psychodynamic theory. Like any other culture, psychodynamic theory and theorists are embedded in a cultural matrix that is not objective, but rather is embedded in a larger Western, masculine, bourgeois, intellectual culture with its own language, rules of belonging and standards of normalcy (Abramowitz, 1997; Fancher, 1993; Moncayo, 1998; Strickland, 2000). This standard of normalcy is by definition subjective. Psychodynamic thinking emerged out of a modernist and positivist scientific tradition that has tended to ignore its own cultural relativism and bias (Abramowitz, 1997; Leary, 2000). Abramowitz (1997) has argued that early, classical psychoanalytic theory grossly neglected the exploration of the psychodynamics of subjective cultural positioning without which you cannot understand the patient's reality. In the case of African American lesbians, the patients, identities represent a convergence of sexuality, gender, and ethnic role identification and enculturation that can only be truly understood in the context of the sociopolitical reality that constructs the meaning of those identities. For example, if the erotic attraction to the other sex were not a part of our culture's definition of gender normalcy, we would not likely have the same concept of or interest in what we consider sexual orientation. This is not unique to psychodynamic theory. This is true of any other theory of institutional mental health (Strickland, 2000).

No theory of human behavior is culture free or unbiased. By definition and design, our theoretical paradigms are products of the culture from which they emerge; hence, they cannot be unbiased, objective, or neutral. In their practical application we must ask where the limitations and biases are and how can we use new knowledge to improve on those limitations. This is true of therapies and paradigms on the other end of the conceptual continuum as well. Kwate (2002) observes that Cognitive Behavioral and Rational Emotive therapies have been viewed as if they are based on objective assessments of behavior and rational, linear thinking. It is as if the therapist's subjective sociocultural positioning is separate from rather than a part of the equation. The assumption is that they are less vulnerable to cultural bias; indeed, culture does not seem to matter at all. When rational thought as opposed to emotion is viewed as the catalyst for scientific progress and healing with the attendant value of mastery over nature, human interests over the interests of nature or the interest of living in harmony with the natural world, cultural bias is flagrant. Cartesian thinking is not culture free or unbiased. It represents a particular way of viewing the world that is embedded in a specific philosophy or ideas about how the world works. Consider an African world view, "I am, because we are" in contrast to the Cartesian notion, "I think, therefore I am." In the former, relationship and connection is a fundamental ingredient in existence in contrast to the latter. Cartesian philosophies exemplify the mind-body, mind-spirit dualism that is not a given for many cultures throughout the world. The assumption that they represent a form of cultural neutrality is a continued failure to examine the subjective cultural positioning of psychological theorists, their theories and their assumptions about human behavior.

American psychotherapies have been for the most part, ethnocentric, androcentric, and heterocentric. Psychodynamic modalities are no exception. Every theory of psychotherapy has evolved out of theories of human behavior, in a specific cultural context, where women, people of color, members of sexual minorities, people with disabilities, and other socially disadvantaged groups have not been among the teachers, theoreticians, practitioners or architects of that discourse. When members of these groups were present, they represented such small numbers that their voices were often silenced in many ways. Strickland (2000) observes that the contributions of people who are not male, white, and European have not been appreciated. Those contributions are excluded from theory, ignored by method and punished by conclusions drawn from reductionistic experimental paradigms that are not proficient at explaining complex patterns of development or behavior.

Many of those who are and were among a stark marginalized minority who created innovations in this work often practice in a kind of psychodynamic closet. Jordan (1997) observes that breaking from traditional paradigms can leave us feeling doubtful about our expertise, vulnerable to criticism, and threatened with disconnection and isolation from professional peers if we are cut off from our community of professional colleagues. This can be particularly difficult for practitioners and theoreticians who are members of marginalized groups as they may already feel their intellect rendered suspect and their acceptance contingent on their going along with the status quo.

My own experience as a co-editor of a volume on innovations in psychodynamic and analytic therapies with African American women (Jackson & Greene, 2000) supports this view. Many more authors initially agreed to write chapters for this volume than were actually completed. While many practical and personal realities interfered in the process for many authors, others, including some who completed papers, expressed concerns about actually committing their ideas and nontraditional work to a paper where it was subject to the scrutiny of their colleagues. Many, reported feeling marginalized and devalued professionally because of their identity as women of color citing experiences of being treated since their graduate training as if they had nothing to offer and "no right to be here." Others found that when they raised concerns about the fallacy of cultural neutrality of psychodynamic theory and attempted to raise issues related to the race of the patient, and subjective positioning of the therapist their criticisms were quite unwelcome. Some acknowledged being patronized while others recalled responses that were overtly hostile. Still others expressed concerns about not being taken seriously or not being accepted by African American peers, who felt that psychodynamic approaches were inappropriate for any African American patient favoring more Afrocentric approaches, thus challenging the cultural authenticity of psychodynamic therapists of color. Overall, concerns encompassed being caught betwixt two peer communities with neither support or acknowledgment and sometimes being subject to feelings of disdain.

Members of socially marginalized groups have been historically pathologized by institutional mental health when compared to White, middle class, heterosexual persons, usually men, who are deemed the exemplars of normative/healthy behavior. While the ethnocentric, classist, sexist, and heterosexist practices of traditional psychotherapies have changed over time, it is fair to say that psychodynamic theories and practice have been the slowest to change their views, particularly with regard to sexual minorities.

It is important to consider how we define a theory and the purpose it serves. A useful understanding of a theory might be as a solid hypothesis about something that while *being* stable is flexible enough to respond to the acquisition of new knowledge about what it explains. Strickland (2000) observes that theories and methods were designed to be replaced. Theory must always be a work in evolution that while conceptually stable also possesses the capacity to allow the same information to be viewed or understood from multiple perspectives. Psychodynamic thinking emphasizes the importance of being able to view the same data or behavior as something that can have many different origins and, therefore, many different meanings, determinants or explanations. The process of therapy itself involves asking what the issue or symbol means to the individual client with the assumption that the same narrative or story can have multiple meanings and origins depending on the client's history or perspective.

A main task of therapy is to elicit that client's unique narrative or story. The client's history and perspective is by definition going to be "colored" by race and ethnicity and the history of racism, sexism, heterosexism in the United States as well as its manifestations in the life of the client and significant figures in the client's life. Hence, the exploration of this material has never been antithetical to psychodynamic thinking; rather, it is quite consistent. Why then has exploring this material been so controversial?

SOCIAL PRIVILEGE AND THE THERAPIST'S COUNTERTRANSFERENCE

Thompson (1989) writes that the failure to explore sociopolitical realities has been more a function of the therapists' countertransference resistance, and is not an inherent limitation of the theory itself. Competent clinicians do not practice in theoretical lock step or cookbook fashion. While they use their theoretical understandings to guide their work, they also allow their experiences with clients to inform what they have learned theoretically and make modifications accordingly. Those who suggest they must be true to the theory in its most fundamentalist interpretation, with indifference to or at the expense of the patient, should be viewed with suspicion. Theory represents a guide to practice decisions; it is not an absolute determinant.

An additional problem is that changes in theory and pedagogy do not automatically result in changes in practice, for many of the reasons discussed here that are connected to having or identifying with a privileged identity. When the therapist, often a dominant cultural being, fails to allow for sufficient self-examination about his/her own privileged identities, or wish for them and how it affects his/her subjectivity, the problem lies with the therapist not the theory per se. How the therapist is raced, gendered, and sexually oriented affects what they choose to see and what they choose to avoid just as it does in the client. Similarly, theoreticians' understanding of the order of the world, via their subjective cultural lens, informs theoretical explanations they put forth about human behavior and its meaning. It is important to understand the nature of constituents of social power and privileged identities to understand why this is so.

SOCIAL PRIVILEGE, DISADVANTAGE, AND THE THERAPIST'S DENIAL AND SHAME

Discrepancies in social power may be understood as representations of social privilege and social disadvantage. The need to deny the existence and meaning of those power differentials is often a key ingredient in the need to maintain silence around institutional oppression associated with ethnic differences, gender, and sexual orientation. When therapists are required to analyze society's realistic power differentials and injustices, and their meaning in patients' lives, as well as in their own lives, many experience discomfort with the process and avoid it. For many people, acknowledging a locus of disadvantage is much easier than acknowledging a locus of power or privilege.

In this discussion, I connect the subjective cultural positioning of psychodynamic theoreticians, as members of institutional mental health, to their identities as primarily dominant/privileged cultural beings (i.e., White, middle to upper class, heterosexual, and male). These observations may also apply to some members of marginalized groups who identify with and wish for privileged identities. This interpretation may also apply to those who may need to avoid confronting the lack of power and control that can be experienced in acknowledging one's victimization. Their subjective cultural positioning is connected to their inability or reluctance to acknowledge the existence of cultural positioning itself or its influence on their views of what is pathological and what is healthy. Additionally, this positioning contributes to avoidance of or reluctance to explore these issues in the lives of culturally diverse clients.

Social privilege is usually something that facilitates the optimal development of an individual, increases access to societal opportunities, or simply makes life easier, but is not acquired by virtue of merit or personal effort. It is gained simply by being a member of the group that is privileged. It is important to understand the nature of privilege as something that is not based on merit to grasp fully the reluctance of many people to acknowledge that they may have privileged identities. What is noteworthy is that while the benefit or privilege is given regardless of merit, once people have it, they experience it as something they have a right to have and that perhaps others who are not like them do not have an equal right to (Wildman, 1996). Traditional mental health paradigms, that include but are not exclusive to psychodynamic theories, have largely ignored this social equation. They have accepted the myth of the meritocracy or level playing field in the United States. Differences from a dominant culture norm have traditionally been attributed to pathology or erased altogether. Both erasure and pathologizing allow clinicians to avoid the difficult business of challenging some of their own dearly held values, and beliefs about their clients and inevitably about themselves.

African American lesbians are positioned at the juncture of ethnicity, gender roles, and sexual orientation in a society that has been invested in maintaining the dominant cultural status quo. Who they are challenges many beliefs about who people should be, how men and women should behave, and what it means if they do not. Dominant cultural values have historically been reflected in mental health institutions and paradigms. Those paradigms invoked and expressed by dominant cultural beings refused to acknowledge their own subjective cultural positioning and invoked the position of objective scientist instead. In this context, the systemic determinants of social privilege and disadvantage are usually invisible and if materialized are denied by those who are in power and who benefit from them. The therapist who needs to deny their own locus of social privilege may need to avoid recognizing a patient's locus of social disadvantage as a significant contributor to their problems, rather than their personal deficiency.

Johnson (2001) argues that privilege is not just a problem for those who do not have it, but is a problem for those who have it as well because of its relational nature. When someone is unfairly privileged by social systems and gets something they do not deserve, someone else is unfairly disadvantaged and does not gain something they do deserve. Each member of this dyad will have feelings about the inequity. This is implicated in our understanding of the ego ideal of the therapist/theoretician.

The ego ideal is defined as the collection of ideal characteristics that we would like to see in ourselves, and the way that some people do see themselves. The reality of who we are always falls short of our ideal because by definition the ideal is perfection and, therefore, unattainable. When we are confronted with the ways that we fall short of that ideal we experience shame and guilt. Few people want to acknowledge getting something that they did not deserve or even worse, profiting at someone else's expense, whether deliberate or not. This consequence of privilege is not viewed as a positive reflection on ourselves when it occurs; rather it is deemed shameful, makes us uncomfortable about ourselves, and can induce guilt. To avoid experiencing shame and discomfort we must deny the reality that having a privileged identity means that we may profit at someone else's expense. This denial becomes difficult if we hold a social privilege and we encounter people who are disadvantaged around that characteristic. The encounter itself can elicit discomfort even if differences and/or their meaning are never overtly discussed.

When the reality of privilege materializes, it also challenges individual's personal beliefs about how they became successful and perhaps even more fundamentally, who they really are. This can be particularly troubling to people who need to believe that their *ego ideal* is the reality. Most clinicians become therapists because they want to help people. They see themselves as somewhat altruistic, tolerant, and accepting. These are our ego ideals. When we are either invested in believing that sexual orientation, race, or gender represent real and not socially constructed differences and that those differences justify unequal (subordinate) treatment and limited access to the opportunities that others who are privileged have benefited from; or that those characteristics mean nothing and can be erased leaving us with the essence of the person, successful therapy cannot take place. It is unlikely that these issues can be confronted in a client without scrutinizing and challenging one's own sense of self as a mental health service provider. This task can be a painful and difficult but necessary undertaking.

Many of the issues raised in my discussion of privilege and disadvantage arise when therapists are confronted with clients whose life experiences challenge the therapists' sense of who the therapist is in the world. There is little doubt that this has been a phenomenon throughout the history of organized mental health. Psychodynamic paradigms were no more immune to this than any others. Members of the majority or dominant group in the United States have not until recently been challenged to understand the values, beliefs and behaviors of nondominant cultural groups, rather, their differences from the majority were historically deemed problematic minimizing any internal conflict within the majority. Their privilege as dominant group members protected them and their own biases from scrutiny. Espin (1995) observes that a significant part of being privileged is being trained to not see anything or regard anything as important if it does not have to do with you.

SUGGESTIONS FOR GREATER INCLUSION

Moncayo (1998) suggests that it is important to acknowledge that just as there are dominant/majority and nondominant/minority groups in society, those same hierarchical divisions may be found within what can be seen as a psychoanalytic culture as well. Usually the majority voices are most privileged and often deemed to speak for the entire culture. It is also those most privileged who have access to the venues that define the salient aspects of the work itself. This phenomenon has been observed even in psychotherapies that emerged out of a need to reject dominant cultural analyses. For example, Feminist theory emerged out of a need to address the realities and consequences of patriarchy and sexism in institutional mental health for women therapists and clients. It also attempted to challenge traditional therapies with the view that women's subordinate social status was a factor in the mental health problems of women.

Despite these worthy beginnings, early formulations of Feminist theory were developed and articulated by those women who were most privileged (middle and upper middle class, well educated, white, and heterosexual). They were criticized for their failure to represent the full spectrum of diversity among women. Similarly, Afrocentric models of therapy emerged out of an attempt to address the failure of traditional therapies to include a consideration of the role of African cultural derivatives, race, and the management of racism in any attempt to comprehend the psychologies of African Americans. Nonetheless, they too were assailed for failing to represent the full spectrum of diversity among its members. The reality of gender oppression was largely ignored. Hence, the complex gender coded nature of racism for African Americans was inadequately addressed and heterosexism was and continues to be virtually ignored (Greene, 2000; McNair, 1992; Williams,

1999). In both models, theory was articulated from the lens of the groups most privileged members, to the exclusion of many group members whose other identities were not only socially marginalized but were transformed and complicated the meaning of any one identity. In Greene (1997, 2000), I discuss the clinical presentation of these issues as well as ways that different aspects of these approaches and psychodynamic theory may be successfully integrated into the treatment of diverse clients like African American lesbians.

It is fair to say that although they have changed over time, the dominant and most privileged voices within the psychodynamic and psychoanalytic community may be slowest to change. Perhaps this happens because change can mean a loss of privilege. Many disagreements within psychodynamic psychology take place in the pages of academic journals and gatherings that are rarely heard outside of that "culture." Often dominant views and perspectives are presented as if everyone is of like mind about them and as if they are naturally correct. Like any culture or group, not every member of the group is of like mind and not every member subscribes in lock step fashion to all of the traditional beliefs espoused by the group's dominant and most powerful members. It may be more difficult, however, for dissenting voices to find their way into journal forums that are often controlled by gatekeepers that hold views that are more traditional. While new journals, books and other venues emerge, there are still some barriers that prevent dissemination of alternative views.

A major factor that contributes to the silencing of dissenting voices may be a function of being in a culture where the written word defines a knowledge base rather than an oral tradition, found more commonly among the traditions of many people of color. This represents one of the barriers making many innovations in practice slow to find their way into the mainstream or garner any acknowledgment. While the snide saying "those who can do, those who can't teach" suggests that those who practice a craft rather than those who teach that craft have greater expertise that is not what necessarily applies to the development of innovations in theory. In psychoanalytic theory and the development of practice innovations (as well as other disciplines) those who can, do, but those who write about what they do and think define the content of the body of literature that serves as the state of the art.

Those who write serve on editorial and consulting review boards and they determine what is published, who is heard, who is considered legitimate, and who is not. This is how the content of professional literature, the state of the art, is determined. Although alternative journals, books, and venues exist, it is often the most traditional venues that are accorded legitimacy and prestige. Furthermore, in many academic institutions and psychoanalytic institutes only publication and or presentation in the most traditional venues are counted in obtaining tenure, promotions, and certification. This discourages the kind of innovative thinking that characterizes much of the work with ethnic and sexual minorities and other socially disadvantaged groups. This work must be more widely recognized.

Beyond these factors there is a practical reality that those who practice and who often develop innovations in that practice are disadvantaged in an arena that privileges publishing. While practice does not preclude writing about one's art, there are practical realities that leave people who do not work in academic or psychoanalytic institutions at a disadvantage. Access to professional libraries and research material, as well as other concrete forms of assistance (for example, research fellowships) may be limited for clinicians.

Most practitioners' incomes are tied to the number of hours they spend seeing patients and they do not earn income for activities like writing, a professional activity that requires large blocks of time. While many public and private mental health institutions say that they support research among their clinical staff, few actually support and some even punish those who are successful in this activity. In some public practice arenas, success at publishing among professionals of color or other marginalized groups can elicit jealousies expressed in the perception that a clinician does not have enough work to do if they have time to write, and can result in the assignment of additional clinical duties. Writers who challenge the traditional canon may be particularly vulnerable to this treatment. A practical reality of conducting research and writing is that it requires large blocks of time, time that outside of academia is not supported or funded. Practitioners who serve as adjunct faculty are at a disadvantage as well. Their research productivity is generally no match for that of full-time faculty with whom they compete for full-time academic positions. Hence, many find that despite long years of experience, both in practice and training students, experience that can prove very valuable in collaborations with other faculty; they are rarely considered "published enough" to be taken seriously as candidates for full-time positions. This also reinforces the notion that spending time in a practice arena, perhaps learning that craft before pursuing an academic career is disadvantageous. Valuable experience and insight that may be gained from that work is lost as well.

These practices fail to incorporate the rich repository of clinical experience and innovation that can emerge from practitioners as a group into the academic professional knowledge base. It is important that we more actively encourage collaborative work and begin building the necessary bridges between practice and the academy. Academic researchers can share resources with clinical partners in ways that lead to the expansion and perhaps greater inclusiveness of what we consider our state of the art, as well as its diversity. Such work can lead to the development of paradigms that continue to improve our competence and literacy with clients from diverse cultural backgrounds.

CONCLUSION

Psychodynamic paradigms have much to offer the treatment of African American lesbians as well as other members of culturally diverse groups. It is important to understand that the unconscious has the power to free people to be more authentic, to integrate disparate parts of themselves, to be more present, productive, creative and free to make conscious, informed choices about what they do, how they go about life and who they choose to have in their lives. Psychodynamic paradigms can also be useful in understanding the dynamics of power between privileged and disadvantaged groups. Jackson (2000) observes that its focus on how people cope and defend in response to pain and trauma in early life is useful in helping patients who belong to socially disadvantaged groups cope with the trauma of social oppression. Root (1992) discusses social oppression as a form of insidious trauma. This warrants revisiting our concept of trauma and expanding it to include the trauma of negotiating what Franklin (1993) calls the invisibility syndrome. Invisibility includes discrimination in access to housing, jobs, education, and the very basic elements of life, the vigilance required when there is a potential for mental and physical assaults, negative stereotyping, its impact on self-image and the evolution of internalized oppression. In its essence, invisibility involves the management of feelings that are a response to being treated as a stereotype and not as a real person.

All of these dilemmas can characterize the lives of African American lesbians as members of a multiply marginalized and socially traumatized group. Psychodynamic therapy can be a powerful tool when it validates a client's accurate perception of social as well as personal injustice and exploitation as well as the feelings elicited by such treatment. It can help therapists correctly recognize the patient's place in time and culture and the influences of those factors on the development of intrapsychic mechanisms and it can assist patients in consciously developing adaptive strategies for addressing ongoing forms of social trauma. Ultimately, psychodynamic therapies can be useful when they help clients know the difference between what they have been told they are, either by family or social pathology, and who they really are and when therapy is a place for clients to tell their story with all of its uniqueness and have it be heard.

REFERENCES

Abramovitz, S. (1997). A discussion of lesbians and psychoanalytic culture and a response to Kassof's treatment of a homosexual woman. In A. Goldberg (Ed.), *Conversations in self psychology* (pp. 231-243). Hillsdale, NJ: The Analytic Press.

Adams, J. M. (2000). Individual and group psychotherapy with African American women: Understanding the identity and context of the therapist and patient. In L. C. Jackson & B. Greene (Eds.), *Psychotherapy with African American women: Innovations in psychodynamic perspectives and practice* (pp. 33-61). New York: Guilford Press.

Altman, N. (1996). The accommodation of diversity in psychoanalysis. In R. Perez Foster, M. Moskowitz, & R. A. Javier (Eds.), *Reaching across boundaries of culture and class: Widening the scope of psychotherapy* (pp. 195-209). Northvale, NJ: Jason Aronson.

Altman, N. (1995). *The analyst in the inner city: Race, class and culture: Through a psychoanalytic lens*. Hillsdale, NJ: The Analytic Press.

Berzoff, J., Flanagan, L. M., & Hertz, P. (1996). *Inside out and outside in: Psychodynamic clinical theory and practice in contemporary multicultural contexts*. Northvale, NJ: Jason Aronson.

Campbell, R. (1989). *Psychiatric dictionary, 2nd Ed.* New York: Oxford University Press.

Chodorow, N. (1989). *Feminism and psychoanalytic theory*. New Haven, CT: Yale University Press.

Espin, O. (1995). On knowing you are the unknown: Women of color constructing psychology. In J. Adleman & G. Enguidanos (Eds.), *Racism in the lives of women: Testimony, theory and guides to practice* (pp. 127-136). New York: Harrington Park Press.

Fancher, R. T. (1993). Psychoanalysis as culture. *Issues in Psychoanalytic Psychology*, *15*(2), 81-94.

Foster, R. M. P., Moskowitz, M., & Javier, R. Art. (Eds.). (1996). *Reaching across boundaries of culture and class: Widening the scope of psychotherapy*. Northvale, NJ: Jason Aronson.

Franklin, A. J. (1993, July/August). The invisibility syndrome. *Family Therapy Networker*, *17*(4), 33-39.

Glassgold, J. (1992). New directions in dynamic theories of lesbianism: From psychoanalysis to social constructionism. In J. Chrisler & D. Howard (Eds.), *New direc-*

tions in feminist psychology: Practice, theory and research (pp. 154-163). New York: Springer.

Glassgold, J. & Iasenza, S. (Eds.). (1995). *Lesbians and psychoanalysis: Revolutions in theory and practice.* New York: Free Press.

Greene, B. (2003). What difference does a difference make? Societal privilege, disadvantage, and discord in human relationships. In J. Robinson & L. James (Ed.), *Diversity in human interaction: A tapestry of America* (pp. 3-20). New York: Oxford University Press.

Greene, B. (2000). African American Lesbian and Bisexual women in Feminist-Psychodynamic psychotherapies: Surviving and thriving between a rock and a hard place. In L. C. Jackson & B. Greene (Eds.), *Psychotherapy with African American women: Innovations in psychodynamic perspectives and practice* (pp. 82-125). New York: Guilford Press.

Greene, B. (1997, June). Psychotherapy with African American women: Integrating Feminist and Psychodynamic models. *Smith College Studies in Social Work, 67*(3), 299-322.

Greene, B. & Boyd-Franklin, N. (1996). African American lesbians: Issues in couples therapy. In J. Laird & R. J. Green (Eds.), *Lesbians and gay men in couples & families: A handbook for practitioners* (pp. 251-271). San Francisco, CA: Josses Bass.

Hall, M. F. (2002). Race, gender and transference in psychotherapy. In F. Kaslow (Ed. In Chief), J. J. Magnavita (Volume Ed.), *Comprehensive handbook of psychotherapy (Vol. I): Psychodynamic/object relations* (pp. 565-584). New York: John Wiley & Sons.

Jackson, L. (2000). The new multiculturalism and psychodynamic theory. In L.C. Jackson & B. Greene (Eds.), *Psychotherapy with African American women: Innovations in psychodynamic perspectives and practice* (pp. 1-14). New York: Guilford Press.

Jackson, L. C. & Greene, B. (Eds.). (2000). *Psychotherapy with African American women: Innovations in psychodynamic perspectives and practice.* New York: Guilford Press.

Johnson, A. G. (2001). *Privilege, power, and difference.* Mountain View, CA: Mayfield Publishing Co.

Jordan, J. (1997). Relational therapy in a nonrelational world. *Work in Progress, No. 79.* Wellesley, MA: Stone Center Working Paper Series.

Kwate, N. O. (2002). *Assessing African centered mental disorder: Validation of the cultural misorientation Scale.* Unpublished doctoral dissertation, St. John's University, Queens, NY.

Leary, K. (1997). Race, self-disclosure and "forbidden talk": Race and ethnicity in contemporary clinical practice. *Psychoanalytic Quarterly, 66,* 163-189.

Leary, K. (1995). Interpreting in the dark: Race and ethnicity in psychoanalytic psychotherapy. *Psychoanalytic Quarterly, 12,* 127-140.

Leary, K. (2000). Racial enactments in dynamic treatment. *Psychoanalytic Dialogues: A Journal of Relational Perspectives, 10*(4), 639-653.

Mattei, L. (1996). Coloring development: Race and culture in psychodynamic theories. In J. Berzoff, L. M. Flanagan, & P. Hertz (Eds.), *Inside out and outside in:*

Psychodynamic clinical theory and practice in contemporary multicultural contexts (pp. 221-245). Northvale, NJ: Jason Aronson.

McNair, L. D. (1992). African American women in therapy: An Afrocentric and feminist synthesis. *Women & Therapy, 12*(1/2), 5-19.

Moncayo, R. (1998). Cultural diversity and the cultural epistemological structure of psychoanalysis: Implications for psychotherapy with Latinos and other minorities. *Psychoanalytic Psychology, 15*(2), 262-286.

Ratigan, B. (1995, February). Inner world, outer world. Exploring the tension of race, sexual orientation and class and the internal world. *Psychodynamic Counselling, 1*(2), 173-186.

Root, M.P.P. (1992). The impact of trauma on personality: The second reconstruction. In L. S. Brown & M. Ballou (Eds.), *Personality and psychopathology: Feminist reappraisals* (pp. 229-265). New York: Guilford.

Schachter, J. S. & Butts, H. F. (1968). Transference and countertransference in interracial analysis. *Journal of the American Psychoanalytic Association, 16*, 792-808.

Strickland, B. R. (2000, March). Misassumptions, misadventures and the misuse of psychology. *American Psychologist, 55*(3), 331-338.

Thompson, C. (1996). The African American patient in psychodynamic treatment. In R. Perez Foster, M. Moskowitz, & R. A. Javier (Eds.), *Reaching across boundaries of culture and class: Widening the scope of psychotherapy* (pp. 115-142). Northvale, NJ: Jason Aronson.

Thompson, C. (1989). Psychoanalytic psychotherapy with inner city patients. *Journal of Contemporary Psychotherapy, 19*(2), 137-148.

Thompson, C. (1987). Racism or neuroticism: An entangled dilemma for the Black middle class patient. *Journal of the American Academy of Psychoanalysis, 15*(3), 395-405.

Wildman, S. (Ed.). (1996). *Privilege revealed: How invisible preference undermines America.* New York: New York University Press.

Williams, C. B. (1999). African American women, afrocentrism and feminism: Implications for psychotherapy. *Women & Therapy, 22*(4), 1-16.

Yi, K. Y. (1998). Transference and race: An intersubjective conceptualization. *Psychoanalytic Psychology, 15*(2), 245-261.

Building Lesbian Sandcastles
on the Shore of Relational Psychoanalysis

Beverly Decker

SUMMARY. Stephen Mitchell, one of the founders of relational psychoanalysis, wrote two early (1978, 1981) articles challenging the then widely held view in psychoanalysis that love between same-sex persons was inextricably pathological. His writings gave me hope that, as a lesbian-identified therapist, I could actively participate in a psychoanalytic community of ideas and practice. However, in the 1980s, when I entered psychoanalytic training, the sandcastle of hope I had built from Mitchell's papers was destroyed with the incoming tide. I describe here a personal journey related to lesbian identity in various contexts from 1978 and 1981 when Mitchell spoke so authoritatively about psychoanalytic attitudes towards homosexuality to 1996 when he described "the plight of the perplexed clinician" with regard to "gender and sexual orientation in the age of postmodernism." *[Article copies available for a fee from The Haworth Document Delivery Service: 1-800-HAWORTH. E-mail address: <docdelivery@*

Beverly Decker, MSW, is in private practice in New York City. She is on the faculty of The Institute for Human Identity where she teaches a course on "Queer Theory: History, Controversy and Implications for Psychoanalytic Theory and Practice." She is a graduate of the New Directions Program in Critical Thinking and Writing in Psychoanalysis at the Washington Psychoanalytic Foundation.

Address correspondence to: Beverly Decker, 26 W. 90th Street, Suite 1, New York, NY 10024 (E-mail: bevydecker@aol.com).

[Haworth co-indexing entry note]: "Building Lesbian Sandcastles on the Shore of Relational Psychoanalysis." Decker, Beverly. Co-published simultaneously in *Journal of Lesbian Studies* (Harrington Park Press, an imprint of The Haworth Press, Inc.) Vol. 8, No. 1/2, 2004, pp. 79-93; and: *Lesbians, Feminism, and Psychoanalysis: The Second Wave* (ed: Judith M. Glassgold, and Suzanne Iasenza) Harrington Park Press, an imprint of The Haworth Press, Inc., 2004, pp. 79-93. Single or multiple copies of this article are available for a fee from The Haworth Document Delivery Service [1-800-HAWORTH, 9:00 a.m. - 5:00 p.m. (EST). E-mail address: docdelivery@ haworthpress.com].

KEYWORDS. Stephen Mitchell, relational psychoanalysis, queer theory, lesbian identity, homophobia

In November 1999, in the preface to his last issue as the founding editor of *Psychoanalytic Dialogues: A Journal of Relational Perspectives*, Stephen Mitchell remarked that in the ten years that had passed since the journal was conceived, "the term relational has moved from intellectual contraband to almost a buzzword" spawning "fascinating new questions and problems for those of us who love the work" (pp. 717-718). Although only fifty-four when he died suddenly in December 2000, Mitchell is recognized as a standard bearer for the approach which places the quality of relations, internal and external, real and imaginary, at the center of the theoretical and clinical psychoanalytic endeavor.

I never met Stephen Mitchell but his work has had a profound effect on my life. His two early papers on homosexuality inspired and supported me as a lesbian-identified woman at a time when the predominant psychoanalytic view of same-sex love seemed to be based on fear, ignorance, and hatred. My reading relationship with Mitchell's writing began in 1978 and in 1981 when he challenged, with the intellectual rigor for which he would become known, the psychoanalytic presumption that homosexuality was inevitably pathological and should be changed. Relatively unknown in his lifetime, since his death these papers have received a great deal of attention and have been reprinted in the journal *Studies in Gender and Sexuality* (2001, 3, pp. 3-59).

In his first published paper, "Psychodynamics, Homosexuality, and the Question of Pathology" (1978), Mitchell observes that most psychoanalytic approaches stress early developmental contributions and tend to view homosexuality as a deviation from healthy and mature living. He then announces in a highly confident manner that he's going to demonstrate that this is not true:

> The notion that psychodynamic causes and contributions imply pathology is, as I will show, a historical artifact deriving from Freud's original libidinal fixation theory of neurosis. Such an assumption is no longer necessary, but is also inconsistent with more

contemporary psychodynamic understanding of human experience. (1978, p. 260)

The second paper, "The Psychoanalytic Treatment of Homosexuality: Some Technical Considerations" was published in 1981 two years before the then controversial *Object Relations in Psychoanalysis* co-authored with Jay Greenberg–a book which opposed a relational model to the drive structure model of mind and development emerging from sexual and aggressive impulses. Drive theory might be unified and comprehensive, but Mitchell's view as early as 1978 was that it was outdated. In his paper, Mitchell summarizes the traditional psychoanalytic consensus beginning in the 1950s that homosexuality was psychodynamically derived, pathological, and potentially treatable, and evolving in the early 1960s into an approach that entailed deviations from traditional analytic technique (1981, p. 65). He notes the belief propagated most notably by Ovesey, Bieber, Socarides, and Hatterer, that the pathological nature of homosexual relationships necessitated the analyst departing from the traditional position of neutrality to take an educative-directive analytic approach (1981, p. 65). Mitchell denounced this belief as "the totalizing devaluation of homosexually" (1981, p. 65).

Mitchell was concerned that the "greatest toll" of this pathologizing approach was evidenced in the "profound sense of failure, shame, self-hatred and deep cynicism about the analytic process" (1978, p. 267) experienced by homosexuals in analysis. In 1978, he wrote that given the language, metaphors, and presumptions in psychoanalytic theorizing on homosexuality:

> It would be difficult to deny what must be the considerable discouraging impact of psychoanalytic thought on any knowledgeable homosexual person unconvinced about the desirability for change, but seeking an opportunity for open inquiry (1978, p. 287).

Mitchell was right when he when he referred to the "souring" of members of the gay community (1978, p. 263) towards psychoanalysis. In 1973, Jill Johnston, a journalist for the *Village Voice* and a self-proclaimed lesbian-feminist activist, referred to psychoanalytic treatment, which so many gay people had been urged, sometimes forced, to undergo as a condition of not being disowned by their families, as "no more nor less than a form of blackmail" (p. 58).

But perhaps one of the most chilling statements in this regard came from the French writer Monique Wittig in a paper delivered in New York City at the Modern Language association in 1978. Wittig, who would later be a major influence in the work of Judith Butler on gender and sexuality, spoke of the political significance of the impossibility that lesbians, feminists, and gay men faced in the attempt to communicate in heterosexual society other than with psychoanalysts who exploited their need for communication. She compared the oppressed person, the psychoanalyzed lesbian, feminist, or gay man to

> one who (in the same way as the witches could, under torture, only repeat the language that the inquisitors wanted to hear) has no other choice (if s/he does not want to destroy the implicit contract which allows her/him to communicate and which s/he needs), than to attempt to say what s/he is supposed to say. They say this can last for a lifetime–a cruel contract which constrains a human being to display her/his misery to an oppressor who is directly responsible for it, who exploits her/him economically, politically, ideologically, and whose interpretations reduce this misery to a few figures of speech. (1980, p. 433)

This anguished expression of suffering meshed with Mitchell's view that, in the service of the dehomosexualization process, "certain" psychoanalysts were exploiting the "transference and the patient's shame" (1981, p. 70), and that by "deliberately encouraging compliance and submission in their work with homosexuals" (1981, p. 70), these analysts were bringing into sharp focus what seemed to be the "necessary contradiction and bad faith inherent in a procedure which both actively exploits and then claims to analyze the transference" (1981, p. 70).

JUST HOW UNUSUAL WAS HOMOPHOBIA IN PSYCHOANALYSIS?

A big difference between Mitchell and lesbian feminist activists, especially in the 1970s, was that he believed that analysts "who had a homophobic ax to grind" (1981, p. 63) were a vocal minority. Because it violated fundamental principles of sound psychoanalytic practice, Mitchell thought it "highly unlikely that this approach is representative of the broad practice of most psychoanalysts with patients who are homosexual" (1981, p. 63). Mitchell believed that "many psychoanalysts approach homosexual material produced by their patients as they would any other experiences of their patients–simply as material to be inquired into and analyzed" (1981, p. 63). Such analysts are not likely to write about psychoanalytic approaches to homosexuality since they would feel that homosexuality does not pose particularly distinctive or unique features in terms of analytic work. Such a point of view would therefore be underrepresented in the literature (1981, p. 63). He found it "disturbing" that "this misleading impression" contributed to the "extremely negative attitudes toward psychoanalysis found in many sectors of the gay community" (1978, p. 262).

Recently, after the reissuing of Mitchell's papers, there has been more questioning as to what extent Mitchell was correct in his "speculation" that anti-homosexual analysts were really a minority. Sometimes he seems to be of two minds, feeling that most analysts are decent, while admitting that prejudice is so pervasive it would be hard to escape. At other times, it seems that his downplaying of the prevalence of anti-homosexuality in psychoanalysis comes from his political savvy. Others can only reflect on the conditions of that time and the difficulty of trying to remain within the psychoanalytic community while challenging its theories (Chodorow, 2002; Drescher, 2002; Lesser, 2002). Homophobia was certainly prevalent enough in psychoanalysis during this time that great courage was required to deviate from accepted doctrine and would have had negative repercussions on one's professional life, if such views were published at all (Conversation with Margaret Black, 2002; Magee & Miller, 2002). Whatever his motivation, as Magee and Miller (1997) point out, Mitchell was "one of the few exceptional analysts" (p. xxii) who "were critical of prevailing psychoanalytic practice of attributing common denominators of etiology and character to homosexual persons" (p. xxii). If you were a lesbian or gay man reading Mitchell in these early papers it was easy to get the impression that, if he had anything to do with it, this was all going to change.

AT THE INSTITUTE FOR HUMAN IDENTITY: DARING TO HOPE, 1978

In 1978, I was in a psychodynamic training program at the Institute for Human Identity (IHI) in New York City, one of the many "gay affirmative" psychotherapy centers which emerged in the 1970s as part of the gay liberation movement. Most of these centers were staffed by gay therapists and most had the word "identity" in their titles. Gay Liberationists stressed "coming out" and claiming an identity as crucial to self-esteem and social change. Psychoanalysis, as I've said, was not considered gay friendly.

It was, thus, an historical moment when someone brought a copy of Mitchell's 1978 article to an IHI staff meeting and read it out loud. Hearing what he had to say and with what conviction he said it, one could almost believe that soon the presumably unrepresentative but vocal homophobic analysts would understood the significance of contemporary developments concerning interpersonal processes and internal object relations. It would then be clear to them that homosexuality, like heterosexuality, involves more than libidinal drives, more then a defense against castration or an expression of regressive pre-oedipal yearnings. There could be other meanings and motives in homosexual behavior, Mitchell suggested, including even such unheard of "feelings for intimacy on other levels" (1978, p. 259).

It's hard to convey the effect Mitchell had on us sitting in that little room on West End Avenue: Some mix of shock and relief? Here was this young, articulate, courageous, heterosexual psychoanalyst speaking out on our behalf. Not that he knew anything about us of course, but it felt that way. We were still open to being optimistic and willing to run the risk of daring to hope–perhaps not so unlike Stephen Mitchell himself. Somehow we got copies of the 1981 article well before it was published. For me it was the beginning of a sometimes stormy if invaluable reading romance with his writing. One might think that we wouldn't have been interested in what a "straight" psychoanalyst who represented the "enemy" had to say. But Mitchell seemed to know more than most that ideas really can change our lives and he had the gift to convey that belief with rigorous and passionate persuasion. It seemed to me that I, with my own idiosyncratic ways of loving and becoming, was quickened to join in the play of psychoanalytic ideas–ideas that could have this same kind of profound therapeutic effect on the lives of the people with whom I worked.

THE 1980s:
UNFORTUNATE CIRCUMSTANCES

Gradually most of us in that little protected room on West End Avenue would scatter into the "real" world. In the 1980s, the memory and feeling of support that came from those early Mitchell papers on homosexuality would, like the tide, recede and return again in different forms at different times for different people. Several of us went for training at psychoanalytic institutes where, ironically, we would experience for the first time the homophobia that Mitchell deplored and which we naively had hoped was quickly evaporating. It's important to remember that at that time there was no clearinghouse for gays and lesbians to get information on what institutes housed these supposedly neutral, nonhomophobic people Mitchell described. Mitchell's papers that challenged traditional thinking were not available to many students (Roughton, 2002, p. 74). I know now of gay people who had analysts who, in the privacy of the consulting room, supported them and even encouraged them to get training at the more liberal institutes, while advising them not to come out while they were there. There were analysts at institutes who were warmly welcoming on an individual level, but who would never have taken the risk of challenging homophobic views in class, at staff meetings, or at a conference.

Gay, lesbian, bisexual, and transgendered persons have in fact been exposed to a variety of psychoanalytic situations that we are gradually learning about as more people talk about their experiences. The institute where I trained from 1981 to 1984 had an American ego psychological approach crowned by the work of Rubin and Gertrude Blanck in their book, *Ego Psychology: Theory and Practice* (1974). I went there for no better reason than the suggestion of a good friend of mine who was encouraged to go there by her analyst who was on the staff. It would be fun, we thought, to study together. The Blancks, as it turned out, were yet another example of what Mitchell identified as the vocal few who saw all homosexuals as those who "more than any other sexual pathology suffer from having to go against their biological destiny"(1974, p. 300).

Mitchell takes on the Blanck's approach in his chapter on "Clinical Implications of the Developmental Tilt" in 1988 in his first book, *Relational Concepts in Psychoanalysis: An Integration*. He uses a clinical vignette from their book as an example of "developmental tilt" where relational issues are introduced as pertaining to the earliest developmental phase so that their appearance later in life is always a sign of pathology. The patient in the case, Mrs. Fletcher, has separated from her husband "supposedly because he failed to gratify her symbiotic needs to be held other than when they were having sex" (1974, p. 305). Mitchell's purpose is to point out that the therapist in the case pays lip service to the need for tenderness throughout life, and then immediately collapses such a need into the infant's need for tenderness from the mother: "Relational needs which might be regarded as aspects of all adult relationships, the longing to be held and cherished, are depicted as regressive, symbiotic yearnings, unresolved residues from earliest childhood" (1988, pp. 155-157).

Even now when I read that vignette and Mitchell's critique, I cringe remembering my experience of psychoanalysis during that period. In some ways, it seems more devastating now because I'm not in the same state of dissociation I needed to get through the program. When I "came out" in an interview for assignment to a supervisor in 1982, the interviewer seemed surprised that I did not know that the institute believed that homosexuals shouldn't be allowed to be therapists. It was the first time I had ever heard this, but unfortunately, not the last and such attitudes continue to the present day. My interviewer said she was glad to meet one of us (homosexuals). I couldn't tell her that she had already trained a few. I spaced out and wondered if I might be hearing extra-terrestrial news. Imagine yourself as "E.T." landing in the playroom of the wrong family. I was advised to read the psychoanalytic authorities on homosexuality. Mitchell wasn't on the list. No one had heard of him, which now makes perfect sense.

But I wasn't asked to leave and I stayed and finished the program. I've been asked if I didn't think I was being masochistic for coming out, and then once being told what I was told, staying. Probably, especially if we think of masochism as in the question Adrienne Harris asked in 1995 when discussing the long-standing concerns of gay and lesbian analysts around training and questions of treatment–"How to love a practice, a body of thought, theories, or institutions which do not appear to offer love and respect in return?" (1995, p. xiii).

WHO GETS TO DECIDE WHOSE SANDCASTLES ARE "REAL"?

In his 1988 book, in another article entitled "The Wings of Icarus," Mitchell draws on Nietzsche's (1886/1989) metaphor about building sandcastles on the seashore to discuss how the interplay between illusion and reality affects the way we live our lives. At the seashore, we build our castles when the tide is out. When the tide comes in, the sea washes away all signs of our individual constructions. Nietzsche saw three possible responses to the realization of temporality and finitude. In Mitchell's summary, "We can attribute to ourselves and our creations an illusory permanence, like a deluded builder of sandcastles who believes his creation is eternal" (2002, pp. 54-55). These are people who ignore reality, comments Mitchell (1988), and who are "therefore continually surprised, battered, and bruised by it" (p. 195). Others, aware of the "inevitability of the leveling tide" (p. 195), refuse to build anything. Constant preoccupation with the ephemeral nature of one's life and creations leaves one "tyrannized and depleted by reality" (p. 195) with no psychic space in which to live and play. In the third option that Nietzsche proposed, the "tragic"–what Mitchell (2002) preferred to call the "enriching tragic" (p. 54)–the "tragic man or woman," lives life to the fullest, as one who builds sandcastles passionately, "all the time aware of the incoming tide" (p. 54). As Mitchell paraphrases Nietzsche: "The ephemeral, illusory nature of all form does not detract from the surrender to the work; it enhances and enriches it" (2002, p. 55).

In this article, Mitchell speaks of the sandcastle metaphor mainly in individual terms. As a relationist, when he talks about "what determines whether one will be able to negotiate the delicate balance between illusions and reality" (1988, p. 203), he stressed that the key factor resides in character-forming relationships with significant others; thus what is crucial in analysis is the interactive function of illusions within the analysand's relational matrix. The analyst seeks to help the analysand develop a more life-enhancing balance between illusion and reality. However, Mitchell does not talk much about who gets to make the decision about which sandcastles are real and which are illusory in terms of social contingencies. The metaphor of building sandcastles on the shore from which Mitchell derived such inspiration seems to be almost purely existential. As Irwin Hoffman (1998) suggests in a discussion of Mitchell, even if all "social realities are 'sandcastles' jeopardized by the awareness of mortality and the potential meaningless of existence" (p. 154), "there's still the question of whose sandcastles get to count as social realities in what contexts" (p. 154).

With regard to sexual identity, in the "real" world of the 1980s, one of the most popular psychoanalytic authorities on sexual realities was Joyce McDougall who cast lesbian sexuality as "a fictitious identity," questioning how it was "possible to maintain the illusion of being the true sexual partner to another woman" (1980, p. 88). Even though McDougall has attributed these earlier beliefs to inexperience and a limited sample of patients (1995, p. 38), her research and conclusions went largely uncontested by the psychoanalytic establishment until the 1990s when lesbian analysts began speaking publicly about how damaged they had felt by her work. It seems obvious now that such attitudes might have a deleterious effect on a patient confused about the legitimacy of her sexual desires, or on all of the closeted lesbian therapists who read and heard McDougall. In contrast, the view that Sandra Kiersky would express a decade later in her article, "Exiled Desires: The Problem of Reality in Psychoanalysis and Lesbian Experience" that "we feel real because our experience is responded to as real and we are not left alone with our feelings" (1996, p. 132) validates lesbian desire and identity.

In the early 1970s, Jill Johnston had formulated the issue of who gets to decide what reality is in the identity-politics language of the time. "Everybody understood identity," she said. When you filled out application blanks for schools or jobs, you found out who you could and couldn't be, and, in that context, "lesbian identity was a non-identity" (1973, p. 40). Twenty years later, Judith Butler, taking up this theme in "post-identity," "postmodern," "queer" language, would have us ask by what norm are we constrained with regard to what we can become (1990/1999). Writing about the uncertainty with which homosexual love and loss are regarded, Butler asks,

> Is this regarded as a "true" love, a "true" loss, a love worthy of or capable of being grieved and, in that sense, worthy or capable of ever having been lived? Or is this a love and a loss haunted by the specter of a certain unreality, a certain unthinkability, the double disavowal of "I never loved her, and I never lost her," uttered by the woman; the "I never loved him, I never lost him," uttered by the man. (1995, pp. 170-171)

Butler might say that to be called "unreal" is one way to be oppressed but that if you're oppressed, you're already "real" in a certain kind of way even though you might not have access to what is "human" (2001). By the 1980s, lesbian patients had appeared in the psychoanalytic lens as real, albeit, as Mitchell points out, in a distorted, grotesque, inhuman manner, but gay and lesbian analysts, having not appeared there at all, were "unreal" until the 1990s. When in 1989, Richard Isay introduced a proposal to the American Psychoanalytic Association that they go on record as being against the use of homosexuality as a reason to reject applicants for its affiliated training institutes, I recall thinking for the first time that Mitchell hadn't mentioned the analytic training situation with regard to homosexuals in 1978 and 1981; he was talking about homosexual patients in treatment.

SOMETHING "QUEER" HAPPENED IN PSYCHOANALYSIS: THE 1990s

In the mid-90s, lesbian and gay analysts began at last to appear in the psychoanalytic discourse. In her forward to *Disorienting Sexuality:*

Psychoanalytic Reappraisals of Sexual Identities (1995), Adrienne Harris remarks on the baffling situation that had existed in psychoanalysis with regard to homosexuals:

> So in the heady moment when some would proclaim this history of rejection and distortion happily concluded . . . I would still want to inquire as to why psychoanalysis has been so recalcitrant and so impenetrable to internal criticism in regard to homosexuality (1995, p. xiii).

By 1996 when he published his paper, "Gender and Sexual Orientation in the Age of Postmodernism: The Plight of the Perplexed Clinician," Mitchell considered the period encompassing his early papers on homosexuality as "one of the dark episodes in psychoanalysis" (p. 68), acknowledging that issues around sexual orientation were "much more complex" than he had once thought (1996b, p. 68). In contrast with Harris, he attributes the major change in psychoanalytic thinking about sexual orientation from the early to mid-80s to growing sophistication about counter-transference and interaction within psychoanalytic theory and practice. That's certainly part of the story. But it is also true that gay and lesbian theorists and clinicians have made an important contribution to the question of what human relationships in relational psychoanalysis get to count as "real."

The rising influence of postmodernism and queer theory in gay and lesbian studies programs in academia and in other cultural domains was central in challenging the notion of identity as being natural, stable, and coherent. By the 1990s, Judith Butler was charging that gender identities act as regulatory constraints that privilege some kinds of sexuality and punish others. One of Butler's major feats in *Gender Trouble: Feminism and the Subversion of Identity* (1990/1999) was that she managed to connect gender issues in psychoanalysis with issues of sexuality, heterosexism, and sexual orientation. Up until that point, feminists in both psychoanalysis and academia had concerned themselves mainly with issues of gender. Sexuality and sexual orientation, on the other hand, seemed to be left to lesbian/gay and queer studies programs in academia (Rubin, 1997, pp. 96-98) with no counterpart in psychoanalysis where gay and lesbian practitioners were not yet recognized as speaking subjects. The enormous interest in Butler's book on gender helped to support analysts, straight and gay, to bring controversial issues of sexuality to the psychoanalytic table. Consequently, in the last decade of the twentieth century something "queer" happened in psychoanalysis. Given the growing critique of psychoanalytic views on gender and sexuality by visible and vocal queer theorists in the academy and in many other cultural domains, the exclusion of lesbian and gay therapists from the psychoanalytic discourse on gender and sexuality began to look especially "queer"–as in the older definition of queer as in odd, inappropriate, and strange.

One of the areas in psychoanalysis given a boost by queer theory interrogation of influence and authority had to do with the notion of neutrality. In 1996, Mitchell observed that we could no longer rely on any simple notion of the analyst's neutrality as the guardian of the integrity of the patient's autonomy. When it comes to sexual orientation, "neutrality is still crucial in terms of programmatic intent" (1996a, p. 69), but he continues, citing Mark Blechner (1993) and David Schwartz (1993), it is questionable "whether it is possible for any analyst to be neutral about something as deeply personal as sexual orientation" (1996a, p. 69), and that the analyst's biases and preferences with regard to sexual orientation "are bound to be at work in a more subtle fashion in counter transference" (1996a, p. 69). What's remarkable here is that Mitchell is citing from two articles that he published, along with one by Ronnie Lesser (1993), as part of an historic moment for gay and lesbian analysts critically discussing the clinical work of Jeffrey Trop and Robert Stolorow with regard to sexual orientation in *Psychoanalytic Dialogues*, the relational journal of which he, Mitchell, was the editor. It's remarkable in two ways: (a) it took so long after Mitchell's early papers for gay and lesbians in psychoanalysts to be able to come out of "the publishing and presentation closet" (Magee & Miller, 1997, p. 148); (b) Mitchell, now in his powerful position as editor, was contributing to a major shift in the discourse on homosexuality and psychoanalysis in a way that he hadn't been able to 15 years earlier in his 1978 and 1981 papers when he was just beginning his career.

CONCLUSION:
BUILDING SANDCASTLES FOR TWO OR MORE

As lesbian, analytically informed therapists, we need castle making to give shape and meaning to our work. We struggle with various mixes of postmodern, queer, feminist, and relational theories to find creative ways to realize the conviction that "good analytic clinical work (and good analytic theorizing) in our time must both inspire meaning-making and passion and make possible the critical reflection on meaning-making and passion" (Mitchell, 1996a, p. 269; Mitchell, 2002, p. 110). In his last book, *Can Love Last? The Fate of Romance Over Time*, published posthumously, Mitchell (2002) speaks of romance as a sandcastle built for two. Finally now, psychoanalysts are meeting to discuss how our sexual orientations and identifications affect our work. As we build sandcastles for two or more, may we remain fascinated by the ways in which, individually and together, we "generate forms of life" that we "hope we can count on" (2002, p. 201). As we strive to restore spaces for creative communication (Benjamin, 2000, p. 300), may we remain deeply aware and tolerant of the fragility of that hope.

Mitchell (2000) observed that narrative like music, like the flow of rivers and selves, takes time to happen. He quoted Leowald as suggesting that not only is it true that "the present is influenced by the past," but, "also that the past–as a living force within the patient–is influenced by the present" (2000, p. 49). I believe Mitchell would agree that the same process goes on with psychoanalytic writing as a living force in the reader. I still have the memory, transformed and transforming over the years, of Mitchell's welcoming me into the world of psychoanalysis. It remains one of the most beautiful lesbian sandcastles I've ever seen.

REFERENCES

A conversation with Margaret Black, CSW. (2002). *Studies in Gender and Sexuality*, 3(1), 121-103.

Benjamin, J. (2000). Response to commentaries by Mitchell and by Butler. *Studies in Gender and Sexuality*, 1, 1291-308.

Blanck, G. & Blanck, R. (1974). *Ego psychology: Theory and practice*. New York: Columbia University Press.

Blechner, M. (1993). Homophobia in psychoanalytic writing and practice. *Psychoanalytic Dialogues*, 3, 627-638.

Butler, J. (1995). Melancholy gender-refused identification. *Psychoanalytic Dialogues*, 5, 165-180.

Butler, J. (1999). *Gender trouble: Feminism and the subversion of identity* (10th anniversary edition). New York: Routledge. (Original work published in 1990).

Butler, J. (2001, December). *Violence, mourning, politics*. Paper presented at the 10th Annual David R. Kessler lecture in Lesbian and Gay studies, City University of New York. New York, NY.

Chodorow, N.J. (2002). Prejudice exposed: On Stephen Mitchell's pioneering investigations of the psychoanalytic treatment and mistreatment of homosexuality. *Studies in Gender and Sexuality*, 3, 61-72.

Davies, J.M. (1998). Between the disclosure and foreclosure of erotic transference-countertransference: Can psychoanalysis find a place for adult sexuality? *Psychoanalytic Dialogues*, 8, 747-766.

Decker, B. (1995). How to have your phallus and be it too: Reflections of a lesbian therapist from Jill Johnston to Judith Butler. In J. Glassgold & S. Iasenza (Eds.), *Lesbians and psychoanalysis: Revolutions in theory and practice* (pp. 63-89). New York: The Free Press.

Drescher, J. (2002). In memory of Stephen Mitchell, PhD. *Studies in Gender and Sexuality*, *3*(1), 95-110.

Greenberg, J. & Mitchell, S. A. (1983). *Object relations in psychoanalytic theory.* Cambridge, MA: Harvard University Press.

Harris, A. (1995). Foreword. In T. Domenici & R.C. Lesser (Eds.), *Disorienting sexuality:* Psychoanalytic reappraisals of sexual identities (pp. xi-xv). New York: Routledge.

Hoffman, I. (1998). *Ritual and spontaneity in the psychoanalytic process.* Hillsdale, NJ: The Analytic Press.

Johnston, J. (1973). *Lesbian nation: The feminist solution.* New York: Simon & Shuster.

Kiersky, S. (1996). Exiled desire: The problem of reality in psychoanalysis and lesbian experience. *Psychoanalysis and Psychotherapy*, 13, 130-141.

Lesser, R. C. (1993). A reconsideration of homosexual themes. *Psychoanalytic Dialogues*, *3*, 639-641.

Lesser, R. C. (2002). Notes in an elegiac mode on Stephen Mitchell's papers on homosexuality. *Studies in Gender and Sexuality*, 3(1), 111-120.

Magee, M. & Miller, D. (1997). *Lesbian lives: Psychoanalytic narratives old & new.* Hillsdale, NJ: The Analytic Press.

Magee, M. & Miller, D. (2002). [Review of the book *That obscure subject of desire: Freud's female homosexual revisited*]. *Journal of Gay & Lesbian Psychotherapy*, *6*(1) 99-104.

McDougall, J. (1980). *Plea for a measure of abnormality.* New York: International Universities Press.

McDougall, J. (1995). *The many faces of eros account of human: A psychoanalytic sexuality.* New York: W. W. Norton.

Mitchell, S. A. (1978). Psychodynamics, homosexuality, and the question of pathology. *Psychiatry: Journal of Interpersonal Processes*, *41*, 254-263.

Mitchell, S. A. (1981). The psychoanalytic treatment of homosexuality: Some technical considerations. *International Review of Psycho-Analysis*, *15*, 170-189.

Mitchell, S. A. (1988). *Relational concepts in psychoanalysis: Integration.* Cambridge, MA: Harvard University Press.

Mitchell, S. A. (1996a). Constructions of gender and sexuality, Sandcastles on the shore: A response to Mayer and Schwartz. *Gender & Psychoanalysis*, *1*, 261-270.

Mitchell, S. A. (1996b). Gender and sexual orientation in the age of postmodernism: The plight of the perplexed clinician. *Gender & Psychoanalysis*, *1*(1), 45-73.

Mitchell, S. A. (1999). Looking back . . . looking forward. *Psychoanalytic Dialogues*, 9, 717-719.

Mitchell, S. A. (2000). *Relationality from attachment to intersubjectivity.* New York: Analytic Press.

Mitchell, S. A. (2002). *Can love last? The fate of romance over time.* New York: Norton.

Nietzsche, F. (1989). *Beyond good and evil* (Trans. W. Kaufman). New York: Vintage Press. (Original work published in 1886).

O'Conner, N. & Ryan, J. (1993). *Wild desires & mistaken identities: Lesbianism & psychoanalysis*. New York: Columbia University Press.

Roughton, R. (2002). Opportunities missed. *Studies in Gender & Sexuality*, 3(1), 73-82.

Rubin, G. with Butler, J. (1997). Sexual traffic: Interview. In E. Weed & N. Schor (Eds.), *Feminism meets queer theory* (pp. 68-108). Bloomington: Indiana University Press.

Shoenberg, E. (1995). Psychoanalytic theories of lesbian desire: A social constructionist critique. In T. Dominici & R. C. Lesser (Eds.), *Disorienting sexuality: Psychoanalytic reappraisals of sexual identities* (pp. 203-223). New York: Routledge.

Schwartz, D. (1993). Heterophilia–The love that dare not speak its name. *Psychoanalytic Dialogues*, 3, 643-652.

Wittig, M. (1980). The straight mind. In S. Lucia-Hoagland & J. Penelope (Eds.), *For lesbians only: A separatist anthology* (pp. 431-438). London: Onlywoman Press.

ONGOING CLINICAL ISSUES

Disclosure and the Development of Trust in the Therapeutic Setting

Darla Bjork

SUMMARY. This essay describes my personal path towards becoming an openly lesbian therapist, the internalized homophobia that interfered with this evolution, and the impact of this process on my patients. I then explore the interplay between when and how the therapist and/or the patient disclose in therapy, the link between homophobia and shame to the fear of disclosure, and the subsequent development of a more trusting therapeutic relationship that results from disclosure. *[Article copies available for a fee from The Haworth Document Delivery Service: 1-800-HAWORTH. E-mail address: <docdelivery@haworthpress.com> Website: <http://www. HaworthPress. com> © 2004 by The Haworth Press, Inc. All rights reserved.]*

Darla Bjork, MD, is in private practice at a location close to Ground Zero, New York, NY. She is also a painter who exhibits her work at SoHo20 Gallery in NYC. Her life partner, Nancy Azara, is also an artist.

Address correspondence to: Darla Bjork, MD, 91 Franklin St., New York, NY 10013.

[Haworth co-indexing entry note]: "Disclosure and the Development of Trust in the Therapeutic Setting." Bjork, Darla. Co-published simultaneously in *Journal of Lesbian Studies* (Harrington Park Press, an imprint of The Haworth Press, Inc.) Vol. 8, No. 1/2, 2004, pp. 95-105; and: *Lesbians, Feminism, and Psychoanalysis: The Second Wave* (ed: Judith M. Glassgold, and Suzanne Iasenza) Harrington Park Press, an imprint of The Haworth Press, Inc., 2004, pp. 95-105. Single or multiple copies of this article are available for a fee from The Haworth Document Delivery Service [1-800-HAWORTH, 9:00 a.m. - 5:00 p.m. (EST). E-mail address: docdelivery@haworthpress.com].

KEYWORDS. Lesbian, therapist, disclosure, psychoanalysis, transference, countertransference

INTRODUCTION

When I decided to explore issues of disclosure in the therapeutic setting, I began a review of the current psychoanalytic literature about lesbians. However, I immediately developed acute anxiety attacks, very similar to those I had experienced thirty-five years ago during my psychiatric residency. Since that time, unaware of the underlying reason, I found myself resisting reading almost any psychoanalytic literature. As I struggled to plow through the literature this time, I realized that I was still afraid that Freud (1905/1961), Deutsch (1932/48) and the other early psychoanalysts might be right after all in describing homosexuality as "inverted," borderline, immature or at a pre-oedipal stage of development. It wasn't until I started reading the postmodern, feminist theories of psychosexual development and gender identity (Butler, 1990; Goldner, 1991; Suchet, 1995) that deconstruct the classic psychoanalytic theories and provide alternative views did I make the link between my difficulty in reading this literature and the psychological trauma I had experienced so long ago.

In 1965, I was a 26-year-old closeted lesbian, graduating from the University of Minnesota Medical School and starting my psychiatric residency at Kings County/Downstate Medical Center in Brooklyn. This program (as I only learned later) was one of the most conservative, Freudian residencies in the country, and consequently, I was force-fed the negative theories then in vogue about homosexuality. Their deleterious impact on me was reinforced indirectly by innuendo and directly by didactic lectures in which the psychopathology of homosexuality and the accompanying psychoanalytic treatment with its "pessimistic outcome" were described, in torturous detail. As I sat through those lectures, I still vividly recall my fear that I was a defective and incomplete person for being a lesbian.

Prior to the 1980s, it was next to impossible for a lesbian or gay man to be accepted into a psychoanalytic institute (Drescher, 2002; Martin 1995). The only way was either to lie about sexual orientation or to be in total denial. I was no longer in denial about being a lesbian and had trouble lying about anything, so I ruled out the possibility of becoming an analyst early in the residency. I was simply in the wrong place at the wrong time. Had I been in training 10 years later, but also in a more liberal residency program (not an easy task even in the 1970s), I think that I would have applied to an analytic institute. For many years, I regretted that this door was closed to me.

During the second year of my residency, convinced that being a lesbian was an illness, I went into my own personal analysis with a heterosexual male analyst with the goal of realizing a "cure." When I finally broke off with the woman with whom I had been having an intense but stormy relationship, that "cure" seemed close at hand. When I soon became involved with another woman, my analyst rather suddenly announced that we should terminate the analysis. Looking back on the situation, I never even considered the possibility that this abrupt dismissal may have been due to my analyst's own countertransference; in any case, I was left feeling like a dismal failure. Interestingly, I also felt a deep relief that I no longer had to try to say and feel whatever it was that would make me seem "normal" and I could go back to simply being myself.

I opened my private practice in 1969. With the development of the women's movement in the 1970s, I started reading the emerging feminist and lesbian literature and subsequently identified myself as a feminist, gradually in the process becoming more comfortable with myself as a lesbian. Around 1980 I came out to some of my heterosexual friends and began to meet other gay and lesbian therapists who initially sent me referrals for medication evaluations, usually of patients who had actively requested a lesbian psychiatrist. At that time, the older patients often seemed relieved that their request had been fulfilled, while women who had come out during the women's movement assumed that they would be able to see a lesbian psychiatrist, as though society had always offered them this option.

PRACTICAL ISSUES IN DEALING WITH DISCLOSURE

General Issues

By the 1990s, I had many lesbian referrals and was learning about the interrelation between my patients' issues centering on being lesbians and my own issues in the same area. For instance, I observed that most of my younger patients (roughly under 30 years of age) were more comfortable with their lesbian identity and even seemed to take this identification for granted, something that I would never have dreamed possible when I was a young adult. Young lesbians now have a better sense of themselves and are more comfortable being "out" (Crespi, 2001). The patients referred to me for either medication evaluations and/or long term therapy commonly present with depression and/or anxiety, but didn't connect these symptoms with the fact that they were lesbians–any more then heterosexual patients associate such symptoms with their sexual identity. In their initial interview, patients revealed their sexual identity in a variety of ways, often indirectly after I asked about any close relationships–past or present. Patients quite casually related their status, such as, never had a girlfriend but wants to have one, has a wonderful girlfriend, has a former girlfriend who follows her around, tormenting her, etc. One young woman said that she "was married, but only in Vermont," while another blurted out that, her "wife" was a pharmacologist. Generally reflecting the status of their relationships, younger lesbians tend to use the euphemism "lover," while older women use "partner." A frequent way to disclose is with a pronoun, as in "my partner is a teacher but she doesn't like teaching." Once patients have disclosed and see that I am comfortable with what they have revealed, their body language transforms as they drop their guard and relax. We then begin the therapeutic process of working together.

A more challenging and at times more troublesome issue for me have been the referrals (from non-gay or non-lesbian sources) of lesbians who did not know that I am also a lesbian. Patients assume that their therapists are heterosexual because of the dominance of heterosexuality in our culture (Isay, 1991). Over the years, I have felt uncomfortable with this false assumption, but as long as I was still entrenched in the traditional analytic attitudes, I did nothing to correct it. O'Connor and Ryan do not advocate direct disclosure and give examples of the challenges involved when the lesbian patient knows that her therapist is a lesbian (1993, pp. 257-262). Kassoff who describes neutrality as a fiction, works with women who have sought her out because she is a lesbian, and frequently deviates from the standard frame, viewing this as necessary as often lesbians experience a lack of mirroring and idealizing functions (Kassoff, Boden, de Monteflores, Hunt, & Wahba, 1995). My own work had brought me face to face with these same issues, and the endless variety of circumstances that come into play as a result.

Case Examples: Disclosure with Lesbian Clients

Case One: Therapist Inaction and Internalized Homophobia

Several years ago, a 20-year-old student, referred to me by her insurance company, was very conflicted as to whether or not she was a lesbian. Jane would bring up this topic but would then quickly change the subject with an uneasy laugh. When I would attempt to bring her back to this issue, she would say that she really didn't want to talk about it. I wondered if I should share my sexual identity with her but never found the "right" opportunity due to my fear (a fear that I was barely aware of at the time) that she might reject me as being less qualified as a lesbian therapist. Unfortunately, she abruptly stopped treatment saying that she was too busy having just started graduate school.

Perhaps she suspected something was going on that she couldn't quite put her finger on, making her mistrustful of the therapeutic process and leading her to quit. On the other hand, if I had found a way to disclose early in therapy, perhaps Jane would have remained in therapy. Would taking the risk with what would have been a premature disclosure have been better than to lose the patient all together? I will never know the answer and deeply regret that I did not disclose to her. Since that time, I have taken that risk with other patients and found that while its timing is always challenging, the act of disclosure nevertheless can lead to an opportunity for a mutual sharing and to the development of a trusting relationship.

I agree with Gabriel and Monaco who have pointed out that when working with lesbian patients premature disclosures make it difficult for the patient to utilize, process, or integrate this information optimally, it is clearly not a question of whether or not to disclose but how and when (1995, p. 171). The ground rules for lesbian and gay therapists are different in that refusal to confirm amounts to a denial that confuses the patient and can in turn destroy trust and authenticity (Magee & Miller, 1997, p. 208). I have found that not to disclose with lesbian patients can interfere with or delay the development of the therapeutic relationship. Disclosing at the proper time (and sometimes even at the "wrong" time) can establish a new level of intimacy between therapist and patient that allows the patient to deal with issues previously hidden.

Case Two: Disclosure and Healing

Frances, a 42-year-old woman who had a childhood history of sexual and physical abuse by both parents and only unpleasant sexual experiences with men in the past, guessed that I was a lesbian and was quite anxious over this possibility. She revealed that she had fantasies and dreams about women and thought that perhaps she was a lesbian. She had broached the topic with a former therapist who was heterosexual and had felt that the therapist had avoided the issue. After several weeks of exploring with her what other meanings my being a lesbian might have for her, I came out to her and she was delighted that she had been right. In later sessions, however, she became annoyed when I did not then tell her how to become a lesbian (as if there were a magical way to accomplish this) or reveal anything else to her about the intricacies of my relationship. Over the next year, though, her ability to trust me grew as we explored her fears of having an intimate relationship with anyone. She gradually became able to separate her childhood associations of sex and violence as linked at least intellectually and then began having lesbian fantasies with less or no violent content. She met a few women at a gay and lesbian center that I had told her about. As of this writing, she has established a tenuous friendship with a gay man, and is still talking about establishing a relationship with a woman; whether or not she ever actually does develop such an intimate relationship is still to be seen. Nevertheless, she is more comfortable and less conflicted about herself than when she started therapy, and my role modeling, I believe, has been of value to her.

Case Three: Patient Resistance and Therapist's Own Issues

After working with me for several months, Wendy, a 33-year-old lesbian executive who was usually evasive about her rather isolated personal life, saw me at a lesbian film preview and asked me in her next session if I had actually been there; she wasn't sure if it had been me or not. I told her that indeed I had been there, but left it at that. She avoided directly asking me if I were a lesbian and then moved onto another topic.

I thought later that the fact that I didn't return to her question for further exploration was another example of my internalized homophobia. I colluded with her evasive style and reinforced her need to stay hidden in her work situation. Was asking about the film her indirect way of looking for affirmation for a more open lifestyle from me and/or her way of trying to determine if I were indeed a lesbian? Questioning her further, as to why she asked me would have led to the fact that I was a lesbian and could have given her a greater sense of confidence in her identity. Kassoff has described her work with lesbians in which she deviates from the standard "boundaries" frame by readily sharing information about lesbian issues and events with her lesbian patients (Kassoff et al., 1995, p. 258).

Case Four: Disclosure and Couples Issues

While heterosexual therapists are possibly more open about their marital status (by wearing wedding bands or displaying family photos on their desks), this is not a privilege that most lesbian therapists can afford. My lover and I share the same office space, and the door to the waiting room has both of our names on it. Patients rarely ask about that other name, but some learn about our relationship through contacts in the lesbian community here in New York City and often ask about her either directly or indirectly. For the patients who do know about my partner, this information often finds its way into the therapeutic setting and can be another area for exploration.

For instance, as they were coming up the block towards my office, Alice and Olivia, a lesbian couple in their early 40s whom I had been seeing for several years, saw my partner walking our dogs and stopped to talk to her about them in a manner that seemed to me to be their way of including her in our sessions. From our examination of this event, issues around the wish for both parents to have been more emotionally available for Alice emerged. Her mother was a raging alcoholic and her father was aloof and formidable, so Alice felt she never had a "real family." She was disappointed that Olivia, who avoided contact with her one remaining brother, was not interested in sharing their pets as a family unit. Talking about how my partner and I interact with our dogs enabled Alice to request that Olivia take a more active role with their dogs. Alice was then able to be more assertive in other areas, such as when dealing with Olivia's volatile temper, not unlike her mother's mood swings that had terrified her as a child.

Case Five: Transference and the Difficult Patient

While most patients, who know that I have a partner, are pleased or at least neutral about her, one rather troubled patient, Mary became openly hostile when she realized I had a partner and left a verbally abusive message on my partner's answering machine. She was a borderline patient who had once been an artist and often made very contemptuous remarks about my partner's artistic career. Her parents favored her older, hated sister so she resented any competition. My negative countertransference was especially intense following the answering machine episode, much worse than when she jammed my answering machine with many aimless phone calls. As a result, I felt the strong urge both to protect my partner and to confront Mary. When I did question her (gently I hoped) about that phone call, Mary was defensive at first but gradually was able to become in touch with the pervasive jealousy she had previously been denying. At this point in her life, she was very socially isolated, with no friends and a volatile relationship with her family. Through our discussions, she was eventually able to see some connections to her childhood rivalry with her sister and acknowledge that her acting out was a function of her wanting me all to herself by getting rid of my partner.

Disclosure Issues with Heterosexual Patients

Case One: Reducing Shame

Although I have been identified as a lesbian therapist for several years, I find that I tend to forget that not all of my patients know that I am a lesbian. Most of my heterosexual patients assume as a matter of course that I am heterosexual. It was therefore jarring when Mark, a 24-year-old heterosexual man, made a homophobic remark while talking about another man who lives in his apartment building. I did not confront him because I was simply stunned. Reflecting later, I recognized my silence was once again due to unresolved homophobia. In the next session I disclosed (much too abruptly) that I was a lesbian. He was quiet for a few minutes and then apologized for the slur. Because of this interchange, however, he then recalled childhood memories concerning his parents who had migrated from Poland as young adults and the shame (previously hidden) that he felt about their broken English. Disclosure for this young man was not about sexual orientation but about his ethnic background (an explosive/loaded issue for many) that he had never explored, as he was totally unaware of the shame that he had unconsciously linked with it. My disclosure of my sexual orientation helped bridge the shame and stigma surrounding his own shame of his ethnic origins and allowed him to resolve it. This proved to be a major turning point in his therapy and established a new level of trust and intimacy between us. He gained a deeper sense of self-acceptance and better understood his own feeling of marginalization that he had projected into homophobia. On the other hand, I was reminded once again that homophobia rears its ugly head at any time and that I had to be more prepared to deal with it as it arises. Silence is not an acceptable response as it masks any lingering shame on my part over being a lesbian.

Case Two: Addressing Personality Issues

Shortly after Ruth, a 61-year-old heterosexual woman with a diagnosis of rather severe narcissistic personality disorder, started therapy with me, a neighbor who knew that I was a lesbian mentioned this to Ruth. In the next session, she confronted me and without exploring the issue adequately, I told her that it was true. She became angry and frightened, stating that she wanted to be referred to another therapist because she was afraid that I would attack her sexually. I almost burst out laughing at that old stereotype of lesbians, but calmly told her that was not going to happen. Fortunately, she had already developed enough trust in me so that she did not immediately walk out and instead accepted my reassurance that we would "just" talk. As she had very fragile ego boundaries, I had initially felt that any disclosure on my part would have been inappropriate until much later in therapy, but when her neighbor co-opted the issue, I discovered that it was possible to work through the issues in spite of the timing. As we explored the many issues around trust she got in touch with the fact that her mother, who didn't love her and had never really wanted her, "always pushed" her away. She was afraid that, unlike her mother, I would try to get too close to her but would then turn on her and reject her as she felt her mother had done. She stated, "You can't trust women." I reminded her that one of our goals in her therapy was in fact to help her learn to trust people. She slowly realized that her lack of trust was a major reason why she never got along with women in general. Coming to see that trust and caring were necessary factors in the development of meaningful relationships, she was then able to gain a better understanding of her mother, a frightened, fragile woman whose own childhood was one of abuse and suspicion. We continue to work together on these issues and she has developed some women friends.

CONCLUSION

Many issues concerning disclosure have evolved for me over the last 35 years as I moved from being a closeted, anxious young psychiatric resident, trying to deny my sexual identity, to the person I hope I am today, open about being a lesbian (most of the time, but not all of the time), willing to disclose this identity in therapy, and even willing to give advice and suggestions to my lesbian patients. I have learned many things from my patients, not the least of which is that I can state my opinion or offer advice with the proviso that people generally hear only what they are ready to hear.

The link to shame that can lurk behind whether and/or when to disclose is one that I, as a therapist, have to be alert to constantly, as I realize that I often hide from myself aspects of my identity that I feel are unacceptable. Disclosing at the proper time (or sometimes taking the chance to do so at the "wrong" time as I have pointed out) can establish a new level of intimacy between my patient and myself that allows both of us to work through the multiple layers of shame over internalized homophobia. In this atmosphere, we are then able to deal more honestly not only with this issue but also with other related issues that also may have been hidden to the mutual benefit of both parties.

I have learned over the years that how and when either my patient or I disclose, whether directly or indirectly, plays a significant role in the development of trust in the therapeutic process. The issue of mutuality–between therapist and patient–is obviously important here in that disclosure by one of us often triggers disclosure in the other with the result of a closer working relationship.

REFERENCES

Butler, J. (1990). *Gender trouble: Feminism and the subversion of identity*. New York: Routledge.

Crespi, L. (2001). From baby boom to gayby boom: Twenty-five years of psychoanalysis in the lesbian community. In E. Gould & S. Kiersky (Eds.), *Sexualities lost and found* (pp. 261-276). Madison, CT: Internal Universities Press, Inc.

Deutsch, H. (1948). On female homosexuality. In R. Fleiss (Ed.), *The psychoanalytic reader: An anthology of essential papers with critical introductions* (pp. 208-230). New York: International Universities Press. (Original work published in 1932).

Drescher, J. (2002). Don't ask, don't tell: A gay man's perspective on the psychoanalytic experience between 1973 and 1991. *Journal of Gay & Lesbian Psychotherapy*, 6(1), 45-55.

Freud, S. (1961). Three essays on the theory of sexuality. In J. Strachey (Ed. & Trans.), *The standard edition of the complete psychological works of Sigmund Freud* (Vol. 7, pp. 125-243). London: Hogarth Press. (Original work published in 1905).

Gabriel, M. A. & Monaco, G. W. (1995). Revisiting the question of self-disclosure: The lesbian therapist's dilemma. In J. Glassgold & S. Iasenza (Eds.), *Lesbians and psychoanalysis: Revolutions in theory and practice* (pp. 161-172), New York: Free Press.

Goldner, V. (1991). Toward a critical relational theory of gender. *Psychoanalytic Dialogues, 1*, 249-272.

Isay, R. A. (1991). The homosexual analyst: Clinical considerations. *The Psychoanalytic Study of the Child, 46*,199-216.

Kassoff, B., Boden, R., de Monteflores, C., Hunt, P., & Wahba, R. (1995). Coming out of the frame: Lesbian feminism and psychoanalytic theory. In J. Glassgold & S. Iasenza (Eds.), *Lesbians and psychoanalysis: Revolutions in theory and practice* (pp. 254-261). New York: Free Press.

Martin, A. (1995). A view from both sides: Coming out as a lesbian psychoanalyst. In T. Domenici & R. Lesser (Eds.), *Disorienting sexuality* (pp. 255-264). New York: Routledge.

Magee, M. & Miller, D. C. (1997). *Lesbian lives: Psychoanalytic narratives old & new*. Hillsdale, NJ: Analytic Press.

O'Conner, N. & Ryan, J. (1993). *Wild desires & mistaken identities: Lesbianism & psychoanalysis*. New York: Columbia University Press.

Suchet, M. (1995). "Having it both ways": Rethinking female sexuality. In J. Glassgold & S. Iasenza (Eds.), *Lesbians and psychoanalysis: Revolutions in theory and practice* (pp. 39-61). New York: Free Press.

Clinical Success, Political Failure?
Reflections on the "Interiority"
of Abusive Lesbian Relations

Jacqueline Neilson

SUMMARY. This paper argues that the dominant language used by the domestic violence movement to conceptualize relationship violence inadequately captures the psychological complexities involved in abusive lesbian relationships. As a corrective, a language based on feminist and psychoanalytic concepts is presented. Against the backdrop of this language, the author reflects on the lived experience of lesbian clients who have come to therapy for relationship violence. It is concluded that a language based on the ethos of postmodern feminism and neo-Kleinian concepts and technique more appropriately addresses the complexities involved in abusive lesbian relationships within a therapeutic context than the polemical language of the domestic violence movement. *[Article copies available for a fee from The Haworth Document Delivery Service: 1-800-HAWORTH. E-mail address: <docdelivery@haworthpress.com> Website: <http://www.HaworthPress.com> © 2004 by The Haworth Press, Inc. All rights reserved.]*

Jacqueline Neilson received her MA in Clinical Psychology from Duquesne University, where she is currently working on her dissertation on lesbian relationship violence. She is the lead clinician for the same-gender domestic violence program at Persad Center in Pittsburgh, PA.

Address correspondence to: Jacqueline Neilson, Persad Center, 5150 Penn Ave., Pittsburgh, PA 15224 (E-mail: jaxneilson@hotmail.com).

[Haworth co-indexing entry note]: "Clinical Success, Political Failure? Reflections on the 'Interiority' of Abusive Lesbian Relations." Neilson, Jacqueline. Co-published simultaneously in *Journal of Lesbian Studies* (Harrington Park Press, an imprint of The Haworth Press, Inc.) Vol. 8, No. 1/2, 2004, pp. 107-121; and: *Lesbians, Feminism, and Psychoanalysis: The Second Wave* (ed: Judith M. Glassgold, and Suzanne Iasenza) Harrington Park Press, an imprint of The Haworth Press, Inc., 2004, pp. 107-121. Single or multiple copies of this article are available for a fee from The Haworth Document Delivery Service [1-800-HAWORTH, 9:00 a.m. - 5:00 p.m. (EST). E-mail address: docdelivery@haworthpress.com].

http://www.haworthpress.com/web/JLS
© 2004 by The Haworth Press, Inc. All rights reserved.
Digital Object Identifier: 10.1300/J155v08n01_07

KEYWORDS. Lesbian, psychoanalysis, abusive relationship, post-modern, Klein, psychotherapy, battered women's movement

Feminist service providers struggle with this on-going tension between honoring women's experiences and working therapeutically to figure out what is really going on. Addressing "internal experiences" perhaps points the way to more psychoanalytic discussions . . .

–Ristock, 2002

The current status of lesbian domestic violence therapeutic services is lacking both quantitatively and qualitatively. In select domestic violence shelters and mental health clinics across the country there are counseling services set up to assist victims of relationship violence, albeit these services rarely assist lesbian victims appropriately. There are also a limited number of same-gender domestic violence programs, mostly in major U.S. cities, which are geared towards treating court and self-referred abusers and victims. There is a common psycho-educational curriculum used by domestic violence programs and service providers, which structures the therapeutic interventions with clients, and the curriculum is usually implemented over a short period of time (i.e., 16-24 weeks). Through working with same-gender abusers and victims in both individual and group therapy, I have become aware of the gaps in services, including the limitations of short-term psycho-educational approaches and the lack of sophisticated therapeutic understanding that surrounds this client population (Ristock, 2002; Kaschak, 2001; Leventhal & Lundy, 1999; McClennan & Gunther, 1999; Hamberger & Renzetti, 1996; Renzetti & Miley, 1996; Renzetti, 1992; Island & Letellier, 1991; Lobel, 1986).

Engaging in "psychoanalytic discussions" is a recent recommendation in the literature on lesbian relationship violence, and appears to be geared towards correcting a tendency in postmodern feminist research and therapeutic approaches to understanding women's experiences as a "top-down process," which assumes identity to be simply the total effect of discursive practices molding subjectivity. The recommendation also appears to be a self-critical moment in Ristock's (2002) postmodern feminist analysis of lesbian relationship violence in which she acknowledges the limits of her research. Ristock's research examines how the linguistic categories of power and control, perpetrator/victim, and other domestic violence speech participate in constructing the experience of women in abusive relationships, and work to inform and re-produce the often-inadequate responses of (feminist) service providers. In Ristock's moment of self-critique she seems to be suggesting that there is "more" to the experience of abusive lesbian relationships than meets the "eye" of the ("top-down"?) language she is using to articulate her analysis. Perhaps meanings of lesbian relationship violence await articulation?

Within the current state of postmodern feminism, giving primacy to language over experience can make it easy to forget the limits of language. Johnson (1999) reminds us of the irreducibility of experience to language, "There is an inner life. It is the life of thought, the life of the heart, the life of dream and memory. These are interiors that encounter lines of exterior force that shape, fold or break them. Exteriority is an outer bound where thought and words unravel in the enigmas of desire, the sublime, forgetting, silence, solitude, suffering, night, death, and nothingness. It is philosophically difficult to speak of interiority in light of the weight of the outside" (p. 25). Although relations between language and subjectivity are emphasized differently among postmodern feminist philosophers and psychoanalysts, there is a general consensus that exteriority and interiority do, in deed, overlap, fold into, co-implicate, and are not simply reducible to each other, and the differences between these thinkers is particularly important when considering the role of "masculine" language in the construction of "feminine" subjectivity (Benjamin, 1998; Kristeva, 1997; Grosz, 1995, 1994; Butler, 1997, 1993, 1990; Irigaray, 1991).

The aim of this paper is, perhaps paradoxically, an attempt to give the interiority of lesbian relationship violence an exteriority of its own. Specifically, I will highlight, much as Ristock (2002) has already done, how the external weight of the dominant speech of domestic violence works to preclude the complexities in abusive lesbian relations *and* I will begin to articulate these complexities within the context of a postmodern feminist psychoanalytic ethics.

THE LANGUAGE OF DOMESTIC VIOLENCE POLITICS

Domestic violence politics has historically been influenced by the view that relationship violence occurs within a context of male domination and hatred towards women. Within this view, men and women are seen to occupy different social positions in culture due to essential characteristics as men (e.g., dominant) and women (e.g., submissive). Interpolating this logic to domestic violence, men are seen to assert their power in abusive ways towards women because they are in a privileged position to do so *and* because maintaining their position as "male" depends on denigrating what is "female." This view of domestic violence is typically understood as commensurate with the parameters of liberal feminist theories, which do not seriously consider the role of language in constructing subjectivity. While a liberal feminist position tends to see the "truth" of the relationship violence as residing in the face-value experience of the heterosexual female victim, a postmodern feminism sees the "truth" of the relationship violence as residing in the way in which the categories of "power," "sex," and "gender" function intersubjectively (Goldner, Penn, Sheinberg, & Walker, 1990; Benjamin, 1995, 1988).

A portion of my analysis is interested in the way in which the experience of heterosexual women victims have been used to generate a theory of relationship violence and a politic for the domestic violence movement without any sophisticated analysis of the function of the language used to articulate heterosexual women experiences. Whereas it was previously discussed how postmodern feminisms are susceptible to a "top-down process" of analysis that can conflate language and experience such that all experience becomes language, the language of domestic violence politics has used a "bottom-up process" for its analysis, which has excluded the role of its own language in the construction of relationship violence (i.e., language does not merely represent experience). The dominant language of relationship violence has also failed to account for the experiences of nonheterosexuals and perpetrators in their analysis.

There are two specific ways the "bottom-up process" of analysis that is contained in the dominant language of domestic violence functions to exclude experiences of lesbian relationship violence. First, the language of domestic violence suggests an essentialist relation between the categories of "woman-heterosexual-victim," and "man-heterosexual-perpetrator" such that within the dominant language all heterosexual men are cited as "abusers" and all heterosexual women are cited as "victims." This essentialist conceptualization makes it easy to talk about heterosexual men "being perpetrators" and heterosexual women "being victims," but discursively impossible to speak of lesbian abusers and lesbian victims without turning them into *heterosexual men* and *heterosexual women*. Second, heterosexual relationship violence theorizes heterosexual women victims' subjectivity, but does not complexly consider intersubjectivity as a precondition of subjectivity. So when domestic violence language is simply applied to abusive lesbian relationships, only the elements of lesbian experiences that are *heterosexual* get articulated and validated; formulating lesbian relationship violence this way erases anything distinctly *lesbian* (i.e., intersubjectivity–woman-to-woman desire) about lesbian relationship violence. For example, a common complaint of lesbians who self-identify as victims and seek help from domestic violence shelters is that they feel as if the institutional and interpersonal pressures in the shelters do not create a space, which would make it permissible to speak openly about being abused by a woman. Female victims can speak as a heterosexual woman, but not as a woman who loves (and hates) another woman. The tension between lesbian experiences and domestic violence language, therefore, is an issue of the erasure of *lesbian desire.*

The silencing of lesbians' experiences in the dominant domestic violence language shows concretely how lesbians' experiences of relationship violence are excluded through the polemical practices of the domestic violence movement. According to Foucault (1984a), "Polemics defines alliances, recruits partisans, unites interests or opinions, represents a party; it establishes the other as an enemy, an upholder of opposed interests, against which one must fight until the moment this enemy is defeated and either surrenders or disappears" (pp. 382-383). The idea is that the other (i.e., anyone not female, not heterosexual, and not victim) is the foundation of the domestic violence movement. Accordingly, domestic violence politics relies on the face-value experience of heterosexual women victims for its legitimacy, and abolishes any dialogue of alternative experiences "not to come as close as possible to a difficult truth, but to bring about the triumph of the just cause" (Foucault, 1984a, p. 382). Lesbians' experiences of relationship violence are neither validated nor included in the conceptualizations of relationship violence, or they are only included in ways that continue to legitimize the face-value experience of heterosexual women. Thus, the way in which domestic violence language-politics has an ethos, that is, a manner of being, is violently exclusionary.

ETHICAL REFLECTIONS ON THE VIOLENT "INTERIORITIES" OF LESBIAN CLIENTS

Ethics is concerned with the processes (i.e., attention, knowledge, and techniques) by which our subjectivity is constituted and reconstituted (Foucault, 1984b). The psychoanalytic situation lends itself to the examination of the sort of processes that go into self-formation. If psychoanalysis can be understood to take the client's speech as its object, it is through the examination of the client's speech that therapist forms and transforms the client's subjectivity (Kristeva, 1989). The ethical means I use to recognize the client's speech and gauge how the client is recognizing my speech involves a heuristic use of Neo-Kleinian terminology and technique (Kristeva, 2001; Phillips & Stonebridge, 1998; Hinshelwood, 1994), and Huntington's (1998) model of asymmetrical reciprocity, which is an elaborated articulation of the ethics of Heidegger (1962), Kristeva (1991), and Irigaray (1984) in which the recognition between self and other is understood as holding the dialectical tension between symmetrical (i.e., similar) and asymmetrical (i.e., different) elements of subjectivity without idealizing similarity over difference or vice-versa (e.g., exoticizing difference or collapsing similarity into sameness). Below, I will elaborate on the elements of Huntington's model of asymmetrical reciprocity, and the Neo-Kleinian terminology and technique used to inform my therapeutic work with lesbian clients who have experienced relationship violence. The case study material I present below consists of the particulars of individual clients and composites of several different clients.

The relationship between the therapist and client is dynamically organized around what is known and unknown. We all struggle to develop a relationship, which is receptive to the unknown in our self and others. However, I have come to discover that some lesbian clients who have experienced relationship violence are relatively closed off to the possibility of exploring what is unknown in themselves and others. These clients appear to have an investment in organizing themselves around who and what they know even if it is at the expense of themselves or others. Exploring what is unknown seems to be associated with the fear that one's internal experience will collapse if articulated in unknown ways. A fear of psychic annihilation often motivates clients to hold desperately onto known patterns of relating.

Let us consider two clinical examples to evaluate the tension between known and unknown parts of experience. A self-identified victim has said to me repeatedly, "I wouldn't know how to live without my pain." The prevailing meaning of her connection to pain is not pleasure, but that pain is what she *knows* to be her reality. Positive feelings and kind behaviors from others are only something to be fantasized about and longed for, but there is no room for them to exist within the reality of pain she was thrown into and that she continues unconsciously to construct for herself.

In another example, a self-identified abuser stated, "I don't want to hurt her, but I don't know how to stop. I just lose my mind and someone else takes over. I don't know who that other person is." This example illustrates the complex issues involved with abusers stopping the violence. For this client there is a desire to be different and not do what she knows, but an inability to think these unknown parts of herself, thus engage with them such that she could be different. These two examples are a reminder that within the context of abusive lesbian relationships it is not necessarily the case that those involved consciously desire to be abused or abusive. Rather, a primary motive of abusing or staying with an abuser is about an unconscious desire to keep one's internal experience intact and organized around who and what is known. Accordingly, what is known about the therapist to these clients is that a kind therapist is really a wolf in sheep's clothing and that all positive feelings generated by or for the therapist are not to be trusted and should be dismissed.

Assuming the client is seeking help because she wants to explore her own psychic life or subjectivity can sometimes be a false assumption on my part. I have found that many lesbian clients would rather me explore and fix their partner than to focus on themselves. Clients can spend entire sessions focused on what could possibly be going on in other people's minds, which functions to keep them organized around a familiar story or perception about themselves. Common statements clients make are: "If my partner would just do (blank) then I wouldn't get so mad at her," and "If my partner wasn't so sick then we could have a good relationship." Both of these examples illustrate how both partners in a violent relationship see the problem as residing *out there* in someone else's mind. Also, there is often much confusion for clients about what is going on inside themselves and others, which is facilitated by a belief that they can read other people's minds and that other people should read their mind. The reading of minds almost always involves the reading of negative meaning into others' behaviors, thoughts, and feelings, which adds to the confusion for the client of whose experience is whose and what is being communicated between client and other. For example, a client told me that it was stupid of me to ask her how she was feeling about the recent death of a relative–I was supposed to guess how she was feeling about the loss. I went ahead and took a guess, telling her that I imagined that she might feel sad about the death. She told me my guess was wrong, and that she did not feel sad, but rather she felt "nothing."

Some of the reasons lesbian clients do not focus on their own minds and choose to focus on what is going on inside others are: (a) They do not believe anything is wrong with them; (b) They believe something is dreadfully wrong with them; (c) They believe it is too painful to think about themselves; (d) They feel undeserving of thinking about themselves, there is no internal permission to explore one's hopes, dreams, fears, fantasies, etc.; (e) There is a belief that they do not meaningfully exist to anyone and are often surprised and/or suspicious when others show interest in them; (f) They believe they can read others minds and others should read their mind.

Additionally, there seems to be two general positions in which some lesbian clients engage with me regarding focusing on themselves. They get either very overconcerned and/or underconcerned about what's going on in my mind. Both positions seem to prop up the view that my mind is something to be ignored or controlled. This observation is consistent with Benjamin's (1995) theorizing about intersubjective recognition between men and women, that is, men tend to overlook or control women's subjectivity so that the threatening other gets absorbed as a part of the self. Ignoring and/or controlling my mind is a common way in which lesbian abuser and/or victims recognize my help, and such recognition appears to be a way to mitigate the client's pain and vulnerability, thereby ensuring inner calm or affective equilibrium, and self-cohesion. The intensity of these clients' pain often escapes words; it is *unspeakable pain.*

Working relationally, by using my separate mind and experience (i.e., subjectivity), can help the client figure out what obstacles are contributing to her suffering. Working relationally allows me to see the problem first-hand. This means that the client will try to get me to do to her or she will do to me what she claims everyone else does to her. For example, one client would begin sessions by *bullying* me around the therapy room by acting out such as sitting in my chair, trying to steal my clipboard or not letting me speak. After doing these behaviors she would often say, "You look angry," and then she would ask me if she could help me with my anger. I quickly became adept at interpreting how she was trying to put me in a vulnerable position and make me mad in order to take care of her own angry feelings, which were very much ignored by the people in her life who had bullied her around. Her bullying was often the result of her fear of recognizing me as the one who could help her with her vulnerable feelings. She put her anger into me in order to keep organized around what she knew (i.e., she knew best how to take care of others' feelings) and to deny the possibility of recognizing me as the one who was there to help her.

Focusing on the therapeutic relationship as a process that constructs and de-constructs meaning requires the participation of both a therapist and a client. Both therapist and client are in this therapeutic process together using both of our stories to create a new story. Although our roles are not set in stone, I keep in mind who is there to be helped and who is doing the helping. This is important for me to remember because so many of the lesbian clients I see for relationship violence try to re-enact with me the roles of *the good caretaker* and/or *the bad one in need of care.* For example, a client who has linked her victimization to the role of caretaker said, "Of course I'm not in a relationship with somebody healthy. Then I would be the bad one." My response to this client's statement was, "So I am imagining it's uncomfortable to be sitting here with me right now." She replied, "Yes, it's scary. I don't know how to be." Most clients believe there is only one way to be in relationships, and their way is the right way.

I have had clients say to me that they try to position themselves as the caretaker in the therapy relationship because they do not want to feel bad about themselves. These same clients have also said they would leave therapy because I *make* them feel bad, and that they would stay with an abusive partner so they don't have to be *the bad one* in the relationship. The flipside is clients who try to position themselves as *the bad client in need of care.* These clients often try to get me to carry their trauma for them, as I describe in an example below.

Focusing on the client's use of me and whether or not this use generates similarity or difference helps to evaluate whether the similarity or difference is facilitating or impeding psychic growth. The way that the client is trying to connect with me gives me information about how she is allowing me to exist for her, and what she sees as my job. I may want to facilitate a therapeutic relationship that allows for the exploration and development of the capacity for the client to encounter herself and others without idealizing or devaluing. However, clients often do not view my job in the same way. For example, a client often stated that I could not understand her because I was a different kind of lesbian than she, and that even if I had survived childhood violence as she had, my experience would not have been as bad as hers. Regardless of the issue, this client always positioned herself as a victim, particularly in comparison to me. She rarely allowed us to have points of similarity because she was terrified of having contact with me as contact represented the possibility of annihilation.

Another client, who identified herself as a child and adult victim of domestic violence spent session after session trying to get me to carry her trauma for her. For example, she often reminded me that my job was to make her feel better, and that I could make her feel better by taking away the pain she felt. When I reminded her that I could not take her pain away, she berated me and told me I was a terrible therapist. However, when she believed I took away her pain, although I would not be any different than I was when she devalued me, she would make idealizing comments about me. This client also dominated sessions, not letting me respond to her. When I spoke she would tell me I was not listening to her, and that I was obviously not interested in understanding her. I felt silenced and coerced by this client and questioned myself, feeling invisible, crazy, and as if I would have to fight with this client in order to be recognized and effective as a therapist. Instead of giving into acting out the fantasies I had of wanting to kill this client, I instead would describe my experience to this client in an effort to show her concretely that her complaints about loneliness and lack of meaningful connections were related to her depiction of me. I would say something like, "You have told me that I don't understand what it was like for you to grow up feeling terrorized, vulnerable and dismissed. However, I think you're showing me what it feels like to be you when you just got upset at me for not understanding you." When she could not connect with me, she would leave sessions feeling lonely and disconnected because her sense of connection was predicated on one person existing and the other person being annihilated, and I was often the one who was killed off. I was not just the container for the part of her that was frightened, dismissed, vulnerable, and misunderstood; I became that victimized part of her that she had to annihilate in order to survive contact with me.

When some lesbian clients are sitting in those painful places inside themselves, it is difficult for them to conceptualize comfort from me through connection. I think because connection itself has been associated with pain, it is difficult for some clients to tell the difference between painful and comforting connections. So connection becomes the equivalent of "You're hurting me," instead of "I'm hurting. Can you sit and talk with me," or "You're going to hurt me, so I am going to disconnect before it happens." As a result of associating connection with pain (i.e., it is contact, not pleasure, which gets associated with pain), these clients often experience intense loneliness. This loneliness cannot be easily remedied with human connection, as it is humans who have been and are the source of pain. Animals are often a big part of the lives of these clients, I think because animals offer the comfort of a preverbal connection, that is, of being understood and connection beyond or before words.

Not taking the client's experiences at face-value allows me to focus on the complexities and contradictions in her stories. Clients in abusive lesbian relationships seem to live in and through their experience to such a degree that they have difficulty reflecting on their experience. Thus, all that is true and real for them is their experience. As a result, clients often have difficulty stepping back and reflecting on themselves as they believe they are totally and completely the stories they tell. When clients begin to say things such as "I never thought of myself that way" or "You mean it's possible to just talk about my feelings to my partner?" clients are considering the possibility that they are complex and have many stories, which constitute their experience.

Attending to process as well as content by focusing on how the client tells her story helps to understand the various levels of meaning in the client's speech. When a client talks about others I think about how she could be talking about herself or about the two of us. It is rare that a client can tell me she has experienced abuse and that she is aware that it has affected her relationship dynamics in a particular way. By focusing on not only *what* clients say, but *how* they say it they *show* me (i.e., clients act out their dynamics in the therapy room) how the abuse in their life has affected them because the abuse is so integral to their identity. This gives me direct access to the relationship dynamics, which are being played out with me. A common dynamic I've encountered with these clients is a tendency to *blow me off* by being late to sessions, leaving sessions early, not speaking during sessions, or only speaking about superficial issues. All of these forms of communication speak to the client's struggle to focus on the *unspeakable pain* that resides inside them. This form of communication also highlights their disbelief that another person can help with the pain, and can provide some comfort. The client has an investment in turning me into a rejecting person they know how to organize around and relate to. As the client shows me her abuse, I am better able to understand her experience and help her see me less and less as a rejecting person.

Focusing on how the client's experience has been discursively constructed works to unpack the client's speech and free up the meanings of her stuck experience. When I talk about discourse, I am talking about an organized body of thought, for example, the dominant language of the domestic violence movement is a discourse. I've noticed that there seem to be several different and overlapping discourses at work in the speech of women who seek help for partner abuse that suggest a resistance to engaging in therapy as a meaning-making process. For example, consumer and liberal feminist discourses are present in lesbian clients' speech. Clients may say things such as "I'm the client you're supposed to tell me what is wrong with me and what to do about it" or "I'm the victim. You're trying to blame me when you ask me that question." Although these are different discourses, they can yield the same effects by positioning the client and/or therapist either as a "know-it-all" or as a "know-nothing." Both positions for therapist and client are disempowering as neither position on its own has the power to explore the possibility of responding to the client's problem. Therapeutic working-through requires two separate and different subjectivities.

Sometimes lesbians who have stayed in domestic violence shelters become very adept at defensively using the dominant domestic violence language to tell me "I'm blaming them" when I'm exploring with them, or to use their victim label in their romantic relationship to harass their partner. Clients who have been given an abuser label often stay organized around their anger, and never go beyond the anger to explore issues of vulnerability because the intensity of the shame evoked by being labeled as "all bad" is unspeakably painful. Also, some lesbian clients get stuck with one story about their lesbianism. For example, some clients link their lesbianism with their identity as abuser or as victim, such that being abusive or being abused is justification or penance for being a fundamentally flawed and evil human being. One self-identified abuser acknowledged how it was *good* that her partner left her for being abusive and added, "God is getting his revenge on me by punishing me for being gay." For this client, it is clear that she believes *victims* and *heterosexuals* are *good*. Additionally, some lesbian clients overtly devalue my lesbianism in an effort to either devalue or idealize their own lesbian identity. Lesbian clients who position themselves *one-down* with me are usually trying to take on the *bad one in need of care* role, whereas those clients who devalue my lesbianism in order to position themselves *one-up* tend to be taking on the *good caretaker* role.

Literature on lesbian relationship violence talks about the use of homophobia as a control tactic. I've observed that homophobia appears to work as a control tactic in relationships where both partners believe that assuming a lesbian identity is fundamentally bad. In other words, homophobia might be an expression of a partner's internalized hatred and disgust for her lesbian desire, but the expression of this hatred outwards onto a partner only seems to work when the recipient believes in the projected hatred. Thus, the recipient of the projected hatred also believes her lesbian desire to be bad and disgusting.

Focusing on the multiple positions from which the client can speak means the client can speak as perpetrator, victim, both, or neither. I am interested in respectfully exploring the meanings that have been linked to all of the parts that exist in my clients' relationships. Lesbian clients in therapy for relationship violence are notorious for splitting certain parts of themselves out of awareness and only allowing the familiar parts of themselves to be known. Everyone has aggressive and vulnerable parts; the acknowledgement of all these parts is necessary if lesbian clients are to organize themselves around a different kind of identity, which is other than *the perpetrator* or *the victim.* For example, the client who bullies me and then wants to help me with my anger showed me at least two important parts of herself: *a bully* and *a helper.* The client's *bully* and *helper* deserve to be engaged in a compassionate dialogue within herself and with me.

Attending to the client self-identifying as victim and/or perpetrator helps to see how she is using these categories to construct and reify her experience. I have already pointed out that clients knowingly and unknowingly identify themselves with both sides of the categories perpetrator/victim, good/bad, heterosexual/homosexual, male/female, right/wrong, and helper/helped. I have learned that clients use the categories of victim and perpetrator to harass their partner or therapist and to justify abusive relations. It is a goal of therapy to help clients learn how to live with all of the different permutations and meanings possible within these categories in an effort to go beyond the reified indexing of experience. For example, I am more interested in how a client is both a *perpetrator* and a *victim* and both *good* and *bad* than I am in how a client is either a *bad perpetrator* or a *good victim.* Instead of punishing "being bad" or extolling "being good," lesbian clients stop abusing and stop returning to abusive relationships when they have been able to develop compassion for both the aggressive and vulnerable parts of themselves and others, as it is this compassion that allows for a transcendence of the rigid and dichotomous indexing of experiencing involved in lesbian relationship violence.

CLINICAL SUCCESS, POLITICAL FAILURE?

In a LGBT health workshop I recently attended, one feminist emphatically referred to postmodern feminist analyses as "intellectual masturbatory horseshit by those ivory tower types." I believe the "intellectual masturbatory" character of postmodern feminism arises out of an obsessive tendency to detach such analyses from lived experience, or to conflate language with experience. In my analysis of lesbian relationship violence I have tried to stay connected to the materiality of lesbians' experiences in order to articulate a language, containing a feminist psychoanalytic ethos, which allows for the complexities of lesbian relationship violence to be heard. What I have shown is that lesbian clients speak their violent experiences in multifaceted ways, and this multiplicity is often organized around an unconscious fear of psychic annihilation.

In sum, this paper leaves us with at least two questions to ponder: Do we try to squash lesbian experiences into a heterosexist model of relationship violence in order to preserve domestic violence politics? Or do we get rid of the model of political language all together? This exposition has shown how it is difficult to understand lesbian relationship violence outside of the theorizing of heterosexual relationship violence. However, through critically making lesbians' experiences of relationship violence visible and heard within the framework of an ethical language, a more compassionate understanding is beginning to develop. I think that this compassionate understanding resembles more of a *lesbian-izing* of the political language of relationship violence than a language of lesbian relationship violence. Above all, this shift from politics to ethics is a reminder of how it is not just the concept of *woman* that is problematic in domestic violence theorizing, it is also *lesbian desire* that is a knotty word for the dominant language of domestic violence.

REFERENCES

Benjamin, J. (1988). *The bonds of love: Psychoanalysis, feminism, and the problem of domination*. New York: Pantheon Books.

Benjamin, J. (1995). *Like subjects, love objects: Essays on recognition and sexual difference*. New Haven, CT: Yale University Press.

Benjamin, J. (1998). *Shadow of the other: Intersubjectivity and gender in psychoanalysis*. New York: Routledge.

Butler, J. (1990). *Gender trouble: Feminism and the subversion of identity*. New York: Routledge.

Butler, J. (1993). *Bodies that matter*. New York: Routledge.

Butler, J. (1997). *The psychic life of power*. Palo Alto, CA: Stanford University Press.

Foucault, M. (1984a). Polemics, politics, and problematizations. *The Foucault reader* (P. Rabinow, Ed.). New York: Pantheon Books.

Foucault, M. (1984b). Politics and ethics: An interview. *The Foucault reader* (P. Rabinow, Ed.). New York: Pantheon Books.

Goldner, V., Penn, P., Sheinberg, M., & Walker, G. (1990). Love & violence: Gender paradoxes in volatile attachments. *Family Process, 29*(4), 343-364.

Grosz, E. (1994). *Volatile bodies: Corporeal feminisms*. Bloomington, IN: Indiana Univ. Press.

Grosz, E. (1995). *Space, time, and perversion*. New York: Routledge.

Hamberger, L. & Renzetti, C. (Eds.). (1996). *Domestic partner abuse*. New York: Springer Publishing Company, Inc.

Heidegger, M. (1964). *Being and time*. New York: Harper Collins.

Hinshelwood, R. (1994). *Clinical Klein*. New York: Basic Books.

Huntington, P. (1998). *Ecstatic subjects, utopia, and recognition*. Albany, New York: State University of New York.

Irigaray, L. (1984). *An ethics of sexual difference*. Ithaca, New York: Cornell University Press.

Irigaray, L. (1991). *The Irigaray reader* (M. Whitford, Ed.). Malden, MA: Blackwell Publishers.

Island, D. & Letellier, P. (1990). *Men who beat the men who love them: Battered gay men and domestic violence*. New York: Harrington Park Press.

Johnson, G. (1999). Inside and outside: Ontological considerations. In D. Olkowski & J. Morley (Eds.), *Merleau-Ponty, interiority and exteriority, psychic life and the world* (pp. 25-34). Albany, New York: State University New York.

Kaschak, E. (Ed.). (2001). *Intimate betrayal: Domestic violence in lesbian relationships*. New York: Haworth Press.

Kristeva, J. (1989). *Language: The unknown*. New York: Columbia University Press.

Kristeva, J. (1991). *Strangers to ourselves*. New York: Columbia University Press.

Kristeva, J. (1997). In K. Oliver (Ed.), *The portable Kristeva*. New York: Columbia University Press.

Kristeva, J. (2001). *Melanie Klein*. New York: Columbia University Press.

Leventhal, B. & Lundy, S. (Eds.). (1999). Same-*sex domestic violence: Strategies for change*. Thousand Oaks, CA: Sage Publications.

Lobel, K. (Ed.). (1986). Naming *the violence: Speaking out about lesbian battering*. Seattle, WA: Seal Press.

McClennan, J. & Gunther, J. (Eds.). (1999). A *professional guide to understanding gay and lesbian domestic violence*. Lewiston, NY: Edwin Mellen Press.

Phillips, J. & Stonebridge, L. (Eds.). (1998). *Reading Melanie Klein*. New York: Routledge.

Renzetti, C. (1992). *Violent betrayal: Partner abuse in lesbian relationships*. Newbury Park, CA: Sage Publications, Inc.

Renzetti, C. & Miley, C. (1996). *Violence in gay and lesbian domestic partnerships*. Binghamton, NY: Harrington Park Press.

Ristock, J. (2002). *No more secrets: Violence in Lesbian relationships*. New York: Routledge.

Transference and Countertransference in Therapy with Lesbian Patients: Contrasting Views from Lesbian and Heterosexual Therapists

Karine J. Igartua

Pascale Des Rosiers

SUMMARY. Like gender, sexual orientation is an important determinant of one's perception of human relationships, therefore influencing the therapeutic process. Through a framework derived from cross-cultural therapy literature, this article explores how lesbian patients' transferences are influenced by their perception of their therapists' sexual orientations and how therapists' countertransferences differ according to their sexual orientations. This analysis took shape through dialogue with heterosexual and lesbian therapists working in a variety of

Karine J. Igartua, MD, CM, FRCPC, is Assistant Professor, Department of Psychiatry, McGill University, Montreal, Canada. She is medical co-director of the McGill University Sexual Identity Centre (M.U.S.I.C.).

Pascale Des Rosiers, MD, is Assistant Professor, Department of Psychiatry, McGill University, Montreal, Canada. She is director of the Community Link Service of the McGill University Health Centre.

Address correspondence to: Dr. Karine J. Igartua, Department of Psychiatry, B6-253, Montreal General Hospital, 1650 Cedar, Montreal, Quebec, Canada, H3G 1A4 (E-mail: karine.igartua@muhc.mcgill.ca).

[Haworth co-indexing entry note]: "Transference and Countertransference in Therapy with Lesbian Patients: Contrasting Views from Lesbian and Heterosexual Therapists." Igartua, Karine J., and Pascale Des Rosiers. Co-published simultaneously in *Journal of Lesbian Studies* (Harrington Park Press, an imprint of The Haworth Press, Inc.) Vol. 8, No. 1/2, 2004, pp. 123-141; and: *Lesbians, Feminism, and Psychoanalysis: The Second Wave* (ed: Judith M. Glassgold, and Suzanne Iasenza) Harrington Park Press, an imprint of The Haworth Press, Inc., 2004, pp. 123-141. Single or multiple copies of this article are available for a fee from The Haworth Document Delivery Service [1-800-HAWORTH, 9:00 a.m. - 5:00 p.m. (EST). E-mail address: docdelivery@haworthpress.com].

Digital Object Identifier: 10.1300/J155v08n01_08

settings, some generic mental health settings and some lesbian, gay, and bisexual identified. *[Article copies available for a fee from The Haworth Document Delivery Service: 1-800-HAWORTH. E-mail address: <docdelivery@ haworthpress.com> Website: <http://www.HaworthPress.com> © 2004 by The Haworth Press, Inc. All rights reserved.]*

KEYWORDS. Lesbian, therapy, transference, countertransference, homosexual, psychoanalysis

INTRODUCTION

In early psychoanalytic writings, transference was considered a purely intrapsychic phenomenon that developed independently of the analyst's characteristics (Freud, 1912/1961). However, the psychoanalytic and psychotherapy literature has evolved to acknowledge that the external reality of the therapist influences the development of the transference. The impact of gender on transference and countertransference has become well established (Mogul, 1982; Raphling & Chused, 1986). Like gender, sexual orientation is an important determinant of one's perception of human relationships and, therefore, has an impact on the therapeutic process. Unlike gender, however, sexual orientation is not necessarily perceptible to an observer. This difference is fertile ground for conscious and unconscious assumptions. Both the therapist's and the patient's sexual orientation will color the relationship.

The approach employed in this article is inspired by the literature on cross-cultural psychology. As Martin (1982) has contended, and others have concurred (Margolies, Becker & Jackson-Brewer, 1987; Igartua, 1998), lesbians, gay men, and bisexuals comprise a minority group similar to cultural and ethnic minorities who suffer unjustified negative acts from the environment. They share with other minorities the character traits resulting from the group's victimization described by Allport (1958). These include obsessive concern with the group stigma, denial of membership, withdrawal, passivity, aggression against one's group and identification with the dominant group, i.e., self-hate. In the lesbian, gay, and bisexual population, the resulting self-hatred has been labeled "internalized homophobia" (Hencken, 1982; Margolies et al., 1987).

Unlike other cultural and ethnic minorities, most lesbian, gay, and bisexual individuals do not share their minority status with their family of origin. They therefore do not grow up with a sense of belonging to a community and have to seek it out. They are not taught strategies to combat discrimination and have to learn them in order to develop pride in their lesbian, gay and bisexual or nonheterosexual identities (Margolies et al., 1987; Igartua, 1998).

Comas-Diaz and Jacobson (1991) stress that both patient and therapist tend to bring their early perceptions of ethnic and racial stereotypes into therapy, and these perceptions play a significant role in the development of transference and countertransference. They advocate that therapists be aware that just as with their patients, their own ethnicity and culture influence their perceptions of norms. This article extends Comas-Diaz and Jacobson's precepts to better understand the influence of sexual orientation on perceptions of norms and relationships.

The cross-cultural paradigm is useful on several levels. First, the two authors of this article have different sexual orientations, thus the cross-cultural approach allowed them to contrast and compare their subjective points of view. Second, the cross-cultural paradigm has been a useful clinical framework when the therapist and the patient have had different sexual orientations. Third, in the cases where both the therapist and the patient belong to a sexual minority, the expertise developed in the cross-cultural approach clarifies how the therapeutic relationship is influenced by the heterosexist culture. And fourth, since societal attitudes towards homosexuality vary tremendously by geopolitical region, the reader may take into account how homosexuality may be treated differently in their own environment rather than in that of the patients and therapists described in this paper, all of whom live in metropolitan Montreal, Canada. Montreal is a rather cosmopolitan city with a tradition of tolerance of all forms of diversity, including sexual orientation. An active lesbian, gay, and bisexual community has gained considerable visibility over the last decade. Montreal will indeed be the host of the 2006 Gay Games. Further, in June 2002, the provincial government modified its civil code to eliminate all discrimination against gay men and lesbians, granting them the legal recognition of their unions and their families. It is, in fact, the most progressive piece of legislation in North America in that regard. Although homophobia is still present on some level, overt homophobic statements or attitudes are frowned upon in Montreal culture.

Since gender and sexual orientation both are influential in the therapeutic relationship, each particular combination of gender and sexual orientation in the patient-therapist dyad will have particular dynamics.

This article will limit itself to female therapists (lesbian and heterosexual) working with lesbian patients.

TRANSFERENCE

General Issues

The influence of the sexual orientation of the therapist on transference is largely dependent on the patient's perception of what that orientation is. In turn, this perception is influenced by a variety of factors among which are the patient's assumptions, the image projected by the therapist, the clinical context, and the way the patient was referred. The following vignette illustrates the complexity of how these various factors can interact to influence transference.

Case Example

> Briana was a 42-year-old lesbian woman who was referred for therapy in the context of a medical clinic where her therapist was a consultant. She was referred for depression. Although Briana was completely closeted, she was in a five-year relationship with an openly lesbian woman. Briana's refusal to come out was a source of tension in her relationship. Initially, she saw her therapist in a rather impersonal office at the medical clinic. Briana immediately assumed that her therapist was straight. Her transference was rather aggressive, accusing her therapist of being homophobic and perhaps even of having the hidden agenda of converting her to heterosexuality. For logistic reasons, the setting was changed and Briana then continued therapy in her therapist's private office. In the office, Briana quickly noticed several books on gay and lesbian psychotherapy. She then changed her view of her therapist and assumed that her therapist must be lesbian: "Why else would a therapist read that kind of literature?" Her transference evolved, unraveling a completely different set of fears. She then, as aggressively, accused her therapist of having a different hidden agenda, namely of wanting to push her out of the closet without an appreciation of the consequences for her professional, social and family life. She repeatedly asked the therapist to disclose her sexual orientation and was quite frustrated at the absence of disclosure. At some point, she noticed a ring on her therapist's left hand, which

she described as "too traditional for a gay relationship ring" and her transferential fear reverted to having a homophobic therapist. She, in fact, kept switching back and forth between her fears of being forced into heterosexual conversion and of being forced into a catastrophic coming out. When the therapist became visibly pregnant, she triumphantly claimed: "Now I know that you're straight!" The therapist pointed out to her that she assumed only heterosexual women could get pregnant, which was a reflection of her own heterosexist assumptions. Briana was quite angry at this interpretation. Nevertheless, it allowed her, for the first time, to start exploring how her projections and her internalized homophobia poisoned her relationships. Briana was convinced that she was unacceptable and unlovable as she was. She therefore engaged aggressively with others to protect herself against the anticipated threats of being forced to change into someone different. In reality, these interactions only reinforced her feeling of being misunderstood and alienated.

An issue frequently debated in the literature is whether the therapist should reveal her sexual orientation to her patients. In Briana's case, there seemed to be more advantages than disadvantages in *not* disclosing it, as it allowed her to express and explore more fully the extent of her fears and projections. In other cases, the issues at stake may be different and a therapist who revealed her sexual orientation could provide a much-needed role model for her patient. Many factors (some belonging to the therapist, some to the patient) influence the therapist's decision to disclose her sexual orientation. A complete exploration of this issue is beyond the scope of this article.

Transference Common to Both Lesbian and Heterosexual Therapists

Women therapists, whether perceived as lesbian or heterosexual, typically are recipients of maternal transference. With a lesbian patient, whether early in her coming-out process or long self-identified as lesbian, unresolved issues around the less than optimal acceptance of her sexuality by her family of origin are often prominent. Even when parents do not reject their daughter's homosexuality, they still frequently lack the information, experience or comfort to appropriately support and guide her. This can result in a role reversal where the child, having come out and sought out information on her own, will then educate and support her parents. Often the balance is never restored and the child remains parentified. When the therapist is experienced as nurturing, knowledgeable, and accepting of a patient's lesbian identity, there is potential for a "corrective emotional experience" or at least a working through of the conflictual feelings.

Though issues of nurturing and comforting can be inherent aspects of the maternal transference, they are not the only issues at play. Erotic elements are frequently present as well. However, the erotic aspects of the mother-daughter relationships have been neglected in psychodynamic literature. Burch (1996) has suggested that this neglect is due to society's relative discomfort with female sexuality. It is our impression that this discomfort with female sexuality has engendered a defensive overemphasis on the pre-oedipal "maternal" transference. Indeed, most psychoanalytic authors equate "maternal" issues with pre-genital issues. However, the fact that transference is "maternal" does not preclude the possibility of it also being erotic (Roth, 1988). In fact, even Freud recognized that genital sexuality in a little girl is not centered exclusively on the father as the object of libidinal aims, and that sexual feelings in children are present for parents of both sexes (Freud 1931/1961). Often forgotten, the two sides of the oedipal triangle play important roles in the children's development. As McDougall (1986) and Benjamin (1988) have suggested, children of both sexes want to be and have both parents. One could easily argue that the genital attraction toward the mother is likely to be more important in the little girl who will develop into a lesbian adult. A complete discussion of the role of the homosexual oedipal aspect of development in lesbians is beyond the scope of this article. Nevertheless, it is our impression that too little attention has been devoted to the homosexual oedipal transference to the mother (unfortunately misnamed the "negative oedipal") and that this relative neglect has contributed to therapists' frequently overlooking or misinterpreting erotic transference between woman.

Whether the therapist is lesbian or heterosexual, the maternal transference can therefore encompass both nurturing and erotic issues. How the therapist's perceived sexual orientation comes into play will be explored in the following sections.

Transference to the Therapist Perceived as Lesbian

When the therapist is perceived as lesbian, the initial transference reaction is often one of identification, especially with younger patients early in their identity formation. This is generally not problematic and can be in fact an integral part of the therapeutic process. For some patients, however, the need for a role model is so strong as to obliterate any perception of difference between the patient and her therapist. This identification may lead the patient to assume that the therapist shares all the same reference points and not to explain situations as carefully. This type of identification tends to have a more defensive component, as it is motivated by the need to avoid anxiety, shame or other painful affects or to restore self-cohesion or self-esteem. Early in the therapy, interpretation of the defensive nature of this identification may be too threatening to the patient, but asking for clarification on the patient's life circumstances may highlight the differences between them and decrease the identification.

Often the identification is colored by idealization as well. The therapist may be seen as strong for having become a professional, for being comfortable talking about sexuality, and for a host of other reasons, real or fantasized. Again, a certain degree of temporary idealization of one's therapist can be adaptive in that it can be reassuring to impute special values and power to someone on whom one is dependant. It becomes problematic when it shows characteristics of a more archaic or primitive type of idealization, i.e., when it implies the conviction that the therapist is omnipotent, omniscient and omnibenevolent. One could describe this type of idealization in Kohutian terms as an idealizing selfobject transference (Kohut & Wolf, 1978). In this type of idealization, imperfections in the self are intolerable and prevented by fusion with an idealized object. The inevitable downside of this type of idealization is devaluation. This devaluation may manifest itself by an abrupt disenchantment with the therapist. Alternatively, the patient may feel that her perfect therapist's success is unattainable to her and thus, may devalue herself and envy the therapist.

Sometimes, identification and idealization are compounded with eroticization. The patient might simultaneously want to be *like* the therapist and want to be *with* the therapist. This particular transference reaction may be specific to the lesbian therapist-lesbian patient dyad the same way that merger has been associated with lesbian couples (Burch, 1986; Igartua, 1998). Identification, though it can occur with people of opposite genders, is more likely and often stronger with members of the same sex. For lesbians then, the object of identification and of eroticization can be the same. Very little has been written on this co-occurrence of identification and eroticization. As is the case with simple identification or temporary idealization, this is not in itself problematic. In therapy, however, it can take a defensive function when it is used as a way to avoid anxiogenic material, restore self-esteem, or distract from a sense of inner deadness. In Kohutian terms, this would be known as alter-ego or twinship transference (Kohut & Wolf, 1978). In order to maintain her sense of self-cohesion, the patient needs to mirror herself through the ideal sexual companion, someone like herself, yet not herself, who would understand her perfectly while also stimulating her sexually.

Case Example

Alexandra was 24-year-old girl who had her first same sex experiences at age 14 when she and her best friend experimented sexually. Since then, she had sex with a handful of women but no men. Still, she did not identify as lesbian because she equated this with "big butchy women without style, finesse or femininity." She chose her therapist after seeing her speak to a gay, lesbian, and bisexual youth group where the therapist was known to be lesbian. Immediately she identified with and idealized the therapist as someone who was "pretty, smart, successful and not afraid of being out." She began talking about returning to school to become a psychologist who would work with gays and lesbians. She would often stare at the therapist's diplomas on the wall, replacing in her mind the name to match her own. She became flirtatious with the therapist, and frequently alluded to how she told her friends how gorgeous her therapist was. She, however, resisted discussing directly her attraction or attachment to her therapist. This embarrassed her because "only losers fall in love with their therapists." By admitting to longing for a "real" (i.e., nontherapeutic) relationship with her therapist, she was reminded of the inherent inequality of the therapeutic relationship. This threatened her identification, which she still needed to regulate her self-esteem: "One day I will be happy and accomplished like you." As this was interpreted to her, the erotic aspects of the transference waned. The idealization, however, remained just as strong. Alexandra became able to see her need for nurturing and mirroring. She became quite perturbed by her awareness of her mounting emotional dependence on her therapist, and needed to tests the therapist's omnibenevolence. She pushed the limits of therapy with multiple phone calls between sessions, and by throwing herself into her therapist's arms. When the therapist refused to change the therapeutic frame, devaluation was instantaneous. In Alexandra's psyche, the therapist had shifted from "caring, competent and cool" to "incompetent, inhumane, cruel and in it for the money." Fortunately, the therapeutic alliance was strong enough to withstand this shift and Alexandra could continue to work through her need to be taken care of and her desire for intimacy with her therapist.

Patients who are at earlier stages of identity formation, still disavowing homosexual feelings or admitting to them while believing they are wrong and should be eliminated, may devalue a therapist who they believe to be lesbian. They may feel the therapist will try to coerce them into a "gay lifestyle" and thus become reticent to discuss any same-sex eroticism. Normalizing bisexual feelings, distinguishing attractions from identity, avoiding labeling, and exploring both heterosexual and homosexual fantasies may be ways to decrease the patient's anxiety to a workable level. In some cases, however, a therapist perceived as lesbian may simply be too threatening and these patients may only be able to explore their sexuality with someone they perceive as heterosexual.

For lesbian patients who are out to themselves exclusively, the fear may be that the lesbian therapist will push the patient out of the closet without a real appreciation of the issues at stake for them personally. The lesbian and gay community canonizes public coming out as a sign of maturity, strength, and mental health. As well, from a political point of view, the more the community is visible, the more successful it can be in demanding equal rights and recognition. For these reasons, patients may get pressure from those close to them as well as from the wider community to come out of the closet. They may therefore assume that their therapist will share this agenda (see the case of Briana described above). Though coming out may indeed be a healthy outcome of therapy in many instances, there remain situations where being closeted is advisable. One must keep in mind Maslow's (1987) hierarchy of needs when determining with the patient what her best course of action is: if food, shelter and physical safety are at risk then disclosure may not be prudent. However, sometimes the patient's internalized homophobia may magnify or indeed create a risk when none exists.

Case Example

Valerie was a 47-year-old lesbian with a unionized customer service job in a large downtown mall. She lived in fear that someone would discover her sexual orientation and thus avoided as much as possible any friendly conversation with co-workers or regular clients. This severely limited her social life, which had become, over the years, virtually nonexistent. She sought psychotherapy for longstanding anxiety that was unresponsive to medication. She explored with the therapist what were the possible consequences of disclosing her sexual orientation or even of not hiding it so obsessively. In her fantasies, she would be ostracized from co-workers and probably even lose her job, all this despite knowing of out gay colleagues who were better integrated than she was, and despite being protected by a union. Valerie's fears were clearly exaggerated and rooted in her own internalized homophobia.

Transference to the Therapist Perceived as Heterosexual

In our heterosexist society, many patients will assume that their therapist is heterosexual unless the context of the referral or a prior knowledge of the therapist's sexual orientation influences them otherwise. Having been surrounded and frequently ostracized by the heterosexist society all her life, a lesbian may tend to fuse in her mind her heterosexual therapist and the society as if they were one, as if the therapist personified society at large. The therapist becomes an internal representation of the hurtful other and is therefore not be trusted until she can "prove herself" trustworthy.

It is not surprising then that feelings of resentment and fear of ostracization may color the initial transference. Ensuing transferential reactions frequently involve distancing and defending against intimacy by overemphasizing differences: *"You cannot understand me; our lives have nothing in common."* Projections of internalized homophobia via accusations of homophobic prejudices (as in Briana's case) are commonly used as a way to create and maintain distance. Fears that the therapist may be trying to "convert" them to heterosexuality are often expressed. At times, projective identification can occur: The therapist, identifying with the anger and hostility, may unwittingly react in ways that will be rejecting to the patient, thereby accentuating the distance and confirming the patient's fear of having an unempathic homophobic therapist. Underlying these fears and projections can be a wish to be in a beneficial relationship with a heterosexual woman. For some patients, this issue can be insurmountable and a therapist perceived to be lesbian may be indeed necessary.

Certainly, this type of reaction will present itself more frequently in cases where social and/or family stigmatization has left painful scars, when the feelings of alienation and rejection have been so strong as to leave overwhelming resentment toward any "representative" of the heterosexist society. However, factors other than previous experiences with discrimination can help explain this reaction. For example, middle stages of gay and lesbian identity development, characterized by exaggerated gay and lesbian pride, are associated with devaluation and outright rejection of anything remotely associated with heterosexuality (Cass, 1979). Psychodynamic factors, such as the need to develop an alter-ego transference can also contribute to this reaction.

Some patients will justify their desire for a lesbian therapist by stating that they do not want to have to "educate their therapist." Although "educating a therapist" can be a genuinely annoying element in therapy, having precise knowledge about the exact context and circumstances of a patient's life is perhaps less important than having the capacity to encourage the patient to elaborate on the personal meaning of these circumstances. Though patients are certainly entitled to their preferences, the preference for a lesbian therapist sometimes represents (and thus can be interpreted as) a preconceived assumption about heterosexual therapists, stemming more from the patient's internal world than from the reality of the therapist.

On the other hand, internalized homophobia can be expressed through an idealization of heterosexuality. As one patient once told one of the authors: "*I would not want to have a lesbian therapist because that would mean that she would be just as messed up as I am.*" A frequent corollary to this idealization is envy, not only of the therapist as an individual, but of the circumstances of her life, which are perceived to be perfectly easy, successful, and satisfying. As is often the case in envy, rage at the therapist "*who had it all so easy*" is not far away and can appear later in therapy. Contempt and devaluation may follow, and can be expressed with phrases such as "*you the breeders*" or by portraying stereotypes of heterosexual men as "*emotional retards*" and heterosexual women as "*dependant and helpless wimps.*" This devaluation tends to occur in the context of exaggerated gay pride, as a way to fend off negative stereotypes and affirm one's identity vis-à-vis a heterosexist culture.

Homoerotic transference with a therapist perceived as heterosexual can have a desperate overtone at times, as the patient may assume that her love and her attraction cannot be shared. Patients may fear that their attraction to their therapist may lead to being rejected by her. The amount of shame associated with the sexual longings can be extremely painful and may lead to concealment of the sexual fantasies and stalemate of the therapy. On the other hand, for some patients, the perceived heterosexuality of the therapist can be seen as reassuring and protective and make the erotic transference more tolerable. As is the case with perceived lesbian therapist, sexual feelings in the transference in and of themselves can be part of a patient's evolution and are not necessarily defensive. If the therapist is able to recognize and validate these feelings and resist the temptation of interpreting these as exclusively pre-oedipal longings, she can help her patient better integrate her sexual orientation.

Case Example

Michelle was a 22-year-old medical student consulting for confusion about her sexual orientation. She had been involved with a woman for two years in the past but was wondering if this "was just a phase that would pass." She was referred to a junior therapist who, upon meeting for the first time, she deemed to be "the most beautiful woman on earth." There was an immediate intense erotic transference that never abated throughout the therapy. Though the initial attraction may have been pure projection, the fact that the transference remained highly erotically charged suggests that an unconscious seduction was playing out in the therapeutic relationship. The therapist may have failed to tone down her usual seductive demeanor, as she would have instinctively done with a male heterosexual patient. Michelle was titillated by the eroticism yet most uncomfortable with it. To soothe her anxiety, Michelle searched for clues of her therapist's orientation, all the while not really wanting confirmation of her suspicion that her therapist was straight. Eventually she came across her therapist's picture in an old yearbook. Her last name had changed. Michelle interpreted this as a sure indication that she must be married and heterosexual. She was relieved that the fantasized relationship with her therapist would never materialize yet she felt that her therapist could not understand or tolerate her attraction to her. She thus avoided exploring any same-sex attractions either to her therapist or to other women, despite the fact that this was her initial reason for presentation. Michelle's therapist colluded with her avoidance by interpreting any remote allusions to sexual yearnings for her as a defensive sexualization of a maternal "pregenital" transference, i.e., as a regressive need for nurturance and dyadic fusion (yearnings for the maternal breast). This further reinforced in Michelle the feeling of alienation from herself. It was only in a second therapy with a more experienced, less defensive (and perhaps less seductive) therapist that Michelle was able to explore these feelings, and eventually become comfortable with her same-sex eroticism.

COUNTERTRANSFERENCE

General Issues

Countertransference surrounding sexual orientation depends not only on the therapist's sexual orientation, but also on how open she wishes to be about it. Choosing to reveal one's orientation, and how and when to do this with patients will depend on many factors external to the therapeutic relationship, such as treatment setting, safety and comfort in the work environment, life stage, degree of visibility in the community, and the therapist's own level of internalized homophobia, as well as theoretical and ideological issues such as type of therapy and school of thought.

Given the prevalence of heterosexist messages in our society, neither lesbian nor heterosexual therapists can ever be absolutely certain of being exempt of heterosexism and homophobia. Occasionally, even the most enlightened therapists will be surprised by their heterosexist assumptions.

Case Example

A lesbian psychiatry resident working in a crisis intervention unit was assessing a disheveled, woman in her 50s. Nicole was agitated and had disorganized, pressured speech. She wore flamboyant and sloppy makeup and had one black eye. When the resident inquired how the patient had injured herself, she was informed that it was a case of domestic violence and that Nicole had taken out a restraining order on her lover. The patient pulled out a tattered piece of paper that she handed to the resident. It was indeed a court order taken out against another woman. The resident's immediate assumption was that, in the patient's excitement and confusion, she had taken out a restraining order on the wrong person. When she noted aloud that the court order was against a woman, the patient put her hands on her hips, sat up and stated, "Well Madame, I am a lesbian. She is my lover and she did this to me!" and pointed to her black eye. The resident was surprised at her heterosexist assumption that a male lover must have abused this woman. She realized that she had denied the mere existence of female to female violence, and automatically equated violence with males.

Countertransference of the Lesbian Therapist

Therapists from minority groups may initially tend to identify with their minority patients (Comas-Diaz & Jacobson, 1991). Similarly, lesbian, gay, and bisexual therapists may identify with their lesbian, gay, and bisexual patients (Cabaj, 1991). This identification is most likely for therapists working and living isolated from other lesbians. Identification may become problematic if it veils the differences between patient and therapist, thus creating blind spots. If the therapist fails to see the patient as an individual different from herself, she may be tempted to push the patient to resolve her issues in the same way she did. She may either encourage coming out or closetedness based more on her own comfort with disclosure than on the patient's situation.

Therapists who choose to remain closeted about their sexual orientation for reasons peripheral to the therapeutic process may fear displaying their knowledge about homosexuality. If they appear too knowledgeable, patients may assume, or question them directly about their sexuality. However, feigning ignorance is not conducive to the therapeutic process.

In some cases, therapists who are open about their identity may serve as well needed role models for their patients, and in so doing alleviate the isolation some lesbian patients may feel. It takes courage, attunement and generosity to disclose aspects of one's life and share oneself for the benefit of the patient. Consideration must be given to whose needs disclosure would meet (e.g., the patient's need for role modeling vs. the therapist's need to be idealized or validated). Therapists may overly display their knowledge and/or interest in the happenings of the gay community. If they do, their curiosity puts them at risk of being seduced by gossip on mutual acquaintances or community politics at the expense of working through intra-psychic conflicts.

Case Example

> Since Alexandra (case described earlier) planned to become a psychologist herself, she had become involved in support groups in the community, including the youth group for whom her therapist had given the lecture. Alexandra spent many sessions giving her therapist "the dirt" on the various community organizations. By seducing her therapist with this "valuable" information, she made the sessions feel more like a coffee break with a colleague than a therapeutic encounter. This promoted her sense of equality. When

the therapist put her own curiosity aside and understood the defensive nature of this discourse, she was able to bypass the defense by simply asking Alexandra "what is it that you are avoiding talking about today?" This led to an exploration of the complex transferential feelings that Alexandra harbored for her therapist.

When the patient develops an eroticized transference, a lesbian therapist may be more or less likely to tolerate and explore these feelings depending on her own comfort with her own sexuality. Likewise, erotic countertransference may be more conscious in the lesbian therapist than in her heterosexual colleagues, but may also feel more threatening to her role as a therapist. Experience in psychotherapy, a satisfying personal life, and colleagues with whom she can debrief openly without fear of reproach, will help solidify her confidence so that she can remain therapeutic.

The lesbian therapist's own personal history, beliefs, and experiences may play a role in her response to her patients. When a lesbian therapist notes that one of her patients has had a relatively easy coming-out experience, with good family and social support, the therapist may feel envious. However, if a patient has faced hardships and discrimination that the therapist herself was spared, the therapist may feel a form of survivor guilt. Some patients, whether heavily discriminated against or less so, blame *all* their personal shortcomings on discrimination. For therapists who value integration of lesbians into mainstream society, these attitudes may evoke anger. The therapist may feel that these people "cry wolf,' give "gays a bad name" and hinder the social harmony between gays and straights. Therapists who may have more of a separatist political view may support and, at times, collude with this anger.

Countertransference of the Heterosexual Therapist

In order to be effective in working with a lesbian patient, a heterosexual therapist must feel reasonably free of at least conscious homophobic prejudice and she should be comfortable with her own psychic bisexuality.[1] In being so open, it may be tempting to deny the differences between the lesbian, gay, and bisexual and the heterosexual experience. This is likely to lead to a superficial pseudo-understanding, which in the end can be frustrating for patients. Acknowledging the differences with honesty and being able to question patients on aspects of their life that may be less familiar will bring more reward for both patient and therapist. With this type of approach, an empathic heterosexual therapist can effectively work with lesbian, gay, and bisexual patients, just as an empathic lesbian, gay, or bisexual therapist can effectively work with heterosexual men or women.

Reaction formation can be a frequent pitfall. This may happen when the heterosexual therapist wants so much to be open that she fails to confront patients with some obviously inappropriate or self-defeating behavior. This may be rooted in a form of "survivor's guilt," by which the therapist, being aware of the prejudices and hardships that her lesbian and gay patients face, feels uncomfortable with the relative ease of her life. She may tend to collude with her patients' blaming of societal homophobia, as the cause for their difficulties while it would be more useful to help them see their own contribution to their difficulties.

Case Example

> Alice was a 45-year-old woman who presented to therapy for work-related difficulties. During therapy, she was quite aggressive, extremely sarcastic and demeaning toward her heterosexual therapist. She complained that she had lost her job as a receptionist in a large company because of homophobia. Although the therapist was struck by the patient's provocative leather outfits and multiple body piercings, she hesitated to suggest that the patient's refusal to comply with the usual business dress code, while at the same time applying for positions in very traditional milieus, may be a way of setting herself up for failure.

Another pitfall that may await the heterosexual therapist may be elicited by homoerotic transference. Some therapists may be uncomfortable with their own homoeroticism and may become quite anxious when a patient expresses such fantasies. Denial of homoeroticism may similarly lead some heterosexual therapists to fail to notice flirtatious behavior in themselves. Indeed, conscious or unconscious flirtation amongst women occurs frequently as a way of connecting with each other. When both women are heterosexual, the seduction does not become highly erotically charged. A heterosexual woman may be surprised by the level of eroticism she can elicit through her flirtatious interactions with a lesbian. In the context of psychotherapy, an unconsciously flirtatious heterosexual therapist will have to deal with the eroticism and may be tempted to "analyze it away" by labeling it as "pre-oedipal" (see the case of Michelle). Women who are conscious of the flirtatious aspect of interactions may choose to tone it down when treating a lesbian patient in the same way they might when treating a heterosexual man. Reaction formation may cause some therapists to minimize the complexity of the human sexual psyche in order to exaggerate their comfort with the sexuality of their lesbian patient.

Case Example

> Sandi was a 32-year-old openly lesbian woman who consulted a heterosexual therapist. During the course of the therapy, she developed a homoerotic transference toward her therapist. Given Sandi's history of poor boundaries, the therapist was reluctant to address the eroticism directly. She feared that Sandi would not be able to explore her fantasies without misconstruing them as reality. Instead, the therapist normalized and minimized the importance of the homoerotic transference. Overwhelmed by her anxiety and fearing loss of control, Sandi turned toward a male medical professional, who then appeared to her as ideally empathic and soothing. As she sought solace in this man's company and understanding, she quickly developed toward him equally strong sexual feelings as she had experienced toward her female therapist. Far from relieving her anxiety, her feelings for this man awakened other insecurities, as she felt it threatened her whole identity as a lesbian. The therapist, rather than helping her explore her feelings and fantasies toward this man, found herself again minimizing the importance of Sandi's heterosexual fantasies, and over-reassuring her of the solidity of her lesbian identity. The therapist realized that her reluctance to explore the initial erotized transference had left Sandi overwhelmed. Although the therapist believed that Sandi's heterosexual feelings were probably mostly defensive against the erotic transference, she found it equally difficult to explore them. She realized she was afraid to be perceived as trying to "convert" Sandi or influence her toward heterosexuality if she allowed her to explore in greater depth her heterosexual fantasies.

Finally, although rarely talked about, the heterosexual therapist can feel envy. The sense of community in the lesbian and gay world can appear as enviable. Also, from the point of view of a heterosexual individual, there appears to be a greater freedom in androgynous behavior in a community that has, at its very foundation, a rebellion against the established order of the traditional division of the sexes.

CONCLUSIONS

Working with sexual minority patients can be similar to cross-cultural psychotherapy. Both patient's and therapist's perceptions of human relationships are colored by each one's experience of life, including gender and sexual orientation. Despite the best intentions, therapeutic work can be fraught with conscious or unconscious pitfalls. It has been the authors' experience that in order to work effectively with lesbian patients, a therapist must be genuine and honest about her countertransference, but most importantly, she must have a capacity to tolerate the patient's psychic bisexuality as well as her own. Further, she must be able to help the patient tolerate her confusion and decipher internal from external homophobia and heterosexism. Discussion with a peer group of heterosexual, lesbian, bisexual, and gay therapists is very useful in working through the difficulties and rewards of doing therapy in a world of diversity.

NOTE

1. Although Freud initially conceived of the concept of psychic bisexuality as a child's belief that s/he is of both sexes, the concept has evolved to denote the potential for conscious and unconscious bisexual attractions. This latter definition is used here.

REFERENCES

Allport, G. (1958). *The nature of prejudice*. Garden City, New York: Doubleday.
Benjamin, J. (1988). *The bonds of love*. New York: Pantheon.
Burch, B. (1986). Psychotherapy and the dynamics of merger in lesbian couples. In T. Stein & C. Cohen (Eds.), *Contemporary perspectives on psychotherapy with lesbians and gay men* (pp. 57-71). New York: Plenum.
Burch, B. (1996). Between women: The mother-daughter romance and homoerotic transference in psychotherapy. *Psychoanalytic Psychology, 13*(4), 475-494.
Cabaj, R. (1991). Overidentification with a patient. In C. Silverstein (Ed.), *Gays, lesbians and their therapists: Studies in psychotherapy* (pp. 31-39). New York: W. W. Norton & Co.
Cass, V.C. (1979). Homosexual identity formation: A theoretical model. *Journal of Homosexuality, 4*, 219-235.
Comas-Diaz, L. & Jacobson, F. M. (1991). Ethnocultural transference and countertransference in the therapeutic dyad. *American Journal of Orthopsychiatry, 61*(3), 392-402.
Freud, S. (1961). The dynamics of the transference. In J. Strachey (Ed. & Trans.), *The standard edition of the complete psychological works of Sigmund Freud* (Vol. 2, pp. 312-322). London: Hogarth Press. (Original work published 1912).

Freud, S. (1961). Female sexuality. In J. Starchy (Ed. & Trans.), *The standard edition of the complete psychological works of Sigmund Freud* (Vol. 21, pp. 225-243). London: Hogarth Press. (Original work published 1931).

Henken, J. (1982). Homosexuality and psychoanalysis: Toward a mutual understanding. In W. Paul, J.D. Weinrich, J.C. Gonsoriek & M.E. Hotvedt (Eds.), *Homosexuality: Social, psychological and biological issues*. Beverly Hills, CA: Sage Publications.

Igartua, K. (1998). Therapy with lesbian couples: The issues and the interventions. *Canadian Journal of Psychiatry, 43*, 391-396.

Kohut, H. & Wolf, E. S. (1978). The disorders of the self and their treatment: An outline. *International Journal of Psychoanalysis, 59*, 413-25.

Margolies, L., Becker, M., & Jackson-Brewer, K. (1987). Internalized homophobia: Identifying and treating the oppressor within. In Boston Lesbian Psychologies Collective (Ed.), *Lesbian psychologies: Explorations and challenges* (pp. 229-241). Chicago, IL: University of Illinois Press.

Martin, A. D. (1982). Learning to hide: The socialization of gay adolescent. *Adolescent Psychiatry, 10*, 52-65.

Maslow, A. H. (1987). *Motivation and personality* (3rd Ed.). NY: Harper & Row.

McDougall, J. (1986). Eve's reflection: On the homosexual components of female sexuality. In H. Meyers (Ed.), *Between analyst and patient* (pp. 213-228). Hillsdale, NJ: The Analytic Press.

Mogul, K. (1982). Overview: The sex of the therapist. *American Journal of Psychiatry, 139*(1), 1-11.

Raphling, D. L. & Chused, J. F. (1986). Transference across gender lines. *Journal of the American Psychoanalytic Association, 136*, 77-104.

Roth, S. (1988). A woman's homosexual transference with a male analyst. *Psychoanalytic Quarterly, 52*, 28-55.

Lesbian Tomboys
and "Evolutionary Butch"

Lee Zevy

SUMMARY. Lesbian tomboy development occurs within a psychosexual experiential field on a continuum from childhood gender dissonance to "evolutionary butch" in adulthood. Through the process of integrating gender development, sexual orientation, and identity development, tomboy lesbians learn how to maintain a sense of self and organize desire within a complicated familial/socio/cultural/context. Traversing these complications usually brings adolescent and adult lesbians into therapy where they need clinicians who understand this unique course of development. *[Article copies available for a fee from The Haworth Document Delivery Service: 1-800-HAWORTH. E-mail address: <docdelivery@haworthpress.com> Website: <http://www.HaworthPress.com> © 2004 by The Haworth Press, Inc. All rights reserved.]*

KEYWORDS. Lesbians, tomboys, sexuality, gender, gender identity, therapy

Lee Zevy, CSW, received her MSW from Fordham School of Social Welfare and is a past President, a graduate, and current faculty member of New York Institute for Gestalt Therapy. She is a founder, trainer, supervisor and past Clinical Director of Identity House and the past President, New York City Coalition for Women's Mental Health.

Address correspondence to: Lee Zevy, 171 West 23rd St. #2C, New York, NY 10011 (E-mail: lzevy@cs.com).

[Haworth co-indexing entry note]: "Lesbian Tomboys and 'Evolutionary Butch.'" Zevy, Lee. Co-published simultaneously in *Journal of Lesbian Studies* (Harrington Park Press, an imprint of The Haworth Press, Inc.) Vol. 8, No. 1/2, 2004, pp. 143-158; and: *Lesbians, Feminism, and Psychoanalysis: The Second Wave* (ed: Judith M. Glassgold, and Suzanne Iasenza) Harrington Park Press, an imprint of The Haworth Press, Inc., 2004, pp. 143-158. Single or multiple copies of this article are available for a fee from The Haworth Document Delivery Service [1-800-HAWORTH, 9:00 a.m. - 5:00 p.m. (EST). E-mail address: docdelivery@haworthpress.com].

INTRODUCTION

Lesbian tomboy development occurs within a psychosexual experiential field from childhood gender dissonance to "evolutionary butch" in adulthood. Unlike heterosexual tomboys whose tomboy qualities diminish or refocus at puberty, the lesbian tomboy journey to adulthood is a complicated pathway, one having few or no role models to assist in integrating gender and identity with sexual orientation into a whole organization of self and desire. Without adequate mirroring of role models, lesbian tomboys maintain desire, capability, and power sub Rosa through fantasy, heroic imitation, and inchoate longing. In adolescence and adulthood as lesbian tomboys come out, these early forms of desire can be externalized and shift from fantasy and inchoate longing into conscious sexual awareness and experience. This process of integration occurs through the experiencing of various fluid forms of being, a process I call "evolutionary butch."

Although much of this process may be manifest through the assumption of various roles as performance play, they are tried and examined in the service of the development of a more defined integrated sense of a lesbian self. Since lesbian psychological development can be so traumatic because of a social, cultural and familial homophobia (in addition to the confusions of sorting out gender, identity and sexuality), many lesbians turn to psychotherapy at some point in their lives in an effort to find ways to understand these complicated processes and untangle the healthy creative aspects from those that are rigid and may be a response to the lack of choice or a sign of early trauma. Yet because of the unique quality of this experience, clinical understanding is often too narrowly defined to accommodate the fluid creative adjustment necessary to evolve from lesbian tomboy to "evolutionary butch." Understanding this experience will not only expand the potential for treating this population, but will go a long way toward opening up a clinical perspective that views all forms of sexuality in a more creative fashion.

TOMBOYS AND SOCIAL CONSTRUCTION

As a rule, tomboys occupy an imagined space created by diverse cultural and familial definitions of gender. The term according to the *Compact Oxford English Dictionary* (1994), which became defined in the late 16th century, originally meant a rude, boisterous boy, and then evolved into a "ramping, frolicsome, rude girl." As "cultural rebels" resisting social restriction, Secrist (1996) maintains that tomboys are able to manipulate this more fluid space existing between the gender determinations for both girls and boys. In this way, they create new possibilities containing excitement and risk for the girl who dares being the ongoing creator.

In societies or families where assertive attitudes and behavior are seen as a factor in success at sports or business, the acquisition of male attributes in young girls merits praise and encouragement and the space between male and female is extended. Yamaguchi and Barber (1995) contend that because tomboyism is often patronized and devalued, it has often been overlooked as a valuable place for learning for girls. Girls not only learn the nurturing and social skills that will gain them acceptance into a female world. Girls, also by imitating boys, learn about adventure, activity, irreverence, fighting, competition, and bonding. These tools acquired from this period of their life will translate into power, mobility and visibility, and adult forms of achievement and satisfaction.

Although, the space can be very limited or quite open as determined by cultural norms for behavior, dress, role and function, as long as the tomboy exists in play and imagination she is relegated to a place of little significance because it is usually regarded as a "phase, a condition that girls pass through on their way to growing up and becoming women" (Yamaguchi & Barber, 1995, p. 13). The difference, between those tomboys who will grow up to be heterosexual, or even femme lesbian, and tomboy lesbians, is a difference in intensity of the need to use and manipulate space to match the boys and men who are being used as models. These models are used not only in terms of the eventual attainment of relationships with woman, but also as examples of power, capability, and agency, which will support organic need. Contrary to what Harris (2000) maintains, that genders are constructed and exist only in terms of social matrix, almost all societies as they are currently constituted, are constructed as binary male/female systems and lesbian tomboyism is not a "soft assembly." Underlying all the external imitation and activity, sexual/emotional desire for women fuels this process providing the energy behind the unconscious longings that become manifest in a different form from those tomboys for whom tomboy life is not as intensely goal driven.

For example, one client reported anonymously that as a child, she would wheel her doll carriage to the ball field, then play games, and run with the boys, and when she was finished, she would wheel her doll carriage home and play dolls with the girls. For another woman, a tomboy lesbian, playing with dolls was unthinkable. She would, against family prohibition, sneak out a pair of high top sneakers, run without a shirt with a gang of boys who were her buddies and steal her father's fencing swords to play pirate capturing the princess as a reward.

Tomboys are allowed by adults and boys to exist. In a previous article, Zevy (1999) notes that being a tomboy means that a girl has left the safety and security of socially expected behavior and entered a creative but potentially dangerous play space, a "warning zone" whereby she can create herself as long as she is wary of approaching the dangerous boundaries designated as "all male territory." The degree to which a tomboy will be tolerated or disliked is the degree to which she attends to and keeps a distance from the boundary of all male behavior that is always bound up in sexuality and the male ownership of sexual difference.

Creed (1995) has pointed out that historically, the penalty for role transgression has ranged from admonition to death, and is tied to genital differences between men and women. Up until the 1700s, only a one-sex model was thought to exist, with the ovaries and vagina being thought of as undescended testicles and penis. "Given the conceptualization of a woman's body as a thwarted male body and the clitoris and labia as penis and foreskin, it is no wonder that desire was also thought of as masculine"(Creed, 1995, p. 91). Once it was discovered that two sexes did in fact exist, Freudian theory (1931/61), based on the principal that biology is destiny, determined that women were psychologically castrated males and, by defining the point by moving the site of pleasure for the "mature" woman from the clitoris to the vagina, preserved once more, through the differences in physiology, the boundaries of gender. It was only in the 1970s that, in Western thought, these ideas gradually changed to include physiological difference and sexual parity for both men and women.

In keeping with this shift in understanding in Western thought, the role of tomboy–for girls who become heterosexual at least–has broadened considerably. In many places gender role rigidity has been reduced, and has been replaced by mutual success and independence for both sexes in many areas of significance. In contrast, Desquitado (1992) offers quite a different perspective, one that dominates in many parts of the world, when she writes of the Philippines where the word tomboy means lesbian, and girls are subject to the harshest limitations of gender role with dangerous consequences for minor transgressions. Regardless of the changes, paradigms for power continue to pervade human existence even where there is great laxity. For example, if one examines children's television with particular attention to action shows, even though women are now allowed to fight and join forces with men to best the enemy, they are only in rare exceptions allowed to be in the top power role. The alpha position is always accorded to a man. Although the play space may have changed, the boundaries now require more vigilance because they are now so variable.

LESBIAN TOMBOY DEVELOPMENT

Although positive changes have meant greater equality for heterosexual tomboys, for lesbian tomboys who by definition transgress the boundaries of sexual difference the situation is still quite different. Although it is usually a given for heterosexual women who wish to attract men and marry that they relinquish or refocus many tomboy freedoms in adolescence, for tomboy lesbians it is precisely these traits that will guide their sexuality. Even though the boundaries of lesbian tomboy life are defined by sexuality, a word that always conjures up trangressive play and potential sexual transgression, that period of childhood is still regarded as an asexual time. Tomboy as a constructed category signifies a presexual time, demarcating nonthreatening masculine behavior before it signifies a change to lesbianism, a warning space perhaps that designates an approach to "Biblical abomination."

However, although the term tomboy is socially constructed, theories of lesbian development that focus on social constructionism are insufficient. For example, the difficulty with using Kitzinger's (1987) ideas of the social construction of lesbianism is that like the construction of tomboy, as a category, it is too limiting to explain a lesbian childhood where lesbian sexuality is a continuum from childhood to adulthood. Although it is quite clear that labels are socially constructed, the notion that lesbianism is only constructed by cultural definitions leaves out the genetic, biological and psychological aspects of sexuality that are specific to lesbian development.

All sexual development, including lesbian, begins in infancy, continues throughout the lifespan, and is bound up within a matrix of emotional reciprocity containing desire, admiration, adoration, specialness, pleasure, understanding, reflection, and excitement. A theory of lesbian sexual desire that begins around adolescence and object choice is inadequate to explain lesbian sexual development. Such a theory excludes those lesbians who evolved defined as lesbians with a recognized masturbatory sexual object choice from their first memories; those whose early lesbian sexuality, also sometimes masturbatory, was expressed through heroic fantasy; those whose sexual orientation developed within intense exclusive girlhood friendships and inchoate yearnings; or those women who retained pleasurable memories of infant female connection that led to lesbian relationships later in life. Many tomboy lesbians report quite early that they were aware of their own sexuality through masturbation and childhood sexual games and that it was directed toward girls and women (often baby sitters, neighbors, and teachers). During these games, they were always the male counterparts of a female role having limiting heterosexual choices to imitate. Later on, at latency, sexual experimentation with girls was not a pathway toward relationships with men, but was usually a painful experience of being outside and feeling that something was wrong with them.

The desire to be desired by someone who one desires is a need originating at birth when reciprocated desire between maternal figures and children begins. Wrye and Wells (1994) illustrate how maternal erotic desire forms the foundation of the experience of sexual desire and is always embedded within nurturing and caretaking.

> The beginning of relating is evident in babies as young as three days: they show distinct preferences for their mothers and select by smell the breast pads of their own mothers . . . Much attention has been given to the sensual bonding of feeding, bathing, cooing and holding the first year of life . . . This sensual, erotic attachment proceeds developmentally and included reciprocal visual, tactile, olfactory, taste, and auditory behaviors, cues and fantasies. (1994, p. 34)

Wells and Wrye further elaborate upon the eroticism involved with daily care through the exchange of fluids and bodily contact and further stipulate that " the early sensual bond between mother and baby . . . becomes the basis for all loving relations and all eroticism . . ." (1994, p. 34).

Although most psychological theory insists that in normal development girls must relinquish the maternal figure as an erotic object and transfer these needs to fathers and eventually other men, some feminist analytic work, namely Benjamin (1988) and Chodorow (1978), argue that theory should be more inclusive of the maintenance of maternal erotic love throughout life. However, even these current positive developments do not take this idea far enough, beyond heterosexuality, into what seems to be another logical theoretical extension, that of lesbian development. While the relinquishing of the mother is often an inadequate substitute for heterosexual women, for the lesbian child it is confusing and harmful as she tries to integrate an erotic representation of self and other into the physical/emotional experience of daily life.

The requirement that children relinquish the maternal erotic object is reinforced repeatedly as most children are predominantly exposed to media images of a one-dimensional heterosexuality and taught a similar brand of gender appropriate social/sexual behavior. The recognition of lesbian identity for girls who felt "different" from early childhood does not always occur, as is usually thought, at the point where object choice is consciously identified. This felt "difference" is actually a continuous and changing process from early childhood onward, as recognition of how one is like or not like others within a kaleidoscope of changing images brings into focus new realities of self and other. Each time a fragment of mirror is twisted a new pattern of recognition occurs as multiple representations in turn are experienced and then dissolve into new possibilities of identity. For girls who will become lesbian, tomboy is simply part of the evolutionary process of establishing that within a gendered world sexual/emotional excitement will be directed toward women and that one's active relationship to the world, embedded in a concept of self and identity reflecting this reality, will be altered in both subtle and profound ways to accommodate this desire. As Harris aptly points out, "both agency and masculinity still come from the father" (2000, p. 243) and if these qualities are prized by women then imitation and appropriation of these qualities will begin much earlier in life than has been acknowledged.

Tomboy is an adult appellation for that prepubescent period where tomboy lesbians can learn to negotiate the shifting spaces between excitement, activity, and danger before they become sexually active as adults. Within this period lesbians try on all sorts of male/female combinations trying to arrive at workable images that are acceptable to those significant adults while preserving the integrity of self. Some lesbians, like Feinberg (1993), incorporated masculinity in all aspects suffering great hardship, while others wore their hair and dressed in feminine attire, but ran with the boys for games, activity and fun, fitting in externally and resisting internally. In actuality, tomboy life is never simple, stories of early lesbian development vary considerably from woman to woman as the contingencies of cultural location, familial identity, and individual need intersect. Julia Penelope makes this point when she writes,

I decided that something I'd done in a past life (my karma) had dictated that I would spend my life as a male soul "trapped" in a female body, as punishment for some transgression . . . I was uncomfortable with my femaleness (at least what I was told I was supposed to be as a "female") because I couldn't accept the weakness, passivity, and powerlessness that such "femaleness" required.

Since I refused to be "female," as I understood it, I concluded I had to be male. (1992, p. 6)

Penelope clearly points out a child's understanding of the internal and external meaning of transgression, clearly illustrating how the creative adjustment to such a closed system can recreate again other bounded systems that at the time seem freer but ultimately imprison. Since boundaries can be both defined and amorphous, a developing skill in lesbian tomboy life is to develop, most often through painful trial and error, sensitivity to approaching transgression. However, an intrinsic problem for lesbian tomboys is that because they can only perceive and imitate boy behavior from an *external* vantage point they are caught unawares when that behavior reveals the *internal* physical/emotional/sexual male experience that dictates male behavior.

One client reported that as a young girl, she would hang out only with the boys and they would roam around the neighborhood and into the woods and fields. She was accepted into the group, and looked, acted and played as they did. One day they were heading through a field to a creek when they encountered an older group of boys. One of the boys made a sexual reference to her and suddenly her group was laughing and shifting loyalties. She was suddenly alone in a recombined larger group of jostling, sexually bonded boys. She ran home alone; recognizing that what she thought was acceptance was only skin-deep.

Stories abound in Mullins (1995) book of lesbian tomboys who trespassed and were punished with violence and actual or threatened sexual domination. Yet, learning to negotiate these sexual systems early in life is a skill that paves the way for adult lesbians who will have an easier time maintaining their adventuresome spirit as the ground of safety and danger in lesbian life shifts. In keeping with cultural prohibitions toward lesbian sexuality, Zevy (1999) describes how lesbian tomboys secretly develop other skills that help them maintain their erotic/emotional desire through childhood into adolescence and adulthood when they can officially "come out."

Living within a heterosexual matrix, they must negotiate an "outsider position," while at the same time holding on to identity and desire, and maintaining often competing relationships with enough flexibility to meet ongoing needs. Then these lesbian tomboys must find adults or images to model where freedom of desire is expressed and realized. These models in childhood used to require the acquisition of behavior of heroic male figures whose attributes would be transposed into female role, but now a sufficient number of female role models exist, although because of the paucity of examples of lesbian desire the search continues. In addition to the search for models, lesbian tomboys need to develop emblems, scripts, and symbols of a future fantasy life that will help project them out of a heterosexually embedded childhood into a future where desire and longing (conscious or unconscious) of being sexually desired by a woman can be realized. All of these skills are braided into the creation of an internal gendered representation of maleness/femaleness that will evolve over the period from childhood through adolescence and eventually in adulthood transform the lesbian tomboy into some form of "Butch."

"EVOLUTIONARY BUTCH"

For lesbians, "Evolutionary Butch" like sexuality in general, is a complicated multidimensional creation that continually reinvents itself over the lifespan. Unlike most of the literature, such as Vance (1992) and Stein (1993), that portrays butch as a unitary entity or as submerged within the Butch/Femme dyad, butch evolves not only within culture but also internally and externally within the individual. Since cultural constructs change as society changes in its flexibility toward sexuality in general, the understanding of butch has split many times in language, meaning, and activity. In the 50s, for example, when lesbian social existence dictated that one had to be butch or femme, the range for butch was limited to butch, bulldyke, bull dagger, diesel dyke, dyke, stone butch, truck driver, etc., all close approximations of certain limited types of maleness. Today, there are as many names, incorporating both masculine and feminine aspects, as there are combinations, each one designating a variation of the theme. Although these new images of butch are more narrowly focused, they can be traversed more easily as individuals change and grow. These new names range from babybutch, bois (gender identity leaning toward male), guppies (designated by materialistic acquisition) dykes, queers, and the even newer labels of psychobutch, powerbutch or blazerdyke. Then there are the many categories signifying trans (transgender) and the possibilities of transsexual so that the variations have become endless. Contrast these multiple categories with the concept of femme, which up until very recently was a single entity to which power femme and barracuda have now been included. It is clear how these inventive names, as performance, mirror cultural constructs, but do not truly signify the intensity of organic drive beneath. Butch, as an internal representation of the continuum of masculinity, is not an appropriation of maleness, but a transformation of maleness into female form incorporating aspects of both in highly inventive and changing ways. Schwartz makes the point that "A 'butch' woman, a man in drag, calls into the question the very nature of the binary gender system and destabilizes phallic privilege" (1998, p. 30).

In doing so, Schwartz challenges Butler's (1990) notion that the gendered body is largely performative existing on the surface of the body. Halberstam (1994) also limits the conception of butch to a superficial reading, "Butch is a belief, a performance, a swagger in the walk; butch is an attitude, a tough line, a fiction, a way of dressing" (1994, p. 226). She further fragments lesbian development when she writes, "The postmodern lesbian body is a body fragmented by representation and theory, overexposed and yet inarticulate, finding a voice finally in the underground culture of zines and sex clubs" (Halberstam, 1994, p. 226). The notion that "gender is created as fiction" (Butler, 1990) is too insubstantial to explain the layered facets of "evolutionary butch" development leading to an internal sense of self from which performance, as play, lends fun and excitement to a committed way of life.

In a female form and separated from femme, butch takes on its own new meanings. In its external form butch can be a style of dress, attitude, sexual stance, activity, action, and means of relating to the world. Internally, as a part of self and core identity, butch can bind the shaded meanings of male/female into other forms until an integration of internal/external experiences of power, capability, and sexual entitlement provide a substantive ground that will support life experience. During this process these creative forms can vary widely ranging from designating various body parts as male or female; inventing new names for what one is. One client disclosed creating a completely new image; she declared that she was a third sex because the male/female categories did not fit.

Although many of these forms are temporary in nature dissolving and reforming as the need arises, others are more enduring having been established in childhood and arising out of biological predisposition and personality in combination with familial and social learning. The categories and labels of butch individuals apply to themselves are ways of externalizing internal desires, so that a means is created whereby the internal representations of self can be brought into a social/relational field and be tweaked through exploration and experimentation. Tomboy lesbians grow up being defined by externally determined boundaries so that until adulthood they are in a process of resistance to what does not fit.

It is only after "coming out" in adult life that the freedom exists to create their own definitions of self, and it is often a complicated process to untangle the healthy creative aspects of these combinations from those that are rigid and developed because of the lack of choice or in response to trauma. Because lesbians tend to be hidden or restricted during adolescence, they often learn about dating and relationships after coming out through serial relationships. This process, in combination with role experimentation, new friendships, and community paves the way for awareness to develop in regards to psychological inhibitions and anxieties that may be a part of a fear of being gay or an indication of early trauma that block greater fulfillment. For this reason, at some point in the search of psychological meaning and the need for a witness, most lesbians turn to therapy.

THERAPY

Therapy has been a route many lesbians have sought to untangle the confusions derived from such a complicated path. Although the psychiatric nomenclature changed in the 1970s to remove homosexuality as a diagnostic category, the current *Diagnostic and Statistical Manual*'s (4th Edition, 1996) diagnosis of Gender Identity Disorder equates the evolution of "Butch" with pathological process. Although most non-lesbian therapists no longer see homosexuality per se as pathological, they are not yet familiar with the evolutionary process of sexual identity formation in all its shadings, nor are they familiar with the language and action of female-to-female sexuality as a multifaceted experience. Schwartz describes a common experience "One particular identification that surfaces often but not exclusively among lesbians is the feeling that they are "not female like (their) mothers." Then these "Identities based on being not female like (their) mothers often coincided with negative body images, as their bodies are perceived to be out of synchrony with gender stereotypic icons" (1998, p. 11).

Initially, many lesbians enter therapy to reconcile this dilemma and supported by the weight of psychotherapeutic theory, believe that if they reconcile their "feminine" side the problem will be solved, but this approach does not go far enough nor deep enough toward the formation of new individual representations. The process of separating from gender stereotypes *is* the work of becoming lesbian, but after separation when adult sexuality and relationship occur new needs arise, those that are often unfamiliar to the therapeutic community.

Two experiences reported anonymously by a "butch" lesbian, who had been in a successful long-term therapy with a male analyst, offer examples of the kinds of therapeutic ruptures that emanate from a lack of knowledge and a more traditionally distant stance. In the first example, she reported a dream she brought in to therapy one day describing that she is seeing a soft cloth striped in many soft colors lying in a cart with other fabric; the fabric is bunched and raised in the center. The therapist interpreted the image as phallic, but the client said she laughed and pointed out, it was clitoral, and the cloth was about women. At that point, she needed him to mirror the softer feelings, emerging out of the toughness she usually expressed, and which were reserved for her relationships with women.

Although the dream had multiple meanings embedded within a variety of affectual responses, the client restricted her discussion of them because the therapist could not move away from traditional theory. More importantly, he could not accept the softness she was trying to give him as a way of deepening the intimacy of the therapeutic relationship. Many approaches would have opened the discussion to include the meaning of softness of both the cloth, and its colors; the many colors might have represented gender, role, and identity possibilities that she was experimenting with at that time. A helpful response might have been for him to say, "That's a wonderful dream, so soft and colorful it must have a lot of meaning for you about your feelings for women."

In the second example, she reported that the therapist came in with two fingers bandaged and the client said, laughing, "that would be my form of castration." The therapist did not respond but sat and waited. At that time, she was trying to open a dialogue about her sexuality. Although she already had a successful ongoing relationship, she felt fearful that he would be angry and shaming at any overt attempt at bonding with him over a commonly held desire. Kaufman and Raphael note, "To proclaim oneself openly as gay is, above else, to come out of shame–profoundly, to break the silence. This is why the term 'coming out' is a shame metaphor" (1996, p. 11). In both of these situations the therapist was not aware of the subtleties of shame and discomfort in regards to her relationship with him that were the foundation of these disclosures.

It was not that she was questioning her sexuality, which had been laid to rest before she came into therapy, but she was trying to find a way to bring her intense pleasurable feelings about women out of hiding, and she needed him to understand and help her.

Without a warm inclusive response, the sexual meaning along with its concomitant affect and potential symbolic representation was not encouraged to emerge using mirroring and attunement, and the opportunity was lost. In addition, the therapist could have just moved beyond what he thought he already knew and simply joined her in her fun of the moment. What the therapist was not aware of was the way in which in both of these situations, the client was approaching what was for her a boundary of potential transgression, testing the limits of safety and danger and looking for a way to discuss deeper meaning with someone, whom she already knew from previous allusions loved women as she did. Many areas of lesbian life relate to the holding on to desire and sexuality within a foreign system and most lesbians initially feel therapists to be part of that foreignness. They come to therapy with a hope that this time they will find a person who can help them heal the split between their "outsider" position and the "foreign" culture.

Significant issues like that of the "closet," or "coming-out-of-the-closet" are poorly understood by non-gay/lesbian/bisexual therapists. These issues are very meaningful parts of everyday lesbian and gay life where clothing and attitude play important roles in the creation of agency and competency. Thus, therapists often fail to examine the meaning of creating an image that supports identity. Falco (1991) addresses the differentiation that must be made between lesbian identity (who am I as a gay person), lesbian sexual activity (who do I sleep with), lesbian erotic interests (where are my sexual fantasies, daydreams and excitements directed), and lesbian attachments (who do I actually have relationships with). Understanding these differences would offer a deeper knowledge of lesbian life as well as the interplay between these important issues. Because so much of the theory about homosexuality is based on pathological functioning, as evidenced by works like McDougall (1980), therapists, who have not read the more recent lesbian affirmative work (O'Connor & Ryan, 1993; Glassgold & Iasenza, 1995; Magee & Miller, 1997; Schwartz, 1998), often mistake the interweaving of fear and desire and the ways that these are overcome through fantasy and sexual play as problem signs. They often fail to see the ways in which altered states of consciousness using costuming, fantasy, and sexual games are creative tools that help lesbians and gay men overcome fear and anxiety and propel them forward into the realization of sexual contact and relationships. For lesbian and gay therapists, a problem can occur if the specific individual meanings are missed because of the use of shared terms and culture.

Even where clients are able to discuss their lesbianism it is often accompanied by diminished emotion and limited relatedness (poor eye-contact, uncomfortable body movements, avoidance of contact) because of the level of fear and/or a first time experience of bringing themselves into dialogue with another person. The fear and shame cannot be underestimated. A lesbian acquaintance, who had recently gone into therapy, described how as late at the 1980s and 1990s she would lie on the floor with her ear to the radio and play the gay station very softly so her family could not hear.

In another example, a butch lesbian colleague reported a dream to a male analyst in which she is eating a melted tuxedo cat with a spoon. He sagely asks, "What does eating pussy mean to you?" She is delighted he is giving her permission to enter into dangerous territory, but cannot reveal this to him because she would be in open competition with him (she knows he is heterosexual) and becomes flustered with excitement and fear. He is unaware of how thrilled yet endangered she feels as she backs away. Erring again on the side of traditional analytic unintrusivness, he does not create a safe foundation for her to continue to explore the dream. Instead, he could have asked how she feels about his comment or the dream elements; how she feels about oral sex with a woman; what the meaning of "cats" and "pussies" is to her; and how oral sex fits into lesbian life. However, the most important absence is that he does not offer to explore the nature of competition with him or men. In addition, she needed him to explore the transferential aspects of the dream where she felt she was melting because she was changing and was afraid she would be eaten up by him. She definitely felt that he offered her a supportive opening, but she needed him to enter the space between them with more active interest and to provide reassurance that he would not be angry, rejecting, or need to assert power over her.

Buloff and Osterman offer an explanation for the way in which a lesbian client might interpret silence by writing of lesbian childhood experience, "Mirrored back are grotesque and distorted images reflecting back in words like perverse, sinful, immoral, infantile, arrested, inadequate, or she sees no reflection at all–a peculiar silence–an invisibility" (1995, p. 95). This is particularly meaningful for lesbian tomboys, and in particular, those whose mirrors became increasingly distorted the further out from convention they traveled.

Lesbians seek therapy to find new mirrors within safe environments in the form of therapists who not only encourage them to re-live the excitement of risk taking and the adventure of creating themselves, but who reflect back excitement, admiration, and approval. Bollas writes that, "Generative mutuality in human relations depends amongst other things on an assumption that the elements of psychic life and their different functions are held in common. If A talks to B about grief over the loss of a parent then he should be able to assume that B knows what grief is and will share A's problem with him" (Bollas, 1987, p. 157). Lesbians need to know that a therapist understands the elements of their psychic life, not simply as it is constituted emotionally in common human terms, but as it revolves around an erotic foundation existing from childhood that gives centrality to relationships with women. It is only within this kind of context, that the complexities of their experience will be revealed to them and the processes of self-creation will open and continue in new ways.

REFERENCES

American Psychiatric Association. (1996). *Diagnostic and Statistical Manual of Mental Disorders (4th ed.)*. Washington, DC.

Benjamin, J. (1988). *The bonds of love*. New York: Pantheon.

Bollas, C. (1987). *The shadow of the object: Psychoanalysis of unthought known*. New York: Columbia University.

Buloff, B. & Osterman, M. (1995). Queer reflections: Mirroring and the lesbian experience of self. In J. M. Glassgold & S. Iasenza (Eds.), *Lesbians and Psychoanalysis: Revolutions in Theory and Practice* (pp. 93-106). NY: Free Press.

Butler, J. (1990). *Gender trouble: Feminism and the subversion of identity*. New York: Routledge.

Chodorow, N. (1978). *The reproduction of mothering: Psychoanalysis and the sociology of gender*. Berkeley: Univ. of California Press.

Compact Oxford English Dictionary (2nd ed.). (1994). Oxford: Clarendon.

Creed, B. (1995). Lesbian bodies: Tribades, tomboys and tarts. In E. Groz & E. Probyn (Eds.), *Sexy Bodies: The Strange Carnalities of Feminism*. NY: Routledge.

Desquitado, R. M. (1992). A letter from the Philippines. In J. Nestle, (Ed.), *The Persistent Desire: A Butch Femme Reader*. Boston: Alyson.

Falco, K. L. (1991). New York: Brunner Mazel.

Feinberg, L. (1993). *Stone butch blues*. Ithaca, NY: Firebrand Books.

Freud, S. (1961). Female sexuality. In J. Strachey (Ed. & Trans.), *The Standard Edition of the Complete Psychological Works of Sigmund Freud* (Vol. 21, pp. 223-243). London: Hogarth Press. (Original work published 1931).

Glassgold, J. M. & Iasenza, S. (1995). *Lesbians and psychoanalysis: Revolutions in theory and practice*. New York: Free Press.

Halberstam J. (1994). F2M: The making of female masculinity. In L. Doan (Ed.), *The Lesbian Postmodern* (pp. 210-228). New York: Columbia University Press.

Harris, A. (2000). Gender as soft assembly: Tomboy's stories. *Journal of Gender and Sexuality, 1*, 223-250.

Kaufman, G. & Raphael, L. (1996). *Coming out of shame: Transforming gay and lesbian lives.* New York: Doubleday.

Kitzinger, C. (1987). *The social construction of lesbianism.* London: Sage Publications.

Magee, M. & Miller, D. (1997). *Lesbian lives: Psychoanalytic narratives old & new.* Hillsdale, NJ: The Analytic Press.

McDougall, J. (1980). *Plea for a measure of abnormality.* New York: International Universities Press.

Mullins, H. (1995). Evolution of a tomboy. In Y.L. Yamaguchi and K. Barbara (Eds.), *Tomboys: Tales of Dyke Derring-Do* (pp. 40-49). Los Angeles: Alyson.

O'Connor, N. & Ryan, J. (1993). *Wild desires and mistaken identities: Lesbianism and psychoanalysis.* New York: Columbia University Press.

Penelope, J. (1992). *Call me lesbian: Lesbian lives, lesbian theory.* Freedom, CA: Crossing Press.

Schwartz, A. (1998). *Sexual subjects: Lesbians, gender and psychoanalysis.* NY: Routledge.

Secrist, J. H. (1996). Choices of midlife tomboys: A narrative study (girls, adolescents, and women). (Doctoral dissertation, University of California, San Diego, 1996). *Dissertation Abstracts International*, Section A, 57-04, 1881.

Stein, A. (Ed.). (1993). *Sisters, sexperts, queers: Beyond the lesbian nation.* New York: Penguin.

Vance, C. S. (Ed.). (1992). *Pleasure & danger: Exploring female sexuality.* London: Pandora Press.

Wrye, H. K. & Welles, J. K. (1994). *The narration of desire: Erotic transferences and countertransference.* Hillsdale, NJ: The Analytic Press.

Yamaguchi, L. and Barber, K. (Eds.). (1995). *Tomboys: Tales of dyke derring-do.* Los Angeles: Alyson.

Zevy, L. (1999). Sexing the tomboy. In M. Rottnek (Ed.), *Sissies & Tomboys: Gender Nonconformity & Homosexual Childhood* (pp. 180-198). New York: New York University Press.

NEW THINKING ON SEXUALITY AND GENDER

The Queering of Relational Psychoanalysis: Who's Topping Whom?

Betsy Kassoff

SUMMARY. The author argues that queer theory and relational psycho-analysis have influenced each other in significant ways. These include the designation of "queer" superceding the essential identity categories of lesbian, gay, bisexual, and transgender; multiple implications for gender and sexual orientation developmental theories; the necessity for the analyst to

Betsy Kassoff, PhD, is former Department Chair of the Feminist Psychology Graduate Program at New College of California, San Francisco. She teaches and has a private practice in San Francisco, CA.

Address correspondence to: Betsy Kassoff, PhD, 45 Franklin Street, Suite 320, San Francisco, CA 94102.

[Haworth co-indexing entry note]: "The Queering of Relational Psychoanalysis: Who's Topping Whom?" Kassoff, Betsy. Co-published simultaneously in *Journal of Lesbian Studies* (Harrington Park Press, an imprint of The Haworth Press, Inc.) Vol. 8, No. 1/2, 2004, pp. 159-176; and: *Lesbians, Feminism, and Psychoanalysis: The Second Wave* (ed: Judith M. Glassgold, and Suzanne Iasenza) Harrington Park Press, an imprint of The Haworth Press, Inc., 2004, pp. 159-176. Single or multiple copies of this article are available for a fee from The Haworth Document Delivery Service [1-800-HAWORTH, 9:00 a.m. - 5:00 p.m. (EST). E-mail address: docdelivery@haworthpress.com].

foreground countertransference issues in relation to gender; and a less defended relationship to erotic transferences and countertransferences. *[Article copies available for a fee from The Haworth Document Delivery Service: 1-800-HAWORTH. E-mail address: <docdelivery@haworthpress.com> Website: <http://www.HaworthPress.com> © 2004 by The Haworth Press, Inc. All rights reserved.]*

KEYWORDS. Queer theory, relational psychoanalysis, gender development, erotic transference, erotic countertransference

INTRODUCTION

Queer theory and relational psychoanalysis are unlikely bed partners. They are barely at the age of consent, as they are both historical phenomena of the theoretical shift towards postmodernism of the last twenty years. Queer theory is a descendant of lesbian/gay studies and feminist critiques of heterosexuality and patriarchal gender relations as a norm (Jagose, 1996). Relational theory is an outgrowth of a theoretical shift from a one-person to a two-person psychology, in which the analyst is not just an observer of the patient, but an active participant in co-constructing the analysis with the patient (Mitchell, 1988). Each critiques the modernist assumption of an "objective" reality to be known by the expert, neutral scientist. Queer theory highlights the way individual sexual experience has been marginalized by the dominant narrative of heterosexuality, imposed in part historically by psychoanalysis. Relational psychoanalysis focuses on how the impact of the relationship inside and outside of therapy has been minimized by the classical Freudian dominant narrative of intrapsychic life untouched by context.

In addition to, or because of, being unlikely bed partners, queer theory and relational psychoanalysis are capable of passionate connections that can illuminate some of the shadowy corners of our ideas about both gender and psychoanalytic psychotherapy. In the last decade, an emergent group of psychoanalytic clinicians and cultural theorists who have been steeped in feminism and hermeneutics (Benjamin, 1988, 1998, 2000; Butler, 1993, 1995; Corbett, 1993, 2001a, 2001b; Davies, 1994, 1998; Dimen, 1991, 2001; Harris, 2001; Layton, 1998, 2002; Sedgwick, 1993) have begun to articulate new approaches to contradictions between increasingly fluid ideas about gender and normative ideas about mental health which underlie clinical practice.

In this paper, I will argue that queer theory and relational psychoanalysis have influenced each other in a number of ways. First, I suggest that queer has superceded the designations of lesbian, gay male, bisexual and transgender as "essential" psychological (if not sociopolitical) identities, and includes "nominally" heterosexual experiences (Butler, 1993, 1995; Sedgwick, 1993). Second, there are multiple implications for gender and sexual orientation development theory (Corbett, 2001a; Harris, 2001; Hansell, 1998; Elise, 1998; Layton, 2002), including the principle of multiple and shifting identifications and outcomes, and gender development as a compromise formation that reflects cultural splitting (Chodorow, 1989; Dimen, 1991; Harris, 2001; Layton, 1998, 2001; Corbett, 2001a; Frommer, 1994). Third, relational analysis foregrounds the issue of the therapist's countertransference as both critical to and influencing, the course of the therapy (Mitchell, 1993; Mitchell & Aron, 1998; Stern, 2002). When countertransference is combined with the issue of gender, the therapist is required to examine her own sexual feelings, identifications, dominant and submissive impulses, biases, and anxieties as they interact with those of the patient and create unique therapeutic stories and outcomes (Burch, 1993; Kassoff, 1997; Kassoff, Boden, de Monteflores, Hunt, & Wahba, 1995; Layton, 2002; Frommer, 1994, 2000; Iasenza, 1995; Weille, 2002). Fourth, the particular intersection of gendered introspection and relationship in relational psychoanalysis has profoundly changed clinical discussions of openness to, the usefulness of, and the possibility of judicious self-disclosure in erotic transference and countertransference (Davies, 1994, 1998; Dimen, 2001; Elise, 2002; Frommer, 2000; Gould, 1995; Maroda, 1999). In each section, I will use a clinical vignette from my practice as an example of applying these theoretical ideas to patients.

FROM LESBIAN TO DYKE TO QUEER

Having been heavily influenced by American 1970s lesbian-feminism, I identify myself as lesbian-feminist first, then Jewish, then middle-class. It would not be my first impulse to describe myself as queer; I call myself a dyke in friendly company. I wouldn't call myself an analyst for a number of reasons—not having completed the institutional legitimization associated with that designation, political and personal concerns about the contradictions implied in being a "queer analyst"—but most therapists outside of the psychoanalytic community would see me as decidedly psychoanalytic. What postmodernism, and its elaboration in queer theory, has shown me is that my own identifications say more about my own frames of reference than about who I "really" am. My younger friends and clients think of me as queer, and "dyke" as a quaint '70s anachronism. Relational theory helps me understand my internal elaborations of my identifications, and how they might be enacted in relationship: what I hope for, what I dread, and how I repeat these expectations (Mitchell, 1993). It means something to me that I am both outside and inside the identity of queer analyst, but what it means to me has everything to do with my class and ethnic background, my lesbian-feminist culture and values, my specific experiences inside and outside the power hierarchy of various institutions, and my fantasies and fears related to these identities. All of which influence my behavior and construction of meaning.

Just as queer theory pulls apart my dykeness and relational theory elaborates on my conflicts about being a queer analyst, queer theory (Sedgwick, 1993; Butler, 1993, 1995) helps us unpack our "commonsense" ideas of what is unconsciously collapsed into the designation of sexual identity. Sedgwick notes that dozens of variables are expected to align along binary poles of male and female, including: chromosomal sex, self-perception of biological sex, masculinity and femininity, being the opposite on all these dimensions of your partner, preferred sexual acts (insertive or receptive), procreative choice (yes if straight, no if queer), sexual fantasies (dominant or submissive), and locus of emotional bonds (should be consistent with sex and sexual orientation). If these identities are not seen as not strictly consistent to these assumptions, "that's one of the things queer can refer to: the open mesh of possibilities, gaps, overlaps, dissonances and resonances, lapses and excesses of meaning when the constituent elements of anyone's gender, of anyone's sexuality, aren't made or can't be made to signify monolithically (Sedgwick, 1993, p. 8).

From the perspective of queer theory, my comfortable identification as a lesbian has little meaning as an ongoing construct. How do I understand that I have sexual fantasies, past sexual experiences with men? How do I explain my own transient identifications as a man? What about the fact that I am a mother, which for many in the dominant culture is incompatible with lesbian identity? Does my lack of makeup and unwillingness to wear dresses in public reflect a masculine identification? A cultural signifier that I do not want to be viewed as a heterosexual female, a hangover of the androgyny debates, my primary bisexuality, or fear of glamour? From the perspective of queer theory, these "inconsistencies," within my identity, are expected, and become a window into my personal construction of gender identity at a particular moment in time. My commonalties with heterosexual women, which in early psychoanalytic feminism were seen as primary, diminish; but so do my similarities with gay men, who are comrades in identity politics but may share little in common with my sexual identity.

THE QUEERING OF SEXUAL IDENTITY STORIES

In classical analysis, core gender or gender identity, gender role, and sexual object choice are often conflated, or at the least expected to be congruent. One of the most powerful effects queer theory has had on relational psychoanalysis is what I call the queering of sexual identity stories. Instead of traditional analysis' psychosexual stage model culminating in normative heterosexual genitality, queer theory has incorporated Chodorow's (1989) and Benjamin's (1988) analyses of the process of "achieving" heterosexuality through rigid splitting of masculinity and femininity, heterosexuality and homosexuality, assertion and recognition. Goldner (1991) and Dimen (1991) go further to suggest that gender identity is a universal false self in compliance with a culturally required two-gender system. In response to earlier models that argue that gender identity must be fixed, Harris (2001) argues that gender identity can be coherent but can also mutate over time. In addition, a number of other authors (Corbett, 2001a; Frommer, 2000; Layton, 2002) continue to unpack the many subjective experiences of gender, which are collapsed into a binary system of male/female, homosexual/heterosexual, masculine/feminine, active/passive, at the cost of articulating diversity and multiplicity.

Queer theory describes gender and sexual orientation as culturally scripted performances of dominant norms, which are often unconscious (Butler, 1993). In this process, how we become men and women, straight or gay, is constructed by not only whom we are allowed to love, but also in whom we are *not* allowed to (Butler, 1995). Male and female identities are established in part through cultural prohibitions *against* certain sexual attachments (boys become men through sex with girls, not boys; girls become women through sex with men, not girls or women). In addition to this "accomplishment" of gender through heterosexual positioning, Butler suggests there are losses that accompany mandatory heterosexuality that are not grieved. This results in a "culturally prevalent form of melancholia," or disavowed grief, which can result in a defensive form of gender anxiety. Butler implies that the more rigidly defensive a person presents as masculine or feminine, the fiercer is the disavowed grief. Becoming a man or woman requires, in this way of thinking, finding a "right" direction for desire.

MOVING PAST BINARY:
EXPLOITING CHAOS IN DEFINING GENDER

The shift from the modernist "hard wiring" of Newtonian physics to the "softly assembled" postmodern metaphors of general systems theory (Thelen and Smith, 1991) has supplied a number of nonbinary, nonmechanical metaphors for gender. In Harris's words:

> A general systems approach would see phenomenon like gender not as structural but rather as "softly assembled" sets of behavioral attractors whose form and variability would be quite variable, depending on the task at hand, the context, and the individual's life history and experience. With this approach variability of pathway and experience are privileged . . . Gender saturation varies across situations and tasks, and no doubt across cultures and historical time. It is not that all persons have fluid and multiple gender experiences, it is only that this is expectable and would alter (although not dispense with) the normative qualities and features of psychoanalytic theory. (Harris, 2000, p. 231)

Harris uses the stories of tomboys, including herself, as an example of gendered soft assembly. She describes the tomboy as both playing and being imprisoned by gender conventions as both gender conformist and outlaw. There is enormous variability in the tomboy experience of gender identity across person and within person over time: boy in a girl, boy and a girl, girl and more then a girl, and girl whose "phallus" may be dystonic or syntonic. Some tomboys are heterosexual, some bisexual, and some butch lesbians. For some, the tomboy experience was defined as masculine, for some ungendered, and for some feminine.

Another author who calls upon systems theory in attempting to conceptualize a queer-positive model of sexual development is Corbett (2001b). He points out that traditional developmental models are dominated by normative logic of centrality, discounting the necessity of marginality. However, postmodern theories of subjectivity overvalue the potential of the margin and fail to account for the significance of similarity and coherence. He suggests five "quasi-axioms" towards a new model of development. These include describing development as a process rather than a state, invoking the metaphor of position rather than stage theory, which avoids the dilemma of "more health" being associated with any particular sexual developmental position. He also suggests thinking of developmental hierarchy as a multidimensional topology (rethinking of developmental *lines* as multiple *spirals*; using the metaphor of a *web* of selves rather than a *core self*). A new developmental theory of multiplicity, instead of normality and variance, implies there are many routes to sanity, maturity, and sexuality.

PENETRATING AND PENETRATED: BUTCHY FEMME OR FEMMY BUTCH?

Relational therapists who work with lesbians, gay men and bisexual patients from a "queer" perspective comment upon how their patients provide them with new insights into the nature of gendered experience through the ways these "marginalized" (read: not heterosexual) sexualities remake traditional gender scenarios in new configurations.

Our understanding of gender expands through close attention to how language is used by those attempting to redefine aspects of their gendered experience. For example, Elise (1998) describes the words used by a bisexual woman patient in an effort to show how this patient's "gender repertoire" was influenced by her experience with partners of different sexes. The patient reconstrued her heterosexual sexuality as "passive," in response to a different kind of sexual initiative she felt was required of her in sex with women. She experienced women as more "penetrable" than men both bodily and psychologically, and took pleasure in "playing" (in a Winnicottian sense) with these different aspects of sexual and psychic penetration and receptivity. Elise uses this client's metaphor to point out the cultural splitting (Benjamin, 1988) of masculinity and femininity and penetrating and penetrated. She uses bisexuality, both psychic and object-related, as a site of deconstructing these binaries, similarly to Frommer's (1998) ideas about gay male sexuality as deconstructing the myth of sexuality requiring the tension of difference.

Queer theory gives us some rhetorical tools in order to help us deconstruct narratives of masculinity and femininity. Burch (1993) uses this type of inquiry to analyze her interviews of lesbian subjects for concepts of masculinity and femininity in lesbian relationships. Many of the interviewed women were aware of having internalized the dominant narrative of the lesbian as a failed woman and the butch as a failed man. However, they also were actively involved in trying to stretch concepts of masculinity and femininity to evoke some semblance of their subjective experiences of gender. Burch's subjects talked about being "femmy butches" and "butchy femmes" in complicated idiosyncratic attempts to describe complexly gendered experiences that were essentially collapsed by language into a masculine-feminine binary. The women were also aware of both conscious and preconscious identifications with parental figures in which both fathers and mothers represented masculinity and femininity, challenging classical formulations that lesbians are identified with (or in reaction to) masculine fathers. If we listen through ears sensitized to the inadequacy of language to name nondominant experiences of gender, we can validate our patient's attempts to create new words to articulate new experiences, and look for ways that existent vocabulary limits expression of gendered experience.

Case: Bev

Bev and I both have struggled with understanding her gender identity throughout the five years of our work together. She has thought of herself as a butch lesbian, as a heterosexual man (when she thinks of herself as a man attracted to women), as a transgendered person, as queer, and as uncategorizable. This difficulty in identity stems from her experience of herself as a "biological" woman who identifies with some masculine characteristics and whose sexual gratification initially relied quite exclusively on penetration of a "femme-identified" woman (straight or gay). She wears male clothes exclusively, favoring an urban gay male aesthetic, which includes jewelry, a high degree of preoccupation with body fat, tailored suits and designer male shoes. She finds the idea of sex with men abhorrent. With women, she deeply enjoys emotional sharing but is periodically quite reluctant to allow them to go down on her or penetrate her, seeing this as "too vulnerable" and professing to exclusive gratification through the experience of being the "inserter" of penetrative acts. In social manners, she is stereotypically male, including feeling required to buy plane tickets, expensive dinners, and gifts for the "women" she plans to have sex with. She hates her breasts, and has had breast reduction, or "top" surgery. We have understood her masculine identification as cultural, given her Latina heritage and her experience of the men in her family having privilege. She also associates her masculinity as a response to trauma in the form of sexual abuse by an older man at the age of nine, as formed in response to her desire for feminine women (feminine women want sex with masculine men), and as a defensive repudiation of her mother, who she initially presented as a saint but soon revealed the depth of her anger and revulsion at her perception of her mother's weakness and dominated status.

Bev went through a period of seeing herself as a man trapped in a woman's body, but in her preliminary forays into the transgender community, did not feel her experience was mirrored there. As I began to explore the ideas of gender rigidity and gender flexibility with her, in order to validate her gendered experience of herself as a creative solution to contemporary gender dilemmas, and to suggest that all of these definitions might be meaningful aspects of a multiple and contradictory gender identity, she appeared to show more ease and flexibility in her gendered experiences and behaviors. She formed a long-term relationship, was able to ask for and receive more mutuality in sex and financial obligations, and even began to fantasize about the possibility of having a child, which to her felt like the most extreme gender transgression possible. Looking at the ways in which Bev's gender world was rigidly complementary and introducing the idea of gender multiplicity helped us both to be able to embrace her unique subjectivity.

CLINICIAN:
KNOW THY QUEER OR NOT-SO SELF:
GENDERED COUNTERTRANSFERENCE

A number of clinicians speaking to the intersection of relational analysis and gender have courageously broken ground in examining their own sexual feelings, identifications, biases, and anxieties in their professional writing. This practice is consistent with the value of relational analysis to examine and use countertransference material in treatment, and to the queer practice of privileging subjective experience and acknowledging that experiences of gender are sexed, classed, and raced. For example, Layton (2000) acknowledges heterosexualizing "nominally" homosexual clients, because of the anxiety engendered in her own stirrings of same-sex desire for a patient. She concludes that we need to examine our own beliefs and behaviors for the presence of the *heterosexist unconscious*, including our tendencies to create theory from the experiences of those classes and categories of people who are most like us (her "us" being heterosexual). She points out how clinicians, even those highly regarded in the intersubjective psychoanalytic community, may ward off uncomfortable feelings of vulnerability by resorting to clinical analysis rife with dominant gender role stereotyping. Images of competency, activity, heterosexual dominance, and autonomy are assigned to male analysts, and allusions to inadequacy, passivity, heterosexual submission, and dependence are allocated to women patients.

If we as therapists are unconsciously enforcing gender norms, Donna Gould (1995) suggests we look at all the ways in which our definitions of pathology reflect bias. She describes the stance of an "ideal" relational analyst who is able to examine her "anti-lesbian bias" or homophobia. She suggests we reflect on our own beliefs about sexuality, notice tendencies to try to influence clients towards gender role or sexual orientation conformity, and welcome same-or-cross-sex erotic transferences on the part of either therapist or patient as relevant and useful clinical information.

Even as we attempt to supplant an old norm, such as attempting to redefine perversion, relational theorists may continue to create new norms to police desire (Dimen, 2001): "When perversion relocates from sex to relatedness, its moral baggage comes along. Wholeness and totality in relatedness are as intimidating as heterosexuality untroubled by the homosexuality it has renounced" (p. 847). Queerness can be seen as perversion or as health in different times and subcultures. Relationality, or the capacity for mutual recognition (Benjamin, 1988), may be exalted as the new dominant norm. From this perspective, any sexual practice may be symptomatic or "healthy" based on the individual and cultural meanings it expresses for its practitioners.

For psychoanalytic clinicians, even as homosexuality may be removed from the perversion category, paraphilias continue to push the envelope. Weille (2002), in her study of consensual sadomasochistic practitioners, describes her subjects as experiencing a powerful agency in "playing with" masochistic or dominant positions. How is this to be interpreted from Benjamin's typology of masochistic-dominant positions as being inextricably embedded in male-dominant power relations? One answer is suggested by Dimen: "not to concern yourself with what perversion means to a particular patient is, in fact, to enact a perversion of your own–to reduce your patient to a non-entity by annihilating his or her subjectivity, to confuse what the patient means to you with what the patient means to himself or herself, and thereby to violate the patient's (emergent) boundaries" (2001, p. 833).

When sexuality is revisioned from a queer perspective, gender is just one of multiple variables shaping sexuality (Iasenza, 1995). If gender is displaced as the primary organizer of sexual desire, other "attractors" emerge, including ". . . gender role (masculinity and femininity), sexual orientation (gay, lesbian, bisexual), sexual agency (activity and passivity), power relations (dominance and submission, top and bottom), sexual act (oral or anal sex, paid sex, group sex, S/M, vaginal intercourse, bondage, leather, costumes), and other characteristics such as age, intimacy, body size, race, ethnicity, class, physical appearance and personality. In other words, some people may desire sexual acts or particular characteristics more than other people" (Iasenza, 1995, p. 367). There is a tension between relatedness and mutual recognition (privileged in the relational story of sexuality), and the multiple attractors that proliferate in the diversity expressed in queer sexuality.

Applying one of the "quasi-axioms" in Corbett's (2001b) developmental model, of using the metaphor of *position* rather than *stage*, I would term the *relational position* being foreground at times in the experience of desire, when intimacy with a particular person becomes primary. The hopes and fears constellated in relationship may oscillate into the background when the *sexual position* gains ascendancy, and a particular sexual characteristic, such as gender, gender role, top or bottom, physical type, or sexual act, becomes the focus of desire. This model avoids the hierarchical equation of subject-subject sexuality with maturity, and "using" the other as a sexual object with immaturity. Instead either position may be symptomatic, healthy, or neither, depending on its intrapsychic and cultural meanings. The ability of the analyst to enter into the significance of internal and sociocultural references depends on the clinician being able to examine how personal anxieties might be affecting her formulation.

Case: Maya

Maya had seen me in couple's therapy seven years previously, and at the conclusion of that therapy had relocated to a different part of the country. She reentered individual therapy with me on her return to the area, which was subsequent to a difficult breakup of a long-term lesbian relationship. She was depressed and having difficulty in a leadership role at work. When she, along with most of the workforce in that organization, was laid off, she was unable to locate a new job for six months due to an economic downsizing in her field. Having counted all her adult life on her stable identities as a successful professional and as a valued relational partner, for the first time she had neither identity to inhabit, and was terrified. Many issues from her early life as the daughter of an addicted mother and physically abusive father began to surface, as her habitual coping strategies as an overfunctioning helper were unavailable. As we explored and attempted to work through this material, Maya was able to integrate her fear and vulnerability into her self-image along with her resilience. After tolerating multiple job rejections as well as experiencing several sexual rejections, and being able to separate these experiences from her own self-worth, she was offered a satisfying job and started several new sexual relationships.

While it would seem from the outside that these were good developments for Maya, I became increasingly uneasy at her developing sexual relationships. Within a few months, she played with the possibility that she might want to pursue the identity of a female-to-male transgendered person and established a reputation in the BDSM community as a new top on the scene. From a relatively vanilla sexual identification in which she had never really identified as either butch or femme, she redefined herself as a butch top and enacted multiple sexual scenes with a number of "play partners." She had a polyamorous agreement with her partners, who were also in multiple sexual and emotional relationships as submissives. Maya appeared glowing and happy, reported being more sexually and emotionally satisfied than she could ever remember, and described with glee how free she felt to only "take care" of these partners in the context of the "scene." She felt entitled to ask for her needs to be satisfied in that context, and spoke with empathy and compassion about satisfying intimate emotional and sexual needs of her partners. However, she was deeply relieved to not be "in love," which she now characterized as a potential re-enactment of her abusive childhood history where she devoted herself to unavailable others. She felt something was being repaired in the consensual exchanges of intimacy and power in her scenes, where she was free to "play" and to leave it to her sex partners to assert their own needs and boundaries.

Although I identified with aspects of Maya's history and defenses, I found it hard to tolerate some of her different solutions. I had clearly prioritized relationship in my own life as mutual. In addition, my therapy work was permeated with the relational bias of relational theory. Here was one case where the values of queer theory allowed me to begin to imagine that there might be other pathways to psychological and sexual healing than my own dominant narrative. As I let go of some of my judgments, Maya appeared to be more willing to examine both the strengths and compromises of her current solutions. She began to imagine that her current identifications might be transient, or that they might be longer term. We both became more interested in her journey, and less anxious.

WHO IS HAVING SEX WITH WHOM: EROTICISM IN THE CLINICAL HOUR

Until ten years ago, discussions of sexual feelings in analytic therapy almost unilaterally focused on the experience of the patient. Any discussion of erotic countertransference on the part of the therapist was rife with prohibitions against self-disclosure. Defense mechanisms such as projective identification were suggested that implied the patient had "inserted" sexual feelings into the therapist to metabolize. The therapist was admonished to contain the feelings until they could be "worked through" away from the patient, in the therapist's own therapy or consultation.

With relational theory's increasing emphasis on countertransference experience as information for the therapist regarding the patient, some analysts (Maroda, 1999) began to name the experience of sexual feelings in the clinical hour as important information regarding the inner world of the patient, but not as relational material to be explored. Davies (1994) was one of the first to describe a judicious use of self-disclosure regarding erotic countertransference as a corrective to potential reenactment of harmful secrecy and defensive disavowal of the patient's experience. Gabbard (1998) points out that the gender constellation Davies describes (female analyst, male patient) can have a different power connotation that of a male analyst for a female patient. "Cultural discourses involving gender and power do not disappear when one enters the consulting room. If a man says to a woman that he has sexual feelings for her, an action is implied by that communication" (Gabbard, 1998, p. 783). Much of the recent writing about "welcoming" erotic countertransference takes place in the nondominant constellations of lesbian analyst, bisexual/lesbian patient (Elise, 1998); straight female analyst, lesbian patient (Layton, 2002); straight female analyst, straight male patient (Davies, 1998); and gay male analyst, gay male patient (Frommer, 2001). Two constellations in which descriptions of sexual feelings are more heavily weighted with fear and caution on the part of the analyst include the straight male analyst and straight female patient

(Gabbard, 1998), and the gay male analyst with the straight male patient (Corbett, 2001b).

Davies (1998) invokes the relational emphasis on the capacity to tolerate ambiguity and paradox in describing the capacities required in "mature" adult sexuality:

> A capacity to move fluidly between experiences of passive surrender and active pursuit; the capacity to supply and take pleasure from nurturing others as well as from the ambitious pursuit of self interest and self satisfaction, a comfort with heterosexual and homosexual forms of passionate excitement, and as Benjamin (1995) has highlighted, a balance between a sadomasochism rooted in non-recognition and one-sided idealization and the mutuality of mature sexual desire. (p. 758)

In Davies description, which we can also apply to the analyst's (symbolic) erotic capacity, we can see the influence of relational analysis in the tension between poles of experience. The impact of queer theory is apparent in equating heterosexual and homosexual forms of excitement and in the emphasis upon the power relations embedded in sexuality. Here again, we see the dilemma Dimen (2001) is concerned with: How "mature sexuality" becomes equated with "mutuality," reflecting a developmental hierarchy with moral overtones.

Elise (2002), in queer theory's tradition of looking at who we are not allowed to love, suggests that the absence of erotic desire and romantic love on the part of the analyst and patient should be examined for its defensive aspects, instead of being taken for granted. She sees a relationship between the capacity for symbolic sexual "play" in analysis and the capacity for creativity.

Case: Maya Revisited or Spiral Developments

> In the process of discussing her developing sexuality, it became clear to Maya that I was familiar with the vocabulary of the BDSM community. In one session, she asked me directly if I had personal experience with what we were discussing. I was flustered but intrigued, and I asked her what her fantasies were about my answer, both because I genuinely believed it would foreclose her experience for me to answer quickly, and because I was conflicted about being so intimate with her. She responded that she thought I was a switch, capable of assuming both top and bottom roles. And what

does that bring up for you, I asked, feeling like we were in dangerous but important territory. "It turns me on," she said. "I can imagine topping you, but I can also imagine you topping me, which could be even better." I became quite aroused, but remained quiet while I reflected on how I was feeling and what to share with her. Then I said, "I can imagine both those fantasies as well, but I'm particularly interested in how different it seems to be that you can imagine me topping you, given how hard it has been for you to allow that lately. I wonder how we can safely play with that energy, here, to learn more about that part of you, without overwhelming either of us." Maya appeared relieved and moved. We were both quiet for a minute. When she spoke, she said, "That was quite good, but your cheeks are red." My hands went involuntarily to my face, which was quite warm. Then we were both able to laugh for a while.

The most difficult part of Maya's sexual explorations for me was the lack of mutuality in her sexual play, and I was concerned that this was a reenactment of a non-mutual relationship history. Intellectually, I agreed with Weille (2002) that many consensual BDSM practitioners were "metabolizing" abusive sexual histories in reparative sexual scripting, and I felt comfortable with Maya's fluctuating gender identity assemblies. However, my edges were pushed around the issue of whether the relational position (where intimacy and a specific partner are foreground) is a "better" way to work through painful sexual and emotional issues than the sexual position (in which a particular sexual characteristic or position is primary). It was clearly Maya's experience that the top sexual position was allowing her to feel aspects of her own vitality and wholeness that were not at this time available to her in a primary relationship. In addition, it seemed important that Maya be able to bring in that vitality to our relationship. In our exchange, I allowed Maya to momentarily top me (in fantasy and symbolic verbal enactment), and she allowed herself to be topped by me. We both felt vitalized and learned something, about her construction of sexual meaning, about my own, and about ours together. We both referred to this moment together a number of times in our subsequent work. In a development which Maya felt was related to this experience, she began to explore "switching," or a more fluid exploration of both top and bottom roles, and found herself also drawn to the relational position with some partners.

CONCLUSION:
WHAT CAN WE KNOW ABOUT GENDER, AND WHO KNOWS IT?

As many of the writers I have cited acknowledge, postmodern discourses such as queer theory are not theories in and of themselves, but critiques meant to destabilize dominant norms, including the norms of mental health and the theories of assisting people towards "more health." At the end point of deconstruction, there can be a skeptical inability for us to "know" anything about the other, or even to believe in the possibility of mutuality in relationship. As Stern (2002) speaks to in his analysis of "what we know first" in relational psychoanalysis, there is an inherent tension between the "construction" inherent in hermeneutic/narrative versions of relational theory, and the deconstruction of what he calls the power/knowledge version of psychoanalysis influenced by feminism and queer critiques. The constructivist position is hopeful that we can free ourselves from old meanings and construct them anew in mutual new stories, experiences, or perspectives. From the perspective of queer theory, we must always doubt that we are capable of constructing new stories or ideas about others and ourselves that is not embedded in dominant power relations.

I have argued that queer theory has profoundly changed the terrain of gender for relational psychoanalysis: in how we designate our gender identities, in the stories we construct regarding gender development, in the introspection required of the analyst regarding her own internalization of dominant gender norms, and in measured openness to the erotic nature of the therapeutic relationship. It is difficult to leave behind some of our old ways of thinking about things, and yet postmodernism creates new ways of thinking, even as the shadows of old constructions are left behind. I believe there is more hope, more room for new voices on both sides of the therapeutic relationship, "more life," as Corbett (2001b) evokes, in the current dialogue between queer ideas about gender and contemporary psychoanalysis.

REFERENCES

Benjamin, J. (1988). *The bonds of love.* New York: Pantheon.

Benjamin, J. (1998). *The shadow of the other: Intersubjectivity and gender in psychoanalysis.* New York: Routledge.

Benjamin, J. (2000). Response to commentaries by Mitchell and by Butler, Roundtable on J. Benjamin. *Studies in Gender and Sexuality, 1*(3), 291-308.

Burch, B. (1993). Gender identities, lesbianism, and potential space. *Psychoanalytic Psychology, 10*(3), 359-375.

Butler, J. (1993). Imitation and gender insubordination. In H. Abelove, D. Halperin & M.A. Barale (Eds.), *Lesbian and gay studies reader* (pp. 294-306). New York: Routledge.

Butler, J. (1995). Melancholy gender–refused identification. *Psychoanalytic Dialogues, 5*(2), 165-180.

Chodorow, N. J. (1989). *Feminism and psychoanalytic theory.* New Haven, CT: Yale University Press.

Corbett, K. (1993). The mystery of homosexuality. *Psychoanalytic Psychology, 10*(3), 345-357.

Corbett, K. (2001a). Faggot = Loser. *Studies in Gender and Sexuality, 2*(1), 3-28.

Corbett, K. (2001b). More life: Centrality and marginality in human development. *Psychoanalytic Dialogues, 11*(3), 313-335.

Davies, J. M. (1994). Love in the afternoon: A relational reconsideration of desire and dread in the countertransference. *Psychoanalytic Dialogues, 4*(2), 153-170.

Davies, J. M. (1998). Between the disclosure and foreclosure of erotic transference-countertransference: Can psychoanalysis find a place for adult sexuality? *Psychoanalytic Dialogues, 8*(6), 747-766.

Dimen, M. (1991). Deconstructing difference: Gender, splitting and transitional space. *Psychoanalytic Diaogues, 1*(4), 335-352.

Dimen, M. (2001). Perversion is us? Eight notes. *Psychoanalytic Dialogues, 11*(6), 825-860.

Elise, D. (1998). Gender repertoire: Body, mind and bisexuality. *Psychoanalytic Dialogues, 8*(3), 353-371.

Elise, D. (2002). Blocked creativity and inhibited erotic transference. *Studies in Gender and Sexuality, 3*(2), 161-195.

Frommer, M. (1994). Homosexuality and psychoanalysis: Technical considerations revisited. *Psychoanalytic Dialogues, 4*(2), 215-233.

Frommer, M. (2000). Offending gender: Being and wanting in male same-sex desire. *Studies in Gender and Sexuality, 1*(2), 191-206.

Gabbard, G. O. (1998). Commentary on paper by Jody Messler Davies. *Psychoanalytic Dialogues, 8*(6) 781-789.

Goldner, V. (1991). Toward a critical relational theory of gender. *Psychoanalytic Dialogues, 1*(3) 249-272.

Gould, D. (1995). A critical examination of the notion of pathology in psychoanalysis. In J. M. Glassgold & S. Iasenza (Eds.), *Lesbians and psychoanalysis: Revolutions in theory and practice* (pp. 3-17). New York: Free Press.

Hansell, J. (1998). Gender anxiety, gender melancholia, gender perversion. *Psychoanalytic Dialogues, 8*(3), 337-352.

Harris, A. (2001). Gender as a soft assembly: Tomboy's stories. *Studies in Gender and Sexuality, 1*(3), 223-250.

Iasenza, S. (1995). Platonic pleasures and dangerous desires: Psychoanalytic theory, sex research, and Lesbian sexuality. In J. M. Glassgold & S. Iasenza (Eds.), *Lesbians and psychoanalysis: Revolutions in theory and practice* (pp. 345-373). New York: Free Press.

Jagose, A. (1996). *Queer theory: An introduction.* NY: New York University Press.

Kassoff, B. (1997). The self in orientation: Issues of female homosexuality. In A. Goldberg (Ed.), *Conversations in self-psychology (Vol. 13).* Hillsdale, NJ: Analytic Press.

Kassoff, B., Boden, R., de Monteflores, C., Hunt, P., and Wahba, R. (1995). Coming out of the frame: Lesbianism and psychoanalytic theory. In J. M. Glassgold & S. Iasenza (Eds.), *Lesbians and psychoanalysis: Revolutions in theory and practice* (pp. 229-263). New York: Free Press.

Layton, L. (1998). *Who's that girl? Who's that boy? Clinical practice meets postmodernism.* Northvale, NJ: Aronson.

Layton, L. (2002). Cultural hierarchies, splitting, and the heterosexist unconscious. In S. Fairfield, L. Layton, & C. Stack (Eds.), *Bringing the plague: Towards a postmodern psychoanalysis* (pp. 195-224). New York: Other Press.

Maroda, K. (1999). *Seduction, surrender and transformation: Emotional engagement in the analytic process.* Hillsdale, NJ: The Analytic Press.

Mitchell, S. (1988). *Relational concepts in psychoanalysis: An integration.* Cambridge, MA: Harvard University Press.

Mitchell, S. (1993). *Hope and dread in psychoanalysis.* New York: Basic Books.

Mitchell, S. and Aron, L. (Eds.). (1999). *Relational psychoanalysis: The emergence of a tradition.* Hillsdale, NJ: Analytic Press.

Sedgwick, E. (1993). *Tendencies.* Durham, NC: Duke University Press.

Stern, D. B. (2002). What you know first: Construction and deconstruction in relational psychoanalysis. In S. Fairfield, L. Layton, & C. Stack (Eds.), *Bringing the plague: Towards a postmodern psychoanalysis* (pp. 167-193). New York: Other Press.

Thelen, E. & Smith, L. (1991). *A dynamic systems approach to the development of cognition and action.* Cambridge, MA: MIT Press.

Weille, K. (2002). The psychodynamics of consensual sadomasochistic and dominant-submissive sexual games. *Studies in Gender and Sexuality, 3*(2), 131-160.

Engorging the Lesbian Clitoris:
Opposing the Phallic Cultural Unconscious

Debra Roth

SUMMARY. This paper argues that colloquial language that casually refers to the male genitals as significations of power and authority (i.e., "having balls," "getting it up," "strapping it on," etc.) has a particularly injurious effect upon lesbian subjectivity because of the critical ways in which lesbians must reject the hegemony of the phallus in order to experience themselves as richly embodied. In working with and against Judith Butler's formulation of the "lesbian phallus," this essay theorizes an "engorged lesbian clitoris" as a way of infusing vernacular language with a form of female genital privilege that is as arbitrary and idealized as its predominating male counterpart. While acknowledging the risks of reification, reductionism, and essentialism inherent in such a formulation, Freud's views on the clitoris and Lacan's on the phallus are examined for their collaborative contribution to an unconsciously held cultural standard grounded in male anatomical metaphor that transmits attributions of influence, fecundity, and capability. The essay argues for the *elevation* of the "engorged lesbian clitoris" to an *unremarkable* position in the everyday language of dominance and desire. *[Article copies available for a fee from The Haworth Document Delivery Service: 1-800-*

Debra Roth, CSW, is a psychoanalyst in private practice in NYC.
Address correspondence to: Debra Roth, CSW, 153 Waverly Place, 10th floor, New York, NY 10014 (E-mail: debraroth@speakeasy.net).

[Haworth co-indexing entry note]: "Engorging the Lesbian Clitoris: Opposing the Phallic Cultural Unconscious." Roth, Debra. Co-published simultaneously in *Journal of Lesbian Studies* (Harrington Park Press, an imprint of The Haworth Press, Inc.) Vol. 8, No. 1/2, 2004, pp. 177-189; and: *Lesbians, Feminism, and Psychoanalysis: The Second Wave* (ed: Judith M. Glassgold, and Suzanne Iasenza) Harrington Park Press, an imprint of The Haworth Press, Inc., 2004, pp. 177-189. Single or multiple copies of this article are available for a fee from The Haworth Document Delivery Service [1-800-HAWORTH, 9:00 a.m. - 5:00 p.m. (EST). E-mail address: docdelivery@haworthpress.com].

http://www.haworthpress.com/web/JLS
Digital Object Identifier: 10.1300/J155v08n01_11

HAWORTH. E-mail address: <docdelivery@haworthpress.com> Website: <http://
www.HaworthPress.com> © 2004 by The Haworth Press, Inc. All rights reserved.]

KEYWORDS. Clitoris, lesbian, lesbian phallus, psychoanalysis, Butler, J., cultural unconscious

My 20-year-old niece tells me that I "have balls" and I know exactly
what she means. I am even flattered by her attribution. My three com-
panions, all feminists, all lesbians, laughingly tell me that I "have
strapped it on" when I return from telling the snooty host in a trendy restaurant that we are tired of waiting at the bar and wish to be seated.
These seemingly inconsequential social anecdotes illuminate the ways
in which references to the male genitals are casually and unremarkably
deployed as significations of power and authority. Linguistic conventions such as these take on a far more serious consequence than it may at
first appear. Because of the myriad lenses through which they can be
unconsciously processed, language used in its vernacular form constitutes important, reflexively applied shadings to the ways in which one
perceives, and then correspondingly relates to, self and other.

In the following essay, I look at the powerful contribution psychoanalysis has made to a set of cultural constructions, both tacit and explicit,
which place the attribution of authority, dominance, and competence
squarely on the head of the phallus. I suggest that the omission of the
clitoris from the range of colloquial terms that refer to endowment and
accomplishment has a distinctly deleterious effect on lesbian subjectivity in particular because of the critical ways in which lesbians must reject the hegemony of the phallus in order to experience themselves as
fully and richly embodied. Otherwise, lesbian sexuality is forced back
under a circular system of references which lead "body and desire back
to the phallus" (Traub, 1995, p. 82).

This necessary identificatory refusal complicates the lesbian experience of self as a subject who penetrates, suffuses, and otherwise im-
pregnates the other, especially since in this case; the other is most often
another woman. A phallogocentric (Derrida, in Evans, 1996) ideational
framework works to severely circumscribe the ways in which lesbians
can grapple with the experiences of embodiment and otherness because
it asks us to reach too far outside our own intrapsychic experience of
self as subject or as object in order to engage and more fully know our
own sexual potency and aliveness.

editorial

The Whitney Biennial is coming.

Carry your ass over there.

It should be good.

See art by the young and the hung

March 7th through May 26th

Whitney Museum of American Art, New York City

The dearth of rich, expansive meanings that can be effortlessly applied to either the clitoris itself, or to words which take the clitoris as its root, point to a significant signification problem for all women, not just lesbians. Within the past several decades, a vital and compelling reconceptualization of the Freudian understanding of the first oedipal period (Grossman, 1986) has been developed through the feminist critique of psychoanalysis. This movement, beginning in the early 1920s with the work of Karen Horney (1924), both challenges and reformulates Freud's thinking when, according to Freud, individual sexual "identity" takes on what is to become its essential form (Freud, 1908/1961, 1917/1961, 1925/1961, 1931a/1961, 1933b/1961, 1938a/1961). According to these paradigm shifts (i.e., Benjamin, 1988; Chodorow, 1978, 1994; Dimen, 2000; Elise, 2000a, 2000b, 2001; O'Connor and Ryan, 1993, and others too numerous to note here) a newly empowered pre-Oedipal mother has usurped some of the developmental authority that had formally resided solely with father. These revisions have contributed to a reconsideration of lesbian subjectivity, unsnarling the reductionist knot that Freud (1920/1961) posited between lesbian desire and male identification.[1] Yet, even with these reappraisals, the phallus continues to function as the absolute signifier of both desire and dominance, although it now moves–as a symbol–more freely among and between the primary gender categories.

In Lacan's influential reading of Freud, he literally refigures sexuality by moving it away from Freudian biology, relocating it in language and culture. This relocation comes with attendant alienating effects or what Lacan refers to as "lack," since for Lacan, desire is always separated from subjectivity by language (Gallop, 1982). According to this line of thought, signifiers[2] or mental sound-images (as opposed to the sounds themselves) become primary since they produce that which is signified. In the end then, the effects of the signifier constitute the subject. In making this shift away from the *internal* drive-based experience–which Freud posited–toward an *internalized* intercalation in culture, Lacan sets up the phallus as the "privileged signifier" or that which itself creates significations or meanings. As Lacan (1958/2000) puts it, "The relation of the subject to the phallus is set up regardless of the anatomical differences between the sexes" (p. 221).

Since the effects of the signifier on the subject constitute the unconscious (Bowie, 1991; Evans, 1996, Dor, 1998; Verhaeghe, 1999), and the unconscious contributes to the formation of conscious perceptions which can be proscribed and regulated through unconscious cultural "memories," this series of interrelated psychic processes creates, as

Lacan (1958/2000) himself acknowledges, an "intractable" interpretive problem for women in general, and I argue, an acutely fractious one for lesbians inasmuch as the distinction between penis and phallus remains murky, at best (Evans, 1996; Dimen, 1997; Gallop, 1982, 1985; Laplanche & Pontalis, 1973).

The discrepancy regarding what the word *phallus* actually signifies has made it a continuously moving psychoanalytic target. For Lacan, the phallus is a signifier which differs from the signifier penis. The Lacanian phallus is a mark of power which cannot be possessed by *either* women *or* men. At the same time, however, the phallus "always refers to penis . . . [since] . . . the attribute of power is a phallus which can only have meaning by referring to and being confused with a penis . . ." (Gallop, 1982, pp. 246-247). Because of this entanglement, it follows that colloquial allusions, either literal, metaphorical or etymological, which derive from the phallus can become seamlessly embedded in the unconscious as significations of potency in ways that are both limiting and confusing, particularly for women who see themselves, as well as other women, as lush, prolific or even engorged, in the sense of being well-filled and flourishing.

In working with and against Judith Butler's conception of the "lesbian phallus" (1993), I am arguing for the metatheoretical, albeit risky, necessity of conceptualizing a specifically lesbian clitoris, one which is characterized by its state of engorgement. Creating a theoretical platform, rooted in female bodily imagery, from which women can experience themselves as both fecund and well-endowed without reference to a phallic prototype, challenges the subtle ways in which "clitoris and 'lesbian' have been mutually implicated as sisters in shame" (Traub, 1995, p. 82).

This conceptual project appears to justify the hazards of reductionism and essentialism that reference to anything specifically "lesbian" or "female" necessarily invites. To this end, theorizing an "engorged lesbian clitoris" is not aimed at either fetishizing the clitoris nor creating or locating a specific lesbian "identity." Rather, this formulation seeks to expand the range of conceptual possibilities available to women in creating a relatively stable, conscious sense of "self," an essential, albeit illusory, ingredient in the ability to function competently (Mitchell, 1993).[3]

In her evocative and penetrating essay, "The Lesbian Phallus and the Morphological Imaginary," Judith Butler (1993) argues against the "naturalized link" of the phallus to male morphology (1993, p. 86). In appropriating the mutable, polymorphous quality of the phallus as it was first adapted from "classical antiquity" by Freud (Laplanche & Pontalis, 1973) and later refabricated and erected as the "privileged signifier" by Lacan (1958/2000), Butler designs a form of conceptual opposition to the phallic patronymic. In doing so, she undermines the designation of the Name [phallus], and thereby the Law [heterosexuality] of the Father as the means through which one attains subjecthood. Through creating an "imaginary" (1993, p. 91) lesbian phallus, she counters the heterosexually grounded, male-privileging principle "which elevate[s] an organ, a body part . . . to the structuring and centering principle of the world" (1993, p. 79). Through her "aggressive reterritorialization" (1993, p. 86) of the phallus as an "imaginary effect" (1993, p. 88), Butler argues for the mutability and, therefore, transferability of the term, along with the privilege that it signifies by definition. By first locating, and next exploiting, the expropriability of the phallus, Butler's argument subverts the distinction made by Lacan between *being* and *having* the phallus.

Lacan locates the woman "in relation to a signifier" (Grosz, 1990, p. 71) or in the position of *being* the phallus (or the object of the other's desire) as opposed to *having* it. For Lacan, *having* the phallus places one at the nexus of discourse which, by his definition, generates meaning, authority and control (Gallop, 1982). In challenging this formulation, Butler deploys her understanding of performativity (1990) to suggest that the claim to privileged signification assigned to the phallus is established through the very act of assignment: "The announcement of that privileged signifier is its performance" (p. 83). In other words, it is the designation of privilege and the subsequent performance of privilege which creates the phallus as privileged.

For Butler (1993), the distinction between penis and phallus cannot be collapsed (p. 61) although it can be refigured. By removing the "penis" from its traditional anatomical location and repositioning it in the register of the Lacanian "imaginary," Butler demonstrates how the imperative to negate the phallus' connection to the penis, paradoxically, binds it to the penis. This results from the nomination of the penis as "that body part that [the phallus] must *not be*" (1993, p. 84, Butler's italics). Through challenging the idealizing (De Lauretis, 1994) structural and logical relations which secure phallic privilege, Butler (1993) "renders [the phallus] transferable, substitutable [and] plastic" (p. 89), making it available for circulation among and between women. In this way, the Lacanian distinction between *being* and *having* is annulled.

Through this series of linguistic collocations and ideational dislocations, resting on "the notion that lesbian sexuality is *as* constructed as any other . . ." (1993, p. 85, Butler's italics), Butler (1993) creates, then justifies, her "theoretically useful fiction" (p. 85) of the lesbian phallus. This concept grounds her argument for the *"displace*[ment]*"* (p. 90, Butler's italics) of the privileged status of the phallic signifier. To this end, Butler posits a set of theoretical contexts in which the phallus is construed as a different *kind* of signifier, one that "exceeds . . . [the] form of heterosexist structuralism" (1993, p. 90) formulated by Lacan. The concept of the lesbian phallus offers "(a set of occasions) for the phallus to signify differently" (1993, p. 90) and with this shift in signification comes the *resignification* of the phallus' heterosexual, masculine privilege.

But does this project of linguistic resignification succeed? I suggest that it does and it doesn't. Butler does an erudite, even masterly, job of first, appropriating masculine phallic privilege, next reformulating it as malleable and transferable and finally, redeploying the resultant theoretical construction, a lesbian phallus, in the service of female, and specifically lesbian, sexuality. Through this formulation she creates "a site where bodies and anatomies" (1993, p. 90) can be continuously refigured and reauthorized.

Yet, the profoundly complicated, exquisitely executed reasoning which produces the lesbian phallus does little to free lesbian bodily imagery from its reliance on a male anatomical and theoretical set of standards. Because of this reliance, the concept of a "lesbian phallus" preserves the alienating convention of using "the male body as the canonical human form" (Laqueur, 1990, p. 96), a practice I am arguing is injurious to lesbian subjectivity.

The Freudian psychoanalytic convention of referring to the female anatomy as a reduced or inferior version of the male's can be traced as far back as the Renaissance (Laqueur, 1989, 1990; Traub, 1995) when the need for language which distinguished male from female organs simply did not exist. The clitoris was first "discovered" in 1559 by Columbo[4] and was soon taken up by anatomists as well as travel writers of the time as the bodily banner for female erotic unruliness.

> [Y]et sometimes [the clitoris] groweth to such a length that it hangeth without the cleft like a mans member . . ., and so strutteth and groweth to a rigiditie as doth the yarde of a man. (Crooke, a 15th century anatomist quoted in Traub, p. 93)

> Tulpius hath a like Story of one that had [the clitoris] as long as half a mans finger, and as thick as a boys Prick, which made her

willing to have to do with Women in a Carnal way. But the more this part encreases, the more does it hinder a man in his business. (Bartholin, a 15th century translator and anatomist quoted in Traub, p. 95)

Considered as "preeminently the seat of woman's pleasure" (Colombo quoted in Laqueur, 1989), manipulation of the clitoris became a threat to male sexual prerogative since it could be stimulated to the point of gratification by a woman herself or, yet more undermining to masculine control, by another woman. By 1653, the clitoris was referred to as *Contemptus viorum* or "the contempt of mankind" (Traub, 1995, p. 96) because it was understood to promote lasciviousness and "tribadism."[5]

Portraits of the clitoris suggest that the organ shrinks in size, portent and importance over time. Whether the clitoris is literally *magnified* as an organ which can be as "big and long as the neck of a goose" (Venette, 1750, quoted in Traub) or metaphorically *minimized* as "the neatest expression of inferiority" (Freud, 1938b/1961), these brief historical illustrations suggest the ways in which the female body's inscription in language has served as a powerful determinant in both the creation and manipulation of female subjectivity.

If "female theorizing is grounded in the body" (Schor, 1981 p. 210)[6] *and* if, as Freud (1923/1961) suggested, "[t]he ego is first and foremost a bodily ego . . . [and] is itself the projection of a surface" (p. 26), then the language, which constitutes the lesbian body, is of the utmost importance in organizing the experience of that body.[7] Perhaps, if while inventing psychoanalysis, Freud (1925/1961) had posited the developing girl's experience as something other than " . . . penis envy, or . . . the discovery of the inferiority of the clitoris" (p. 255), the imperative for constructions like the "lesbian phallus" or an "engorged lesbian clitoris" might have been eliminated.

Instead, through his "rediscovery" (Laqueur, 1989) of the clitoris and by postulating it as ". . . the normal prototype of inferior organs," (Freud, 1927/1961, p. 157), Freud (1938a/1961) made a substantial contribution to the creation of "[a] girl [who] . . . comes to recognize her lack of a penis or rather the inferiority of her clitoris, with permanent effects on the development of her character" (p. 155). Through this construction, he primed the western cultural unconscious for the reception of Lacan's fabrication of the sign of male privilege: the phallus, or as Dimen (2000) refers to it, the "symbol of the permanently erect penis" (p. 31).

My argument for theorizing an engorged lesbian clitoris cannot be complete without referencing some of the compelling viewpoints which oppose the construction of a female analogue to the phallus and its privilege. As Benjamin (1988) states it, "[s]imply finding a female counterpart to the phallic symbol does not work . . ." (p. 125). She suggests, instead, the formation of a new psychic plane from which desire and dominance can be represented; what she calls in another context (Benjamin, 1999) "the thirdness of intersubjectivity" (p. 208). Along similar lines, Shor (1981) points out that "by emphasizing the clitoris, one remains locked into male dichotomies" (p. 215). Traub (1995) is troubled by the potential for "anatomical essentialism" (p. 101) that an association of bodily parts with female desire can engender. From yet another angle, Maroda (2002) expresses a wariness regarding analytic "dogma" and the ways in which new structural concepts can become subject to eventual reification. Finally, there is the persistent threat of transforming the clitoris into a lesbian fetish with the consequent risk of truncating the erotic expansiveness and experimentation[8] that consolidating desire within any particular body organ can generate.[9-10]

Like my own argument, a substantial limitation to all of these divergent positions is their embeddedness in a theoretical register which tacitly authorizes the circumvention of the social processes that all cultural change relies upon for implementation. Cultural theory can stagnate within the realm of the academic unless it is translated into some form of social activity. Therefore, I propose risking bodily essentialisms by inviting you, the reader of this essay, as a member of a community of self-conscious feminists, to begin employing the term "engorged clitoris," even if its use is limited to casual conversational exchanges among friends [i.e., "He didn't have the 'engorged clitoris' to take up my challenge." "Well, you must be feeling your 'engorged clitoris' today, if you were able to say that to her."]. It is only by moving such a psycho-cultural trope out of the realm of the theoretical and into the social that we will come to know its fuller meanings, implications and costs.

In concluding, it is interesting to note that as maligned as the clitoris has been both through time and within diverse fields of thought, it is the *only* sex organ dedicated exclusively to pleasure (Dimen, 2000). Clearly, its possession by women along with its incontrovertible historical link to lesbian eroticism has contributed to this legacy of disparagement. It is this clitoris, which has been regarded as such a powerfully provocative protuberance, that I want to both reclaim *and* elevate to an *unremarkable* place in colloquial language. Following Butler (1993), I am attempting to "promote an alternative *imaginary* to a hegemonic imaginary . . ." (p. 91, Butler's italics) through the formulation of an "engorged lesbian clitoris" . . . one that can take its inconspicuous place in the everyday language of dominance and desire.

NOTES

1. See Freud, (1920/1961) *Case of Homosexuality in a Woman*: "The beautiful . . . girl had . . . her father's tall figure and her facial features were sharp . . ., traits indicating a physical masculinity. Some of her intellectual attributes could also be connected with masculinity, for instance, her acuteness of comprehension and her lucid objectivity, in so far as she was not dominated by her passion . . . What is certainly of greater importance is that in her behaviour [sic] towards her love-object she had throughout assumed the masculine part: . . ." (p. 154).

2. As Lacan (1973) states, "Nature provides–I must use the word–signifiers, and these signifiers organize human relations in a creative way, providing them with structures and shaping them" (p. 20).

3. "We are all composites of overlapping, multiple organizations and perspectives, and our experience is smoothed over by an illusory sense of continuity" (Mitchell, 1993, p. 104).

4. Who is also referred to in other sources (i.e., Laqueur) as Columbus–"Renaldus not Christopher."

5. Synonymous with "lesbian," tribad derives from the Greek *tribein*, or "to rub." Women who engaged in "tribadic practices" were called *Confricatrices* or Rubsters (see Traub, 1995).

6. See also, Harris, A. (1998) for an elaboration of this thesis.

7. See Elise, 1997, for a discussion of the developmentally early sense of self, grounded in the body ego, which is markedly affected by the girl's "actual" anatomy.

8. Alternatively, what Freud (1927/1961) refers to as repression and disavowal. *Paradoxically*, Freud sees the fetish as "[sav]ing the male fetishist from homosexuality, since the fetish "endow[s] women with the characteristic which makes them tolerable as sexual objects" (p. 154).

9. For an opposing perspective see De Lauretis (1994) who purposely calls "the signifier of perverse desire" (p. 231) a fetish.

10. Discussion of lesbian subjectivity and sexuality must include a reference to the use of dildos. See K. Lotney (2000), *The Ultimate Guide to Strap-On Sex*.

REFERENCES

Benjamin, J. (1988). *The bonds of love*. New York: Pantheon.

Benjamin, J. (1999). Afterward to recognition and destruction. In S.A. Mitchell & L. Aron (Eds.), *Relational psychoanalysis: The emergence of a tradition* (pp. 201-210). Hillsdale, NJ: Analytic Press.

Bowie, M. (1991). *Lacan*. Cambridge, MA: Harvard University Press.

Butler, J. (1990). *Gender trouble: Feminism and the subversion of identity*. New York: Routledge.

Butler, J. (1993). The lesbian phallus and the morphological imaginary. In J. Butler (Ed.), *Bodies that matter: On the discursive limits of "sex"* (pp. 57-91). New York: Routledge.

Chodorow, N. (1978). *The reproduction of mothering: Psychoanalysis and the sociology of gender.* Berkeley: Univ. of California Press.

Chodorow, N. (1994). *Femininities, masculinities, sexualities: Freud and beyond.* Lexington: Univ. of Kentucky Press.

De Lauretis, T. (1994). *The practice of love: Lesbian sexuality and perverse desire.* Bloomington: Indiana Univ. Press.

Dimen, M. (1997). The engagement between psychoanalysis and feminism: A report from the front. *Contemporary Psychoanalysis, 33*(4), 527-548.

Dimen, M. (2000). The body as Rorschach. *Studies in Gender and Sexuality, 1*(1), 9-39.

Dor, J. (1998). The return to Freud. In Gurewich, J.F. (Ed. & Trans.), *Introduction to the reading of Lacan: The unconscious structured like a language* (pp. 1-11). New York: The Other Press. (Original work published in 1985).

Editorial/Ad. (2002). Whitney Biennial. *Nest: A Quarterly Magazine of Interiors, 16* (spring).

Elise, D. (1997). Primary femininity, bisexuality, and the female ego ideal: A re-examination of female developmental theory. *Psychoanalytic Quarterly, 66,* 489-517.

Elise, D. (2000a). "Bye-Bye" to bisexuality? Response to L. Layton. *Studies in Gender and Sexuality, 1*(1), 61-68.

Elise, D. (2000b). Women and desire: Why women may *not* want to want. *Studies in Gender and Sexuality, 1*(2), 125-145.

Elise, D. (2001). Unlawful entry: Male fears of psychic penetration. *Psychoanalytic Dialogues, 11*(4), 499-531.

Evans, D. (1996). *An introductory dictionary of Lacanian psychoanalysis.* London: Routledge.

Freud, S. (1961). The sexual theories of children. In J. Strachey (Ed. & Trans.), *The standard edition of the complete psychological works of Sigmund Freud* (Vol. 9, pp. 209-226). London: Hogarth Press. (Original work published 1908).

Freud, S. (1961). The sexual life of human beings. In J. Strachey (Ed. & Trans.), *The standard edition of the complete psychological works of Sigmund Freud* (Vol. 16, pp. 303-319). London: Hogarth Press. (Original work published 1917).

Freud, S. (1961). Psychogenesis of a case of female homosexuality. In J. Strachey (Ed. & Trans.), *The standard edition of the complete psychological works of Sigmund Freud* (Vol. 28, pp. 145-174). London: Hogarth Press. (Original work published 1920).

Freud, S. (1961). The Ego and the Id. In J. Strachey (Ed. & Trans.), *The standard edition of the complete psychological works of Sigmund Freud* (Vol. 19, pp. 13-63). London: Hogarth Press. (Original work published 1923).

Freud, S. (1961). Some psychical consequences of the anatomical distinction between the sexes. In J. Strachey (Ed. & Trans.), *The standard edition of the complete psychological works of Sigmund Freud* (Vol. 19, pp. 243-258). London: Hogarth Press. (Original work published 1925).

Freud, S. (1961). Fetishism. In J. Strachey (Ed. & Trans.), *The standard edition of the complete psychological works of Sigmund Freud* (Vol. 21, pp. 152-157). London: Hogarth Press. (Original work published 1927).

Freud, S. (1961). Female sexuality. In J. Strachey (Ed. & Trans.), *The standard edition of the complete psychological works of Sigmund Freud* (Vol. 21, pp. 223-243). London: Hogarth Press. (Original work published 1931).

Freud, S. (1961). Dissection of the psychical personality. In J. Strachey (Ed. & Trans.), *The standard edition of the complete psychological works of Sigmund Freud* (Vol. 22, pp. 57-80). London: Hogarth Press. (Original work published 1933a).

Freud, S. (1961). Femininity. In J. Strachey (Ed. & Trans.), *The standard edition of the complete psychological works of Sigmund Freud* (Vol. 22, pp. 112-135). London: Hogarth Press. (Original work published 1933b).

Freud, S. (1961). The development of the sexual function. In J. Strachey (Ed. & Trans.), *The standard edition of the complete psychological works of Sigmund Freud* (Vol. 23, pp. 152-156). London: Hogarth Press. (Original work published 1938a).

Freud, S. (1961). Findings, ideas, problems. In J. Strachey (Ed. & Trans.), *The standard edition of the complete psychological works of Sigmund Freud* (Vol. 23, pp. 299-300). London: Hogarth Press. (Original work published 1938b).

Gallop, J. (1982). Phallus/Penis: Same difference. In Todd, J. (Ed.), *Men by women* (pp. 243-251). New York: Homes & Meier.

Gallop, J. (1985). *Reading Lacan*. Ithaca: Cornell University Press.

Grossman, W.I. (1986). Freud & Horney: A study of psychoanalytic models via the analysis of a controversy. In A. D. Richards & M. S. Willick (Eds.), *Psychoanalysis: The science of mental conflict; Essays in honor of Charles Brenner* (pp. 65-87). Hillsdale, NJ: Analytic Press.

Grosz, E. (1990). *Jacques Lacan: A feminist introduction*. London: Routledge.

Harris, A. (1998). Psychic envelopes and sonorous baths. In Aron, L. & Anderson, F.S. (Eds.), *Relational perspectives on the body* (pp. 39-64). Hillsdale, NJ: Analytic Press.

Horney, K. (1924). On the genesis of the castration complex in women. *International Journal of Psycho-analysis*, 5, 50-65.

Lacan, J. (1973). *The four fundamental concepts of psychoanalysis*. (J. A. Miller, Ed. & A. Sheridan, Trans.). New York: W.W. Norton.

Lacan, J. (2000). The meaning of the phallus. In Saguaro, S. (Ed.), *Psychoanalysis and woman: A reader* (pp. 222-230). New York: New York University Press. (Original article published in 1958).

Laplanche, J. & Pontalis, J.-B. (1973). *The language of psychoanalysis*. London: Hogarth Press.

Laqueur, T. (1989). "Amor veneris, vel dulcedo appeletur." In Feher, M. (Ed.) (with Naddaff, N. & Tazi, N.), *Zone, fragments for a history of the human body* (Part III) (pp. 91-131). New York: Urzone Books.

Laqueur, T. (1990). *Making sex: Body and gender from the Greeks to Freud*. Cambridge, MA: Harvard University Press.

Lotney, K. (2000). *The ultimate guide to strap-on sex: A complete resource for women and men*. San Francisco: Cleis Press.

Maroda, K. (2002). No place to hide: Affectivity, the unconscious, and the development of relational techniques. *Contemporary Psychoanalysis*, 38(1), 101-120.

Mitchell, S.A. (1993). *Hope and dread in psychoanalysis*. New York: Basic Books.

O'Connor, N. & Ryan, J. (1993). *Wild desires & mistaken identities: Lesbianism & psychoanalysis*. New York: Columbia University Press.
Schor, N. (1981). Female paranoia: The case for psychoanalytic feminist criticism. *Yale French Studies, 62*, 204-219.
Traub, V. (1995). The psychomorphology of the clitoris. *GLQ, 2*, 81-113.
Verhaeghe, P. (1999). On the Lacanian subject. In Nobus, D. (Ed.), *Key concepts of Lacanian psychoanalysis* (pp. 164-189). New York: The Other Press.

Perilous Crossings:
Tales of Gender,
Identification, and Exiled Desires

Sandra M. Kiersky

SUMMARY. The author argues for an understanding of subjective gender whereby under dichotomous gender conventions people espouse multiple, complex, chaotic, and mutually exclusive feelings, ideas, and actions. Like sexuality, gender is a fluid, ambiguous and contextual aspect of identity. She critiques theory that puts forth a stage related, linear, content-based construction of gender and describes how attachment theory and intersubjectivity can contribute to newer gender theory. Case material is provided to illustrate the intersubjective nature of gender in the analytic process. *[Article copies available for a fee from The Haworth Document Delivery Service: 1-800-HAWORTH. E-mail address: <docdelivery@haworthpress.com> Website: <http://www.HaworthPress.com> © 2004 by The Haworth Press, Inc. All rights reserved.]*

Sandra M. Kiersky is a psychoanalyst in private practice in Santa Fe, New Mexico. She is the author of numerous articles about gender and sexuality, child development, and the clinical process. She is the current President-Elect of the Association for Autonomous Psychoanalytic Institutes, Faculty, and Supervising Analyst at the National Institute for the Psychotherapies, Co-Editor of *Sexualities Lost, and Found: Lesbians, Psychoanalysis and Culture* from IUP and on the Editorial Board of the journal *Studies in Gender and Sexuality* from The Analytic Press.

Address correspondence to: Sandra M. Kiersky, PhD, 44 Alteza Avenida, Santa Fe, NM 87508 (E-mail: Sky@psychoanalysis.net).

[Haworth co-indexing entry note]: "Perilous Crossings: Tales of Gender, Identification, and Exiled Desires." Kiersky, Sandra M. Co-published simultaneously in *Journal of Lesbian Studies* (Harrington Park Press, an imprint of The Haworth Press, Inc.) Vol. 8, No. 1/2, 2004, pp. 191-207; and: *Lesbians, Feminism, and Psychoanalysis: The Second Wave* (ed: Judith M. Glassgold, and Suzanne Iasenza) Harrington Park Press, an imprint of The Haworth Press, Inc., 2004, pp. 191-207. Single or multiple copies of this article are available for a fee from The Haworth Document Delivery Service [1-800-HAWORTH, 9:00 a.m. - 5:00 p.m. (EST). E-mail address: docdelivery@haworthpress.com].

KEYWORDS. Gender, intersubjectivity, psychoanalytic process, sexual identity

INTRODUCTION

It is impossible to think about lesbians, psychoanalysis or feminism without thinking about gender and the ways in which gender conformity has been equated with mental health and emotional maturity in the Western world. Lesbians have always disrupted this comfortable binary thinking about men and women and psychoanalytic theories have labeled them disordered, manly, or simply immature (Kiersky, 2001). In this way, psychoanalysis, like the culture in which it is embedded, exiled lesbian desire and gender richness to the margins of relatedness and acceptable experience.

At the same time, these moving violations seem actually to be moving into new and uncharted territories. That once simple, biologically given fact of being male or female, masculine or feminine is turning up in feminist and post-modern literature in the most complex and contradictory disguises. Suddenly, we all have tales of gender, and have gender crossings: moments when gender is salient and we feel uncomfortably in or out of gender role. As a culture, we install borders between what it means to be a man or a woman, but these borders are no more secure than those are between Texas and Mexico. In reality, we expect unauthorized crossings, though there is a certain pretense by all concerned that these forays are not really taking place. There is a general appearance of structure and unity under which amazing diversity and contradiction pose a constant threat. Our most enduring myths about gender and sexual identities no longer fit the prevailing models of social and scientific inquiry. According to Thelen and Smith (1994), however, there is no cause for alarm, for this is actually how all development, in open systems, goes forward. In line with this, I will argue that it is not gender conformity that indicates emotional health but a fluid and flexible experience of gender that reflects the complexity of our lived experience.

Despite this diversity, myths that privilege some individuals over others give way very slowly and gender crossings are experienced internally in a variety of ways. Some are felt to be perilous, some exhilarating, some are made purely to please others and some to please ourselves. A few are crossings to safety. I once treated, for example, a young woman who was pre-operative but taking hormones as part of the process of becoming a man. She had emigrated here from Israel as an adolescent in an effort to put an ocean between herself and her father. An ocean, however, turned out not to be distance enough. For this youngster, the desire to cross from woman to man was a desperate solution to an unbearable psychic situation. At around three, Ricky's father began to sexually abuse her. If she resisted, she was hung by a rope from a lighting fixture in the bedroom ceiling and beaten. For Ricky, gender was a trap. It was simple, fixed, and straightforward. To be a woman was to be hurt. Psychic survival depended on being a man. Such crossings to safety are rare. They arise in extreme and terrifying conditions in which a child's world is too dangerous to endure and gender becomes a concrete solution.

Most crossings are adventurous, contextual, and desired. We all cross if only in our dreams. One gender tale of my own is of an unsuccessful crossing that occurred in the third grade. I had ridden my bike to school and entering the building, I heard a number of my classmates asserting that boys were stronger than girls were. This seemed to me the most ridiculous statement I had ever heard, perhaps because the only measure of my strength to that point was with my sister who was five years younger. "I am just as strong as any boy in this class," I told them–a statement that was received with a certain amount of laughter and derision. "Well," I added a little less confident, "I could definitely knock down Steven Wolf." Steven Wolf was the shortest boy in school but actually quite stocky, a quality I had not really considered when making this threat. At the end of the school day, I secured my bike and began to leave the school grounds. Suddenly, Steven appeared from nowhere, asking if I had said that I could knock him down, and telling me to get off my bike and prove it.

"You get out of my way Steven Wolf," I answered, "or I will get off this bike and knock you down." Eventually, I did get off my bike and Steven knocked me down. I was saved, from God knows what, by a woman who lived across from the school who began yelling at Steven and threatening to call his parents. I learned from this experience, in a general way, that men are usually stronger than women are. To this day, however, I harbor secret fantasies of unlimited physical strength. I keep them to myself, along with the remnants of an even earlier feeling that I am capable of flying. All these notions float through my subjective experience. I accept certain differences between men and women; that they don't really mean anything except that when they do–I could get myself killed–except that if I *really* tried I could render unconscious any man who tried to attack me. These kinds of contradictory, unrealistic, and constantly changing experiences of gender and physical strength co-exist in my inner world without creating much conflict internally. Most of the time, I don't think about them at all.

As analysts, we are beginning to understand that this is not un-usual–and under all the dichotomous gender conventions people es-pouse are multiple, complex, chaotic, and mutually exclusive, feelings, ideas, and actions that comprise subjective gender. With this recogni-tion, attempts to understand and rethink gender have left many clini-cians reeling. In this sense, psychoanalysts themselves are engaged in a perilous crossing and are currently somewhere between essentialist no-tions of a biologically given, dual gender system and post-modern posi-tions that nothing is as it appears and all is culturally constructed.

FEMINIST ANALYSTS ON GENDER

Recently, Muriel Dimen (1995) argued that we have seen two waves of feminist influence in psychoanalysis and that it is time for a post-modern third. She suggests that Freud's uncritical adoption of cultural norms and conventions was the "First Step" in psychoanalytic theoriz-ing about women and, by implication, men. During this period, woman was defined primarily in relation to man as an envious individual with a weak conscience whose only hope for a happy life lay in her capacity to be a mother. Significantly, Dimen notes that although, for Freud, gen-der was a given, it was also a developmental achievement. He would not have disagreed with Wittig's (1993) statement that "one is not born a woman" –but he emphasized the epigenetic unfolding of gender appro-priate feelings. Freud (1905/61, 1924/61, 1925/61 1931/61, 1933/61), like many current theorists, put forward a stage related, linear; content-based theory with gender at the center of human development. This kind of theory is difficult to dislodge but I hope to show is one reason we have failed to revision gender in a way that retains its complexity and richness.

It was Freud's image of women as inferior, Dimen continues, that ushered in what she calls the "Second Step" in which Horney (1923/67) and Thompson (Green, 1964) immediately critiqued Freud. Horney equated Freud's view of women with that of a little boy who is unable to see any value in femininity at all. She proposed, instead, an innate, de-velopmental line of femininity, currently elaborated in psychoanalysis in the form of primary and secondary femininity. Both Horney and Thompson believed that many of the problems women encountered were socially based and derived from the phallocentric nature of the culture.

What Dimen designates this "Second Step" in psychoanalytic theorizing began in the 1920s and continues in a growing body of feminist theory and research. It consists of attempts to reconceptualize female development, mothering, femininity, relatedness, and gendered identities. During this period, feminists split into two branches—"difference" feminists focusing on the psychology of women (Pollitt, 1994; Dimen, 1995) and "gender" feminists, focusing on masculinity and femininity and the consequences of these constructions both inside and out. The tension between the two, Dimen argues, calls for a new way of thinking—a "Third Step" which is necessarily postmodern. She suggests that this tension evokes a central and necessary contradiction in feminism itself, as well as the sometimes troublesome, but in fact creative, tug-of-war between psychoanalytic theory and clinical practice. Difference feminism represented by theorists like Miller (1976) and Gilligan (1982) argue that Mahler's theory of progressive separation and autonomy reflects the culture's masculine bias. Relatedness, a distinctly feminine quality from their point of view, is as salient as autonomy. In general, these writers believe women to be different from men due to different socialization and experiences—with women emphasizing relatedness and caring for others and men emphasizing autonomy and individual achievement. Chodorow (1978), whose work, Dimen notes, is crucial to both lines of theory, elaborates the complex and overdetermined way in which women come to want to be mothers. At the same time, she stresses the difficulty women experience separating from their mothers, suggesting that the little girl's similarity to her mother keeps her closer and more embedded in relatedness than the little boy does.

Benjamin (1988), taking an entirely different tack, argues that psychoanalysis fails to theorize maternal subjectivity or agency. This failure extends, of course, to lesbian subjectivity as well (Kiersky, 2001). As Benjamin asserts, the psychoanalytic denial of maternal authority creates uncertainty in mothers about their own agency and renders her child unsure of her autonomy and capacity for self-assertion. For Benjamin, recognition of a child's subjectivity and her similarities and differences by both parents are crucial to healthy development.

The core of Dimen's argument, I believe, is very important. From her perspective, difference feminists elaborate an independent line of female development that revalues and valorizes aspects of femininity as traditionally defined, for example, nurturing, empathy, and receptivity. For gender feminists, masculinity and femininity are part of a hierarchical "system of difference" (Benjamin, 1992, p. 90), a dual gender system that divides human possibilities such that what girls are supposed to become boys are not, and vice versa. It is this "system," gender feminists assert, that underlies the denigration of women and the idealization of men. These two lines of thinking, Dimen argues, contradict each other. Rather than tell us who women are, and what they want, one ratifies women's autonomy and self-assertion while the other argues for an innate femininity that centers on mothering, mutuality and caring for others. This contradiction, Dimen asserts, reflects a split in women themselves. Women are often of two or more minds about who they are and what they want. Instead of finding this a problem, she suggests, why not make it the beginning of a solution?

In my view, Dimen arrives somewhere much closer to lived experience than gender and difference theorists have managed. However, we conceptualize the problem, not all women are the same, nor do they want the same thing, nor does the same woman necessarily want the same thing at different times. Dimen rightly believes that clinical understanding can only be undertaken with an image of multiplicity in mind and, I would add, a consistent and steady focus on phenomenological experience. This will take work, for, as Goldner (1992) notes, the very language we use to talk about gender reproduces the categories we want to escape and the moment we move away from gender as purely phenomenological we create categories into which unruly women cannot fit.

One question that comes to mind is whether post-modernism is really the only way or even the best way to capture the contradiction that Dimen highlights. What sort of theory can embrace the multiplicity of meanings gender evokes; the range of emotional experience embedded within it and the uniqueness of each individual's subjective universe? Only a theory, I believe, that focuses specifically on meanings rather than theoretical contents and developmental lines that sees the primary role of affects in human motivation and that explicitly incorporates individual uniqueness into the analytic process. No theory is perfect or, for that matter, even correct. Post-modern positions are useful, for they remind us to question even those things that appear to be unquestionable. Some theories, however, are more useful than others are. From my perspective, attachment theory (see, for example, Slade & Wolf, 1994) and intersubjectivity (Stolorow, Brandcraft, & Atwood, 1987) with their emphases on relatedness, affects and the co-construction of meaning are helpful in understanding gender. For example, when we speak of gender dysphoria, or body-self-hatred or the feeling that one is the opposite sex or somehow inadequate as a man or a woman–these things are best understood as the consequence of insecure or disrupted early attachments and a child's attempt to sustain that attachment without loss of self or other.

Some years ago I was referred a young woman by her surgeon because she had undergone seven surgeries to change her nose, her forehead, her cheeks, her chin, and her eyes and was requesting work to be done on her ears. When I asked her why, she explained that she cared about her appearance, wanted to be perfect and felt that her ears were unfeminine and ruining her face. As I got to know her, I learned that she was a woman who, as a child of six, had been left by her father who moved in with, eventually married, and had a second daughter by another woman in the same small town where my patient and her mother lived. Though the children saw each other at school, the father rarely visited my patient, and she and her mother lived in a rather marginal way while the second family enjoyed increasing financial and social success. As I listened to her describe herself, her parents, and her half sister, it became clear to me that surgery was this child's attempt to become someone her father would not have abandoned. For Maria, perfected physical gender could stave off intolerable loss. She had become a close, physical approximation to the child of her father's second marriage. In her words, she was the perfect girl. Though it was possible for her to see these connections early in her treatment, it took many years and several more surgeries before a sense of herself as an acceptable, even lovable woman took hold. This was possible only after a deep, new attachment had taken root with me allowing for a different organization of gender experience to emerge.

WHAT IS GENDER AND CAN IT BE THEORIZED?

I think of gender as an intersubjectively organized aspect of self-experience. Like sexuality, it is simply one fluid, ambiguous and contextual aspect of any identity. In fact, we have many genders and organizations of desire that co-exist in every individual. Gender is created and sustained in interaction with others and capable of transformation throughout life. Gender and sexuality are not, as analysts have often thought, the same thing, but they are intimately connected and are both mediated through attachment giving them a special significance for affect regulation and self-protective maneuvers. I do not mean by this only that a parent passes on stereotyped notions or anxiety about gender nonconformity. I think it is also the case that in the absence of secure attachment and parental responsiveness, a child relies more and more on gender conventions to understand the world and his or her place in it. Any departure, then, from gender conformity will feel threatening, because for the child gender provides self-cohesion and regulates self-esteem.

From the moment a child is born, she is engaged in an active, relational dialogue with others and gender is being co-constructed (Kiersky and Beebe, 1994). Contrary to a great deal of psychoanalytic thinking, even a child's experience of her body is organized and given meaning in a relational matrix just as that body affects and shapes the parent's response to the child. "What a big guy you are" mother says to her little boy with a Kohutian gleam in her eye and the little boy feels big and emotionally expansive–a feeling that will hopefully develop into satisfaction and pleasure in his body and its positively constructed "bigness." In these early, mutually regulated interactions, the child locates himself in his mother's face, and voice, and actions–seeing there his desirability, masculinity, vulnerability and so on. His mother mirrors and delivers back to him all the things she sees and feels in his face and voice and actions. He can also lose himself, for instance, in her absence or in her fears.

Consider this vignette that describes the experience of a little boy who discovers a litter of kittens and excitedly picking one of them up accidentally drops it. The mother races toward him in horror and outrage, yelling that he is going to grow up to be a "killer." Rather than meet the child's sense of wonder and discovery, she has so imposed her own fears upon the child's experience that she obliterates his original impulse. Only in treatment, does she trace her anxieties back to traumatic physical abuse suffered from men in adolescence (Coates, 1997). Though this vignette is not specifically about gender, from an intersubjective point of view, the mother's belief that men are killers will certainly be organized in the child's experience of himself as a man causing him either to reject his own masculinity or to experience himself as destructive, or to be destructive. And, if men are killers, women are certainly victims. Over time, for this little boy, a world might emerge in which gender is power and violence and relationships are coercive.

When gender is so fragile an aspect of self-experience, we might wonder if it is really possible for parents to avoid communicating stereotypes in a culture that is so gender preoccupied. A group of English researchers has described a particular developmental process that seems, to me, important, to the acquisition of a comfortable and fluid sense of gender. Fonagy and Target (1996) have studied the self-reflective function in children and parents finding that somewhere around age six a momentous change occurs. Prior to this, the child's reality is characterized by two ways of relating internal experience to the external situation. The psychic equivalence mode is defined as when the child expects his internal world and that of others to correspond to what is outside, and the pretend mode, which is defined as when what is inside is thought to have no relationship to external events.

Children keep these two modes of understanding quite separate until, around six when they are integrated into a reflective mode or what Fonagy calls "mentalisation." At this time, a theory of mind develops based on the child's experience of her mental states being reflected upon by others. It is a special form of mirroring the way a child thinks that allows the child to distinguish feelings and ideas and to represent how her own mind and others' work. Through it, the parent provides a link to reality even when the child is pretending and in this way experiences come about which are understood to be pretend but also to have real consequences in the larger world. In this way, a child learns that inner reality can cause a person to distort something in the external world and vice versa.

Some children and adults never successfully integrate these two modes of understanding. Moments of pretend for young children can easily slip into the psychic equivalence mode and a fantasy can cause intense distress because it is experienced internally as corresponding to the actual situation. Aspects of subjective experience like gender and sexuality that are centrally implicated in one's sense of self are, I would argue, particularly vulnerable. For example, the feeling a young woman might have that if she is asserting herself professionally, she is no longer a real woman is precisely this kind of anxiety inducing slippage.

Though Fonagy does not address the construction of gender, it seems to me that the capacity for mentalisation or self-reflection is crucial to healthy gender. Experiences in which child and parent understand gender self-reflectively as something that is different for different people and different for the same person at different times, but also something with real consequences in the outside world are essential to a child's construction of a flexible, self-sustaining sense of gender and gender crossings. Under optimal circumstances, a parent reflects on the child's experience of being male or female and the fact that inner experience does not have to fit some external convention. On the other hand, the transmission of parental anxiety and unconscious fantasies about gender conformity are also clear when we see gender as a developmental achievement rather than given in body or soul.

From this developmental perspective, it is gender rigidly conceived that creates problems for people–not gender conformity or nonconformity. Rigid gender prescriptions and intense distress imply problematic patterns of attachment and a failure to achieve a self-reflective capacity leaving a child or an adult constrained in ways that limit creativity, pleasure, diverse experience. If we cannot experience our genders as mental states that can be reflected upon, they imprison us and our bodies express this constraint. A young boy feels that he is not a man because his penis is too small. A middle-aged woman tells me that since her mastectomy, she is no longer a woman. The little girl, who was sexually abused by her father, wants to be a princess but dreams of herself as a monster. In a world of psychic equivalence, she can only imagine herself as an infantile seductress, unclean and untouchable. If a sense of pretend and imaginative crossing is never integrated into the youngster's experience of a gendered self, subjective gender remains stereotyped. Any nonconformity will be evidence to the child of his or her inadequacy–a state of affairs that is all too familiar to us, as analysts. This thought brings me to gender in the clinical process and how it can be reworked in the analytic discourse.

CLINICAL GENDER

Nowhere is the intersubjective, co-constructed, and contradictory nature of gender more evident than in the analytic process. Psychoanalysis itself is a space for play and what better place for perilous crossings to be evoked, understood and transformed. In analysis, as in life, gender pops up everywhere. It makes cameo appearances in dreams and waking fantasies. One young man, after hearing that his wife was finally pregnant, dreamt that his penis was so large that it took two people to help him stand up every morning.

Some families are very rigid about gender. Others are not. I would like to suggest that the same is true of analysts and every analytic couple. The more constricted the view of gender in the analytic couple, the fewer the possibilities. Here, constraint consists of exiling certain topics, sensations, memories, and desires. Many analysts take for granted that they know what it means to be a man or a woman. Meanings, however, are always uniquely elaborated in the individual psyche and gender meanings are no exception. Fantasies, fears, expectations, and desires around what it means to be a man or a woman inevitably come to pre-scribe and limit the possibilities we imagine for ourselves and for oth-ers. To overcome these limits, a sense of humor and play in an analyst is extremely important. There are as many ways to explore and rework gender as there are gender meanings, but let me give you an example of one kind of gender play in the analytic process. This one began with a metaphor.[1]

A patient I call Lisa, and have written about in other contexts (Lachmann and Kiersky, 1995) had great difficulty seeing herself as both a desirable woman and a capable adult. In fact, her attempts to se-cure a relationship and a profession seemed destined to interfere with each other. During certain periods of her analysis, these aspects of her experience and the meanings she attached to being female entered the analysis through a series of metaphors, which we explored together. Over time, each of us moved back and forth across our gendered bor-ders. Disguises were employed and masquerade, in Riviere's (1929) sense, was the order of the day. At first, each of us is an active and then a receptive presence; at another, two women competing and then support-ive; finally, two women who both have male and female qualities. This last Lisa, the one that she most admired and hoped to become, is a woman who embodies those male and female pleasures and potentials in every woman. What follows is a brief description of part of Lisa's treatment with particular emphasis on the themes of gender and bodily experience.

At a certain point in Lisa's analysis, she began to eroticize her rela-tionship with me. The more I became the focus of sexual feelings and longings, the more she felt that I was distracted and bored with our rela-tionship. These feelings seemed organized by her experience of her fa-ther, a busy and successful academic whom she remembered as always in his study or away. At the same time, however, there was no question that she also experienced me as a woman she desired. "I don't want to be in love with you," she said, "and yet I am. I have images of you close in your chair and yet so distant and unreachable, just like my father." I reflected how difficult it was for Lisa to feel special and unique with someone she loved and she agreed.

Following this, Lisa experienced an upsurge of sexual feelings and concerns that her body was not desirable. She wanted to "turn me on" but feared that I would be angry. She felt disgusted by her body. She was sure her breasts were too large, her body too big and her needs too embarrass-ing. I noted how completely she felt that her desires were too much for other people and for the next several weeks, we explored the various contexts in which this feeling reoccurred. When this was understood, a metaphor emerged and Lisa began to woo "the woman with the pencil."

My possession of a pencil, taking occasional notes during sessions, distinguished me for Lisa as powerful, self-confident, dazzling, and well equipped. She wanted something from me. Perhaps, she mused, it was my pencil. She wondered if she could ever have a pencil of her own. Sadly, she felt that I remained indifferent behind my pencil creating an unbridgeable gap between us. Describing these fantasies, she suddenly became alarmed. She feared that her longings and sexual feelings would never be acknowledged. She wanted me to find her body desirable and was sure I would find her presumptuous. I responded that Lisa expected her sexual feelings to be dismissed or misunderstood. As with her father, she could not imagine my feeling for her something that she felt for me.

These sessions reminded Lisa of adolescence and her first attempts to enter the mysterious world of men and women. Her metaphor of the pencil included both her active sexual strivings and a serious wish to be a writer. For Lisa, it was hard to believe in the possibility of a woman who was comfortable as a woman and competent as a writer. Thinking about this, she recalled her father teasing and mocking her about the shy young men who came to take her out on dates. She felt humiliated in her attempts to be attractive to them and soon withdrew. She stopped dating and began to fantasize herself as a devilishly handsome, mannish lesbian with a beautiful woman on her arm. In this guise, she imagined, she might also be a writer as well. With me, however, she felt, deflated. "I'll always want something from you that I can't have," she said "and I understand that it comes from my relationship with my father, but it still feels unbearable. What I want is my own life. I have a body, but I don't own it." Together, we worked through her fear that I would ridicule her efforts to make a life of her own and express herself sexually in her own way. In one session, she described masturbating with a large eggplant and feeling that it was entering her very deep. Afterwards, she said, "it occurred to me that it was my father's penis because it was so long and big. I've always had the notion that he is very big because he's very tall. In fact, I thought, he probably has the biggest penis in the world and that made me think of little boys comparing themselves to their fathers."

"It would be hard," I commented, "for little boys to compete with the biggest pencil in the world." Lisa laughed and agreed. As the pencil metaphor faded, Lisa began to explore her feelings about her body and being vulnerable to men. At the end of a session one day in the waiting room, she asked if she might borrow a particular word processing program from me to copy in her computer. She wasn't sure, though, whether my disk would fit her drive. I suggested she bring it up in her next session and she began the next session by telling me how excited she became after our last exchange. She was thrilled that she had been able to get me outside my office. She felt she had crossed a line, and that was scary. What if I did give her my discs? Would they fit? Did we have the same drive or were they actually different. It seemed that Lisa and I had entered the heady world of discs and drives, a pretend world in which anatomy, prohibitions, desires, and taboos were prominent, and perilous crossings were the order of the day. We stayed with Lisa's metaphor, though each of us understood the complexity and range of meaning in each exchange. I acknowledged her concern about equipment. Did I have equipment that she did not have, but needed? Would I give it to her? What about the size of my equipment? If Lisa tried to fit my equipment in to her own, would there by any damage?

Lisa and I came to understand that these metaphors expressed, among other things, central developmental themes concerning gender–certain rigid and painful experiences of self and other that appeared in the transference. She recalled being frightened and awed in relation to her large, potentially hurtful father who never spared her a judgmental or penetrating remark. Sexually curious as a child, she was afraid of being hurt, physically and emotionally, though she wanted to be as exciting to her father as he was to her. She never felt, she said, that he saw her as an interesting or beautiful young woman.

As we explored these feelings, Lisa remembered a specific moment that she had completely forgotten. She saw her father once in their bathroom urinating and was amazed at his size. This memory led to the recovery of a sexual trauma when she was six–an age when self-reflection around gender and sexuality is still fragile and easily disrupted. In the woods, near her family's summer home one afternoon, she had gone on her own to have her bicycle repaired. On the way, she met a boy who asked her to come further into the woods and he would show her something interesting. She went with him because he reminded her of her brother and so she felt safe. He pushed her against a tree, took off her pants, and jammed his penis against her. She noticed that his penis was gigantic, like her father's, and she was afraid she would hurt in some way. It was not clear to her how she had been bad, but she felt that she had. She never told anyone about it, especially her father, for she was sure that he would blame her. She was clearly worried about my reaction, anxious that I would judge her. Remembering the scene, feelings of excitement, anxiety, and shame returned in almost equal measure. She also remembered, then, that it was the first time that she had tried to go off on her own and accomplish something and suddenly understood a longstanding feeling that women shouldn't really go off on their own or something bad might happen. Finally, she recalled how consistently the boys in the family were encouraged to achieve intellectually and professionally, while the girls were encouraged to be pretty and helpful. She felt, she told me, freed from something though she wasn't sure what it was. She began to sell some articles she had written and soon shifted from temp work as a typist to a job with a magazine. Today, she is the publisher of a magazine, which actually is her own creation. Around the same time, she began to date, this time quite successfully.

As the seventh year of analysis drew to a close, Lisa recovered the following memory. She remembered once, in the first grade, feeling that she could not do her homework well, becoming very upset, and finally tearing it up. Her father, hearing her, came out of his study and took the time to sit with her and paste it back together so that she would not be embarrassed in school the next day. She was grateful for this occasion in which in her words, her father protected her from a trauma. "Not every father," she reminded me, "would take the time to do that."

DISCUSSION

This brief segment of an analysis, I hope, illustrates a number of things. First, that the analytic process is layered. There are many meanings in play at any given moment and a multiplicity of genders, identifications, and what I call exiled desires–those ambitions, passions, and pretenses that we feel but do not feel entitled to. In this sense, the analytic relationship is an opportunity to accept these cross-gendered aspects of ourselves and experience a greater sense of opportunity. Second, the analyst must maintain a fluid position. The capacity to play and enter the subjective experience of the patient is vitally important to the exploration of meaning and the construction of a new experience. If we hold a rigid, nonreflective theory of gender, we impose meaning on our patients, exiling their uniqueness and our own. If we remain open to the various ways that patients experience us, gender shapes the analytic interaction in complex and surprising ways. Overly rigid notions of gender leave a young man or woman feeling gender-less. One patient who was sexually drawn to other women painfully described herself as neither a man nor a woman–"I am nothing," she told me, "I fit nowhere. I am what the word misfit was invented to describe." Her difficulty lay in the cultural notion that to actively desire a woman, one must be a man.

Freud elaborated this myth in his theory of sexual identities. In reality, subjective gender can mean almost anything–ethnicity, class, sexuality, weight, or the size of a breast. As a field, we must move away from equating gender conformity with mental health.

Finally, I would like to return to my original question for a moment. Can we create a theory of gender that retains the complexity of experience as it is actually lived? I think we can come closer than we have, but purely constructivist theories, or notions of performativity, will probably not take us there. We must be careful not to produce another set of dichotomies that so often gets us into trouble–this time of gender performed vs. gender expressed.

Gender is both performed and expressed–the fact that it is constructed does not make it less a part of the individual's subjective world nor less subject to the limits of biological potential. Nor does this recognition universalize gender experience. All experience is organized in interaction. This does not mean that we are only what we do. It does mean that organizations of experience are capable of transformation over time and in certain contexts. Even biological potentials are always in flux. What may be more important, clinically, is the phenomenological issue of what feels performative and what does not. I would argue that the more we feel we are performing gender, the greater the sense of a perilous crossing and the more we reinstate the conventional stereotype without meaning to. Like mind and body, doing and being a gender are in the end inseparable. We will find more useful ways to conceptualize gender in a theory like intersubjectivity with its consistent focus on meanings, affects, context, and co-constructed experience. These tell us how gender changes and how it affects us as individuals.

NOTE

1. This case description is reprinted here by permission of The Analytic Press. It is part of a longer case description in a paper by Frank Lachmann and myself entitled "Why Can't a Woman be a Man in the Transference?" In *Progress in Self Psychology*, Vol. 11, 1995.

REFERENCES

Benjamin, J. (1988). *The bonds of love: Psychoanalysis, feminism, and the problem of domination*. New York: Pantheon.

Benjamin, J. (1992). The relational self: A new perspective for understanding women's development. *Contemporary Psychotherapy Review, 7*, 82-96.

Coates, S. W. (1998). Having a mind of one's own and holding the other in mind: Commentary on a paper by Peter Fonagy and Mary Target. *Psychoanalytic Dialogues*, *8*(1), 115-148.

Chodorow, N. J. (1978). *The reproduction of mothering: Psychoanalysis and the sociology of gender*. Berkeley: University of California Press.

Dimen, M. (1995). The third step: Freud, the feminists and postmodernism. *The American Journal of Psychoanalysis*, *55*(4), 303-319.

Fonagy, P. & Target, M. (1996). Playing with reality. I: Theory of mind and the normal development of psychic reality. *International Journal of Psychoanalysis*, *77*, 217-233.

Freud, S. (1961). Three essays on the theory of sexuality. In J. Strachey (Ed. & Trans.), *Standard edition of the complete psychological works of Sigmund Freud* (Vol. 7, pp. 125-245). London: Hogarth Press. (Original work published 1905).

Freud, S. (1961). The dissolution of the Oedipus complex. In J. Strachey (Ed. & Trans.), *Standard edition of the complete psychological works of Sigmund Freud* (Vol. 19, pp. 173-181). London: Hogarth Press. (Original work published 1924).

Freud, S. (1961). Some psychical consequences of the anatomical distinction between the sexes. In J. Strachey (Ed. & Trans.), *Standard edition of the complete psychological works of Sigmund Freud* (Vol. 19, pp. 241-259). London: Hogarth Press. (Original work published 1925).

Freud, S. (1961). Female sexuality. In J. Strachey (Ed. & Trans.), *Standard edition of the complete psychological works of Sigmund Freud* (Vol. 21, pp. 221-245). London: Hogarth Press. (Original work published 1931).

Freud, S. (1961). On femininity. In J. Strachey (Ed. & Trans.), *Standard edition of the complete psychological works of Sigmund Freud* (Vol. 22, pp. 112-134). London: Hogarth Press. (Original work published 1933).

Gilligan, C. (1982). *In a different voice: Psychological theory and women's development*. Cambridge: Harvard University Press.

Goldner, V. (1991). Toward a critical relational theory of gender. *Psychoanalytic Dialogues*, *1*, 249-272.

Green, M. (Ed.). (1964). *Interpersonal psychoanalysis: The selected papers of Clara Thompson*. New York: Basic Books.

Horney, K. (1967). Feminine psychology. In H. Kelman (Ed.), *Karen Horney feminine psychology* (pp. 37-53). New York: Norton. (Original work published in 1923).

Kiersky, S. & Beebe, B. (1994). The reconstruction of early non-verbal relatedness in the treatment of the difficult patient. *Psychoanalytic Dialogues*, *4*(3), 89-408.

Kiersky, S. (2001) Exiled desire: The problem of reality in psychoanalysis and lesbian experience. In S. Kiersky & E. Gould (Eds.), *Sexualities: Lost and found: Lesbians, psychoanalysis and culture*. New York: International Universities Press.

Lachmann, F. & Kiersky, S. (1995). Why can't a woman be a man . . . in the transference? In A. Goldberg (Ed.), *The impact of new ideas: Progress in self psychology* (Vol. 11, pp. 99-108). Hillsdale, NJ: The Analytic Press.

Miller, J. B. (1976). *Toward a new psychology of women*. Boston: Beacon.

Pollitt, K. (1994). *Reasonable creatures*. New York: Knopf.

Riviere, J. (1929). Womanliness as a masquerade. *The International Journal of Psychoanalysis*, *10*, 303-313.

Slade, A. & Wolf, D.P. (Eds.). (1994). *Children at play: Clinical and developmental approaches to meaning and representation.* New York: Oxford University Press.

Stolorow, R. D., Brandchaft, B. & Atwood, G. (1987). *Psychoanalytic treatment: An intersubjective approach.* Hillsdale, New Jersey: The Analytic Press.

Thelen, E. & Smith, L. B. (1994). *A dynamic systems approach to the development of cognition and action.* Cambridge, MA: MIT Press.

Wittig, M. (1993) One is not born a woman. In H. Abelove, M. A. Barale, & D. Halperin (Eds.), *The lesbian and gay studies reader* (pp. 3-44). New York: Routledge.

Index

Abramowitz, S., 60
Abusive relations interiority
   clinical practice contexts of, 119-120
   domestic violence politics and,
      109-111
   ethics-related contexts of, 111-119
   future perspectives of, 120
   historical perspectives of, 108-109
   overviews of, 107-109
   reference resources for, 120-121
Adams, J.M., 60
African American lesbians, 57-77. *See
     also* Cultural diversity
     contexts
Afrocentric approaches, 66-67
Agazarian, Y., 48-50
Allport, G., 124-125
Alter-ego transference, 133-134
Altman, N., 60-62
American Psychoanalytic Association,
     88
Apprey, Y.M., 53
Attachment theory and
     intersubjectivity
   feminist psychoanalysis theory and,
     194-197
     vs. clinical practice, 195
     difference feminists and, 195
     of Dimen, M., 194-197
     dual gender systems and, 196
     gender feminists and, 195
     maternal authority and, 195-196
     overviews of, 194-195
     phallocentric culture and, 195
     postmodernism and, 196-197
     relatedness and, 195
   future perspectives of, 205

gender theory and, 197-205
   case examples for, 201-204
   clinical gender and, 200-204
   co-construction and, 198,
     200-204
   developmental perspectives of,
     199-200
   gender definitions and, 197-200
   intersubjectivity and, 197-204
   nonconformity and, 199-200
   nonreflective theories and,
     204-205
   performance *vs.* expression and,
     205
   psychic equivalence and, 200
   overviews of, 191-194
   reference resources for, 205-207
Authority (maternal), 195-196

Barber, K., 145
Benjamin, J., 148,185-186,195-196
Berzoff, J., 62
Bjork, D., 95-121
Blanck, G. and Blanck, R., 85-86
Blechner, M., 90
Boyd-Franklin, N., 62
Burch, B., 128
Butch contexts
   butch/femme dyads, 151-152,
     165-167
   evolutionary butch, 143-158. *See
     also* Tomboy and
     evolutionary butch
     development processes
Butler, J., 88-90,152-153,163,
     177-189